WATER LAW

WATER LAW

William Goldfarb

Professor of Environmental Law
Cook College, Rutgers University
New Brunswick, New Jersey

BUTTERWORTH PUBLISHERS

Boston • London
Sydney • Wellington • Durban • Toronto

An Ann Arbor Science Book

Ann Arbor Science is an imprint of Butterworth Publishers.

Library of Congress Cataloging in Publication Data

Goldfarb, William.
  Water law.

  "An Ann Arbor science book"
  Bibliography: p.
  Includes index.
  1. Water—Law and legislation—United States.
2. Water resources development—Law and legislation—United States.   I. Title.
KF5569.G65   1984   346.7304'691   84-9597
ISBN 0-250-40627-6   347.3064691

Butterworth Publishers
80 Montvale Avenue
Stoneham, MA 02180

10 9 8 7 6 5 4 3 2 1

Printed in the United States of America

For My Parents

William Goldfarb is Professor of Environmental Law at Cook College, Rutgers, the State University of New Jersey. As a contributing editor to the *Water Resources Bulletin*, Professor Goldfarb has, for the past eight years, written a bi-monthly commentary on water law entitled "Litigation and Legislation." He has also published numerous articles and book chapters on various aspects of water law. In his home state of New Jersey, Professor Goldfarb has been a special consultant to state water resources agencies, a draftsman of water resources legislation, and a member of the Governor's Science Advisory Committee. He is an avid fly-fisherman, and also writes articles for fly-fishing magazines.

CONTENTS

PREFACE

The most formidable obstacle to rational water resources management is the failure of communication among water resources professionals and among students in the water resources field. Narrow specialization generates esoteric jargon that impairs effective cooperation in pursuit of desirable policy goals. When scientists, engineers, lawyers, planners, social scientists, and management specialists speak intelligibly only to their disciplinary colleagues and students, the results are misunderstandings, chauvinism, and frustration. All too frequently, disciplinary separations are institutionalized in water resources management and study organizations. However, optimum water resources policy outcomes can be realized only if all aspects of water resources management, i.e., physical, social-scientific, and legal-institutional, are integrated into comprehensive analysis and decision making.

Curing this unhealthy specialization within water resources will require reforms in education and communication. Fortunately, efforts in this direction have already begun. The American Water Resources Association (AWRA) has taken a strong lead in promoting understanding among relevant disciplines. Through national conferences, regional affiliates, and especially its multidisciplinary journal *Water Resources Bulletin*, the AWRA provides a model of interdisciplinary coordination and information exchange.

The idea for this book arose from reader responses to my "Litigation and Legislation" commentary that has appeared in *Water Resources Bulletin* for over five years. "Litigation and Legislation" attempts to convey, in nonlegal language, recent developments in water law to the predominantly nonlegal readers of the *Bulletin*. From time to time, some of these water resource administrators, consultants, educators, and students in university water resource programs have mentioned the need for a handbook on water law, written for a nonlegal audience, to supplement the commentaries. This book is my attempt to satisfy this need. Additionally, the book will be useful to attorneys and law students who desire an introduction to water law or a short compendium of the law relating to water resources.

Readability has been my guiding principle in writing this book. Legal writing, for example, articles in law reviews, is stylistically inaccessible to most nonlawyers because of its copious (some might say excessive) use of footnotes and "legalistic" syntax ("whereas," "provided that," etc.) and terminology. This would be distracting and counterproductive in a book directed to a nonlegal audience. Thus, the reader may assume that the references placed at the end of each chapter do not contain explanatory material. For the most part, these references consist of treatises, cases, administrative regulations, and statutes. The enterprising reader may follow up these sources by enlisting the aid of a librarian in his nearest law school library. Legalistic syntax has been avoided. Any legal terms used are explained in the text.

As far as content is concerned, no prior knowledge of the law or legal system is assumed of the reader. Where necessary, legal concepts, principles, and institutions are explained as thoroughly as space and subject matter permit. It goes without saying that legal topics are treated in a highly selective manner, and that no attempt is made to comprehensively analyze the American law and legal system. Nevertheless, water resources professionals and students should find in these pages the facets of law which most closely touch upon their fields of responsibility and interest.

Writing this book has been more like drilling into and pumping water from a deep aquifer than tapping a convenient artesian water supply. A good deal of help was needed to produce it. In the first place, the book was made possible by funding from the New Jersey Agricultural Experiment Station, where it is listed as publication number A-17413-1-83 supported by state funds. Many colleagues and students at Cook College, Rutgers University, enlightened me about the nonlegal aspects of water resources management. Foremost among these colleagues was Dr. Theodore Shelton of the Department of Environmental Resources at Cook College. It was also stimulating and educational to work closely with, as special consultant, personnel of the Division of Water Resources, New Jersey Department of Environmental Protection. I have Donald A. Brown, Esq., and former dean Grant F. Walton of Cook College to thank for this unique opportunity. My wife Illse Economou Goldfarb, a fellow water attorney, made invaluable comments on the draft manuscript. And Dorothy Cooke, my typist, was more than patient with my murky handwriting. My labors in writing this book will be amply rewarded if its availability improves, in whatever small measure, the quality of water resources problem solving in the United States.

William Goldfarb

INTRODUCTION: Law, Water Law, and Water Rights

WHAT DO WE MEAN BY "LAW"?

For our purposes, "law" is a precept that is written, formally issued by one or more branches of government, and enforceable by governmental sanctions against violators. There are five major sources of law in the American legal system: (1) constitutions; (2) statutes and ordinances; (3) administrative regulations; (4) executive orders; and (5) common law court decisions ("cases"). Each of these has contributed to the development of water law.

Constitutions are referred to as "fundamental law," meaning that they contain basic principles of justice that underlie other legal principles and procedures. There is a Constitution of the United States, applicable to all American citizens, and state constitutions which afford rights only to citizens of particular states. The federal Constitution and its state counterparts are similar but not identical. For example, most state constitutions contain "takings clauses," forbidding the taking of private property for public use without just compensation. It will be seen that the definition of "taking" is central to a determination of whether, and to what extent, government may legally regulate water-related land use. An unusual provision is the clause in some western state constitutions that all unappropriated surface waters are available for appropriation. Because constitutions are generally phrased in broad terms, the role of courts as final constitutional interpreters is a critical one. State supreme courts, with regard to state constitutions, and the United States Supreme Court, where the federal Constitution is concerned, are responsible for applying ambiguous constitutional terms such as "taking" and striking down statutes and regulations that violate constitutions (e.g., that are unconstitutional takings without just compensation).

Statutes, or "acts," are bills that are passed ("enacted") by appropriate votes of state legislatures or Congress. On the county and municipal levels, legislative enactments are referred to as "ordinances." However, a statute does not achieve the force of law until it is signed by the president or governor, as the case may be, or until the chief executive's veto is overridden by the required legislative vote. The federal Clean Water Act of 1972 is an example of a statute that became law when Congress overrode a presidential veto. In an increasing number of states, water law is primarily state statutory law. Although courts interpret ambiguous statutes in accordance with their conceptions of legislative intent, a legislature can always overturn a judicial interpretation by amending the statute, as long as the chief executive agrees or sufficient support can be mustered to override a veto. Courts have the final say regarding the meaning of constitutions, but legislatures are the final interpreters of statutes. Courts are also important in enforcing statutes. For example, violators of the Clean Water Act may receive judicially imposed penalties of up to $50,000 per day of violation, or imprisonment for up to two years, or both.

Because of the need for continuous expert regulation in highly technical areas such as water pollution control and water distribution, Congress and state legislatures enact statutes creating administrative agencies. An "enabling act" or "organic act" establishes a regulatory framework, sets out general rules and standards for the agency to follow, and delegates to the agency the authority to issue rules and regulations carrying the force of law. Thus, where the agency has developed and issued ("promulgated") a rule or regulation in accordance with the applicable administrative procedure act, the promulgated rule can be enforced against violators either by the agency, for example, through an administrative fine, or by a court at an agency's behest. In contrast, administrative "guidelines," issued without the required public notice and comment, are not "law" because they are not directly enforceable. Administrative agencies also "make law" when they issue written decisions adjudicating disputes over licenses or permits, for example, contested claims to priority of diversion in prior appropriation states. Administrative agencies are governmental microcosms in that they exercise legislative powers (i.e., rule making), judicial powers (i.e., adjudication of conflicting claims), and of course, executive powers. The major federal water law agencies are the United States Department of the Interior (DOI), the Environmental Protection Agency (EPA), and the National Oceanic and Atmospheric Administration (NOAA) in the United States Department of Commerce. At the state level, water law activity is centered in state environmental protection agencies and "state engineer" offices.

The power to issue executive orders is inherent in the chief executive's authority to supervise the executive branch and deal with emergency situations. In 1970 President Nixon created the EPA by reorganization plan, transferring powers from the DOI, the United States Department of Agriculture (USDA), and the Department of Health, Education and Welfare (now the Department of Health and Human Services). Some years ago the governor of New Jersey ordered his Department of Environmental Protection to use existing permitting authority to curtail development in the Pinelands in order to protect a massive and vulnerable aquifer from contamination by septic tanks. Executive orders have the force of law, but important legal questions regarding them remain unanswered. What is the legal effect of an executive order on a legislature? Can a private citizen sue to enforce an executive order? Most important, what is the permissible scope of an executive order?

The common law frequently comes into play when a property owner sues a neighbor ("defendant") for polluting or diverting water which the person suing ("plaintiff") is entitled to use. Forestalling a neighbor's drainage water from damaging property is another kind of common law "action" (suit). Common law is present when a lawsuit is designated as based, for example, on nuisance, trespass, negligence, violation of drainage rights, violation of riparian rights, or interference with the reasonable use of groundwater. Unlike statutory law, common law is judge-made law. It is contained in written judicial decisions in specific lawsuits. These decisions are known as "cases." The keynote of common law is precedent: in similar factual situations judges are expected to follow the legal rules established by their predecessors. An excessive devotion to precedent at the expense of fairness is avoided by encouraging judges to distinguish situations factually and by recognizing the power of a state supreme court to change common law rules. A number of states have judicially substituted the "reasonable use rule" for the "common enemy rule" in drainage cases. Although the common law is of limited importance in water quality law, it remains viable in drainage and water quantity disputes, especially in the east. The availability of common law actions in water law conflicts supports statutory water law by bringing novel situations and their judicial resolutions to the attention of legislatures. Common law also offers an individual the ability to recover "compensatory damages" for property damage and personal injury. Most statutes do not offer individuals the right to recover the cash value of personal loss.

WHAT IS WATER LAW?

"Water law" defies precise definition. It overlaps other legal fields such as environmental law, natural resources law, real property law, tort law, public land law, and land use law. Water law is still strongly identified with water quantity (supply) problems. For example, a recent article on prior appropriation, excellent in other respects, begins with the statement, "Water law is the doctrine on which we rely to provide enough water for those who need it."* But this water must be of a *quality* sufficiently high to be useful to those who need it. There should be no doubt that water quantity law and water quality law are of equal importance in water law. In fact, a mature system of water law, stressing the comprehensive management of water resources, would reject the quantity-quality distinction because the two are inextricably interconnected. It is hoped that this book will hasten the decline of this troublesome dichotomy.

The "enough-water-for-those-who-need-it" conception of water law is also excessively anthropocentric. In fact, water law has traditionally been associated with human uses of water, particularly diversions for economic uses. But that is changing too. Instream uses for recreational and ecological purposes are of growing importance. Some of the most crucial western water law court decisions of recent years have involved the legality of instream uses under a prior appropriation system.

Although water law cannot be exactly defined, a loose operational definition will prove helpful for analytic purposes. The following definition is somewhat tautological but valuable nevertheless. "Water law" is here defined as those aspects of law, including the legal aspects of major water resources management institutions, which are of primary concern to the aggregate of water resource professionals and students. Four of these topics, covered by the four parts of this book, are (1) the law of water diversion and distribution, (2) the law of water resources development and protection, (3) the law of nontransformational uses, and (4) the law of water treatment and related land use.

Because of space limitations, another aspect of water law, namely, oceans law and international water law, is incompletely treated here. These issues are discussed only where they clarify the direct focus of this book, which is the law applicable to fresh and tidal waters of the United States, and to those waterbodies which the United States shares with Canada and Mexico.

Even within these limitations, it is clear that the multiplicity of American water resource legal issues cannot be thoroughly analyzed in a single volume. For example, the legal regime applicable to the Colorado River and the legal problems relating to water use in the Colorado Basin deserve a book all to themselves. Instead, this book emphasizes general water law principles and attempts to provide references for those readers who desire to study the legal aspects of local or regional water resources problems in greater detail.

---

*Schaab, W.C. "Prior Appropriation, Impairment, Replacement, Models and Markets," *Natural Resources Journal* 23(1):25 (1983).

WHAT IS A WATER RIGHT?

Water law deals with water rights of various kinds. A legal right is the assurance that an activity will be protected by the legal system. It means that other people have enforceable duties toward a rightholder.

A set of legal rights that a rightholder holds exclusively ("owns") is called "property." Ownership of property entails a group of rights with regard to the subject of property, e.g., a plot of land or an automobile. These property rights generally include the right to possess the subject, use it, dispose of it, and exclude everyone else from interfering with it for an indefinite period of time.

A water right is property because it is unique to the rightholder, but a water right in a natural waterbody is a different mode of property than that in a plot of land or an automobile. Water in a natural waterbody cannot be privately owned. It is owned by each state as trustee for its citizens. In other words, water in natural waterbodies is "common property"; it belongs to all citizens of the state. A private citizen can only own the right to use such water. This is what lawyers call a "usufructuary right." It is not meaningless semantics to say that the subject of a property right in water is not the water itself but the use of water, even though in many American states water rights can be bought and sold. For one thing, the distinction supports extraordinary state powers to regulate water use, powers that a state can assert against the federal government as well as its own citizens. After all, as true owner of the water in natural waterbodies within its boundaries a state should possess greater authority to regulate water use than to regulate land or automobile use.

Nevertheless, state control over use of water in natural waterbodies is not unlimited. One implication of classifying a water right as "property" is to afford it protection under the Fifth Amendment to the United States Constitution and comparable clauses in most state constitutions. No government, be it federal, state, or substate, is entitled to "take" private property for public use without paying "just compensation" to the owner. For example, the municipality in which a person lives could not zone his lakefront property as a public waterfront park without paying compensation for loss of access to, and reasonable use of, the lake. On the other hand, because of the state's role as public trustee its power to regulate the use of water in natural waterbodies is exceptional. An example is a state's power to compel lakefront owners on a "private lake" to obey state fish and game and pollution control laws.

WATER RIGHTS AND WATER USES

A water right is a legally protected use of water. The traditional categorization of water uses is illustrated by this excerpt from *Water Policies for the Future*, the final report of the National Water Commission (NWC) (1973):

> Water use consists of (1) intake uses; (2) onsite uses, and (3) instream or flow uses. Intake uses include water for domestic, agricultural, and industrial purposes—uses that actually remove water from its source. Onsite uses consist mainly of water consumed by swamps, wetlands, evaporation from the surface of water bodies, natural vegetation, unirrigated crops, and wildlife. Flow uses include water for estuaries, navigation, waste dilution, hydroelectric power and some fish and wildlife and recreational uses.
>
> Water uses are measured in two ways, by amount withdrawn and amount consumed. Water withdrawn is water diverted from its natural course for use, and may be returned later for further use. Water consumed is water that is incorporated into a product or lost to the atmosphere through evaporation and transpiration, and cannot be reused. Water consumption is the more important indicator, since some part of withdrawn water can usually be reused, although not always near the point where the first withdrawal takes place [p. 6].

This formulation is seriously flawed, because, as was characteristic of water resources management in the past, it is oriented toward water quantity, not water quality. Use of water for waste removal partakes of all three uses: a cooling tower is an intake use; uptake of nutrients by a wetland is an onsite use; and BOD (biochemical oxygen demand) assimilation is an instream use. Moreover, in terms of water quality, it is unproductive to place hydroelectric power generation in the same category as scenic preservation. As for measuring water uses, the distinction between "withdrawal" and "consumption," as these terms are defined by the NWC, does not help us to evaluate waste discharges or potential development. Pollution and destruction of fish and wildlife or scenic beauty by water resource development are in a very real sense consumptive uses, although water may not be physically lost to the atmosphere.

Instead of redefining "consumptive use" in a tortured fashion inconsistent with tradition and everyday speech, entirely new phraseology is introduced where appropriate in this book. Water uses are spoken of as "transformational" or "nontransformational." A "transformational use" is one which causes a significant change in the existing condition of a waterbody. This includes substantial diversion or waste discharge as well as heavy recreational use. A "nontransformational use" leaves a waterbody in a basically unaltered state. This approach has the advantage of placing all water uses on the same plane. Thus, it deals directly with the fundamental value question inherent in water resources management: Are the social and economic gains produced by water use worth the costs of ecosystem change? In other words, should a particular water use become a water right?

WATER LAW AND SCIENCE

Law and science are different conceptual systems. They have different goals, different notions of truth, and different methods of proof.* Scientists are often amazed that "good science" does not always prevail in court. By the same token, much of water law is based on obsolete science. For example, one of the most meaningful distinctions in water law is that between surface water and groundwater, a distinction which is minimized by modern hydrology. In fact, many states apply different legal principles to surface water and groundwater. Moreover, in some of these states the applicable groundwater rule is based on the assumption that groundwater moves in fundamentally inscrutable ways. How can the law be so retrograde in lagging behind science?

Like all systems for guiding human conduct, including science, law rests uneasily upon a tension between security (predictability) and flexibility (truth, fairness). Our legal framework for containing this tension is the common law and statutes inspired by common law principles. The common law achieves security by its reliance on precedent. Flexibility is retained by allowing judges to apply a range of legal rules to a particular factual situation, and by providing for changes in legal rules by supreme courts and legislatures. But the legal system is inherently conservative in that judges and legislators are reluctant to overturn existing law. In addition to the intrinsic power of precedent, many important private decisions have been grounded on the then current state of the law. It is true that changes in law are generally not retroactive; but modifications nevertheless cause confusion and administrative problems. Consequently, many viable legal rules, some of which have even been enacted by legislatures, are built upon scientific facts as perceived by lawmakers when the rules were originally formulated, but which are now inconsistent with scientific knowledge. Our legal system is replete with "legal fictions," such as the undiscoverability of groundwater movements, which are demonstrably false but are nevertheless preserved in the interests of administrative stability.

How can the legal system command respect if it is underlaid by false constructs? One answer is that legal decision making is flexible enough that rules based on outdated science do not necessarily result in bad decisions. Judges find ways to decide cases equitably, even if it requires sophistry. At the point where the legal stable becomes too augean with untenable rules,

---

*Large, D.W., and P. Michie, "Proving that the Strength of the British Navy Depends on the Number of Old Maids in England: A Comparison of Scientific Proof with Legal Proof," *Environmental Law* 11(3):555–638 (1981).

conflicting rules, and distorted precedents, a supreme court or legislature will step in and wash away the rubbish. With all its faults, the common law system is clearly preferable to ad hoc decision making by legal officials. But it is equally clear that law is more resistant to change than science.

PART I
The Law of Water Diversion and Distribution

The American legal system is not monolithic. In fact, there are hundreds of major legal systems if those of the federal government, the fifty states, and the largest cities and counties are included. The law of water diversion and distribution is predominantly state law. These rights to use water are almost invariably declared in statutes enacted by state legislatures, adjudicated by state courts and administrative agencies, and administered by state agencies. Since states are independent sovereigns in the water law field, different states, even neighboring states, often apply contrasting legal principles to a particular water law problem. Consequently, in water law we regularly refer to "majority" or "minority" state rules, depending on the number of states adhering to that rule.

Where water diversion and distribution are concerned, state law generally reigns supreme unless a state oversteps its bounds and violates a right embodied in federal law. For example, rights of irrigators to water developed by federal reclamation projects are governed by federal statutory reclamation law. State law in conflict with this federal law is null and void. Federal claims to reserved water rights are decided under federal law, even though they may actually be adjudicated in state courts. Moreover, because a water right is treated by the law as "property," under the Fifth Amendment to the United States Constitution no state may "take" a water right for public use without "just compensation" to the rightholder. But these exceptions only prove the rule of state hegemony in matters of diversion and distribution. Indeed, the federal government has always given extraordinary deference to state water law in these areas.

When a water right is violated, i.e., a rightholder is prevented from using water as the law allows, the rightholder can seek a "remedy" from an administrative agency or a court. An agency can order the violator to curtail interference with water rights and, if necessary, impose an administrative fine. Some administrative agencies in the west have their own enforcement personnel to implement administrative orders. The rightholder, or in some situations the agency on his behalf, may go to court if the agency does not provide an adequate remedy, for example, if the violator disobeys the administrative order or the rightholder desires compensation for financial loss. Courts are empowered to grant "injunctions" and "compensatory damages" for water rights violations. An injunction is a judicial cease-and-desist order enforceable by state or federal law-enforcement officials. Disobeying an injunction could subject the violator to heavy judicial fines and even imprisonment for contempt of court. However, courts are not required to grant injunctions against water rights violations. Injunction is a "discretionary" remedy that can be denied if the public interest militates against it. Thus, a water rights violator that employs a large number of people may be allowed to continue the violating conduct if compensatory damages, measured by actual financial loss, are paid to the rightholder. In other cases, compensatory damages for past violations may be issued in addition to an injunction prohibiting future interferences. Where the violator is a governmental entity, a rightholder may be able to recover the fair market value of the right as compensation for a "taking."

Chapter 1

LEGAL CLASSIFICATION OF WATER

Over hundreds of years, and without reliable hydrologic data, courts and legislatures have divided the hydrologic system into numerous classes of waters that are subject to different legal rules. The trend is away from this unscientific set of distinctions, but legal change occurs slowly, especially in a field, such as water diversion and distribution law, that is a function of fifty different state legal systems and federal law.

The fundamental legal classifications of water are groundwater and surface water. Nowadays, when enlightened water resources management requires conjunctive use of waters based on the interconnections of groundwater and surface water, this distinction is a particularly harmful one. The following is a brief introduction to the legal classes of groundwater and surface water.

SURFACE WATER CATEGORIES

Diffused Surface Water

Diffused surface water is the uncollected flow from falling rain or melting snow, or is spring water that spreads over the earth's surface [1]. It follows no defined course or channel and forms no more definite body of water than a bog or marsh [1]. Water loses its character as diffused surface water when it reaches a well-defined channel. In law, diffused surface water is analogized to a wild animal and the "law of capture" is applied to it. "Diffused surface water may be captured by the owner of the land over which it moves, and when captured becomes the property of the landowner" [1]. Unlike water in watercourses, diffused surface water is almost never subject to state permit programs [2]. The reason for this diffused surface water rule is public policy encouraging agricultural impoundment and use [2]. Most legal problems involving diffused surface water arise when a landowner tries to get rid of it. "Drainage law" is covered later in this chapter.

Water in Watercourses

The term "watercourse" generally includes all surface waters contained within definite banks. A watercourse may be running water, such as a creek or river, or a body of still or flat water, typically a lake or pond [3]. In some states, floodwaters which have become permanently severed from the main current when waters recede are treated as diffused surface water, capturable by the landowner, and not water in a watercourse, subject to public water rights. Other states consider all floodwater as diffused surface water [1]. Courts are also sharply divided on how to classify springs, categorizing them variously as diffused surface water, groundwater, or part of a watercourse depending on the facts of each case and the legal rule applicable in a specific state [3]. The same is true with regard to the legal classification of marshes and swamps [3]. It is possible that the same hydrologic swamp located in three different states will be classified in three different ways and subjected to three different legal rules.

Courts frequently distinguish watercourses from diffused surface waters by declaring that watercourses are characterized by regular flow and defined channels. But in many states, especially in the west, intermittent streams have been held to be watercourses [3]. The "defined channel" test appears to be a more reliable one. Artificial watercourses (impoundments, artificial channels) are governed by different legal rules than natural watercourses.

GROUNDWATER CATEGORIES

It is inaccurate and confusing to distinguish among subflows (underflows) of surface watercourses, underground streams, and percolating groundwater. But courts continue to make these distinctions, and important legal consequences depend on them.

Subflow of Surface Streams

This category refers to the saturated zone directly beneath and supporting a river or lake in direct contact with surface water. Where subflow can be identified, it is considered as part of the watercourse itself [4].

Underground Streams

An underground stream is defined as water that passes through or under the surface in a definite channel [1]. In water law a subterranean stream is treated as a surface watercourse. There is a legal presumption against groundwater being an underground stream: that is, a claimant must produce convincing evidence that underground water flows in a definite and known channel, and does not "percolate" as in an aquifer [5]. This evidence might include surface vegetation along its course, test borings, sounds of the water, geologic data, or interconnections with surface streams.

Percolating Waters

These include all waters that pass through the ground beneath the surface of the earth without a definite channel and groundwaters that are not shown to be directly connected to surface water. Percolating waters come from precipitation that infiltrates the soil, streamflow from losing streams, irrigation return flow, or artificial recharge [5]. Storage of percolating waters may be in unconfined (water table) or confined (artesian) aquifers [5]. Rivulets and veins of water within an aquifer are not underground streams but percolating water. In many states, water rights in surface watercourses and underground streams are determined on radically different legal principles than rights in percolating waters.

The state of Colorado makes a further distinction between "tributary" and "nontributary" percolating waters. Groundwater that will eventually reach and become part of a natural stream, either surface or subterranean, is treated as part of that stream for legal purposes (i.e., governed by the rules applied to surface watercourses) [6].

OTHER CATEGORIES

Wastewater

Alternately referred to as "seepage," "leakage," or "artificial water," these are waters which, in the words of a New Mexico statute, are "due to escape,

seepage, loss, waste, drainage, or percolation from constructed works, either directly or indirectly, and which depend for their continuance upon the
acts of man" [1]. Seepage from reservoirs and irrigation ditches as well as
discharges from treatment works are examples of wastewater. Irrigation
return flow ("tail water") is a particular kind of wastewater that is sometimes
subject to different legal rules. The major diversion and distribution law
problem involving wastewater is whether it belongs to the person who
releases it or a downstream, or underground, rightholder.

Foreign Water

This is water that has been imported by a user from one watershed into
another [1]. It will be seen that interbasin transfers of water have caused many
legal problems. Rights to seepage and return flow from foreign water can
also be troublesome.

Storage Water

Impoundment of water is becoming increasingly important for irrigation,
recreational, hydroelectric, and municipal uses. Legal problems include
liability for negligent storage, the question of storage rights versus direct-
flow rights, and the need for environmental impact statements.

Salvage Water

Salvage water is water saved by conservation practices that would otherwise have been lost to seepage or evaporation [1]. Conservation has been
impeded in the west by rules that make water saved by conservation subject
to use by others.

Developed Water

Unlike salvage water, which would naturally be part of a watercourse,
developed water is "new water" made available by human effort. Drainage
into a stream of a mine or wetland are examples of developed water [1].

Chapter 2
WATER DIVERSION DOCTRINES: THE RIPARIAN SYSTEM

The term "riparian," used as an adjective, means "of, pertaining to, or situated or dwelling on the bank of a river or other body of water"[7]. Thus we speak of riparian homes or riparian lands. Used as a noun it refers to one who owns land on the bank of a natural watercourse. A riparian right is one held by a riparian, and the riparian system (or riparianism) is the legal and administrative apparatus for enforcing riparian rights. The riparian system is found in all eastern states except Mississippi, and the prior appropriation system prevails in the west. However, riparian rights also coexist with appropriative rights in those western states that follow the "California doctrine."

The key to understanding the riparian doctrine is to recognize that riparian rights arise only from the ownership of riparian land. Thus, in pure riparian states water from streams and lakes may be diverted only by persons owning land adjacent to these bodies of water. Pertaining exclusively to natural watercourses, riparian rights do not attach to diffused surface waters or on artificial waterbodies [8], although they may attach to artificial channels of natural watercourses [3]. There is some question about whether downstream riparians have rights to "artificial flow" from reservoirs.

As inherited from the common law, riparian rights were originally defined by the "natural flow doctrine": each riparian owner was entitled to have a stream flow through his land in its natural condition, not materially retarded, diminished, or polluted by others [8]. The so-called natural uses of

7

water (domestic bathing, drinking, gardening, and household stock-watering) were unlimited. But major "artificial uses" (irrigation, manufacturing, power generation, mining, and stockwatering) were restricted to the mouths of waterways [8]. A lower riparian owner could play "dog in the manger"—not using the water but depriving upstream owners of its use by insisting on the maintenance of natural flow [8]. Because it was inherently antidevelopment, the natural flow doctrine has generally been replaced by the "reasonable use rule."

Under the reasonable use rule, every riparian owner has a privilege to use the water for any beneficial purpose if the intended use is reasonable with respect to other riparians, i.e., does not unreasonably interfere with their legitimate uses [8]. Thus, riparian rights on a watercourse are said to be "correlative," mutually interdependent and not merely based on benefit to a single user. Whether a use is reasonable is a question of fact to be resolved by courts on a case-by-case basis. Various factors may be considered, including climate, season of the year, local custom, size of diversion, velocity and capacity of the watercourse, consumptive or nonconsumptive use, place and method of diversion, type of use and its importance to society, and reasonable needs of other riparians [8]. The reasonableness of a particular use may also be affected by its location on the stream. "The riparian owner at its mouth may capture all he can, while the uppermost riparian must consider the needs of downstream users" [8].

As in many fields of human endeavor, there are disparities between the theory and practice of riparianism. For example, since riparian rights are based on comparative reasonableness it is thought to be a rule of riparianism that in times of shortage some uses, otherwise beneficial, may be deemed unreasonable under the circumstances and prohibited. Moreover, since riparian rights, arising as they do from riparian land ownership, are supposedly unaffected by use or nonuse of water, temporal priority of use ought not to be considered in determining reasonableness. In theory, a new consumptive use may displace an old one. But Professor Davis has pointed out that during periods of water shortage courts do not actually reallocate water among consumptive users, but expect consumptive users to share the burden of shortage proportionately, subject to a practical preference for prior consumptive users [2]. As Professor Trelease tells us, "Almost without exception, in every case in which a riparian plaintiff has been using water by diverting or impounding it for a reasonable beneficial use and a riparian defendant began a new upstream use that took the water supply of the plaintiff, the use has been called unreasonable and the defendant has been enjoined or made to pay damages" [9]. Davis's "functional analysis" reveals that during drought periods courts in riparian states appear to decide cases as follows: (1) There is a preference for nonconsumptive as against consumptive uses (upper consumptive users must allow a minimum flow for lower nonconsumptive users). (2) Between nonconsumptive users, e.g., upstream storage versus downstream recreation, a minimum flow principle serves as a standard for resolving disputes. (3) Among competing consumers there is proportionate sharing and a preference for priority of investment as against new uses. (4) "Natural" consumptive uses are preferred to "artificial" ones, but municipal suppliers cannot take advantage of the domestic preference. (5) Some riparian states accord preferences to agriculture and mining [2].

Nonriparians generally cannot exercise riparian rights. In most riparian states water rights are not transferrable apart from riparian land, although a few states have allowed water rights to be severed from the land and sold independently [2]. The general rule is that a riparian cannot use water on nonriparian land, even his own land [8]. In other states this is not an outright prohibition but depends on evidence of injury to downstream riparians [8]. A number of states also have restrictions on the extent of connected land which may be benefited by the use of water. For example, some states have adopted the rule that water cannot be used outside of a watershed, even where it is part of a single tract bordering a watercourse [8]. The "watershed limitation" is a rare example of law conforming to geohydrology.

Theoretically, a municipality cannot divert water off riparian land for purposes of domestic water supply even where it owns riparian property [2]. However, legislatures normally give municipalities the power to acquire water rights by eminent domain, and once water rights are acquired municipalities may sell water to nonriparians and are not bound by watershed limitations. *Privately owned* water companies diverting water for public sale have been given water rights under the doctrine of "prescriptive rights" [2]. A prescriptive right to water arises when a nonriparian or riparian uses water, to which he is not legally entitled, as if it were his own. The adverse use must be open and continuous for a period of time fixed by statute, often fifteen years, in order to become a prescriptive right [8]. The true owner can terminate the adverse use by suing to stop it before the prescriptive period expires. In order to establish a prescriptive right the riparian owner must be capable of recognizing that his rights have been invaded, and so prescriptive rights do not run upstream. One reason for the decline of prescriptive water rights is that modern state legislatures also give private water companies powers of eminent domain [2].

The riparian system favors flexibility over security. By and large it has worked well in the humid, water-rich eastern states. But during shortages the riparian system suffers from grave disadvantages. In theory, a use that is initiated under a particular flow regime may be adjudged unreasonable during a drought period or when new upstream uses are begun. More realistically, a consumptive user may be required to share the burden of drought and reduce water use proportionately, or be allocated a smaller share than a preexisting user. Neither outcome is economically optimal nor does either create the climate of security needed to stimulate investment. Moreover, allocation decisions in pure riparian states are made by the courts, an institution lacking the expertise and administrative continuity to ensure a predictable diversion rights system. Court decisions on water rights are ad hoc and preclude comprehensive record keeping and water supply planning. As a result, eastern states, beset by drought and increasing demands for water, have moved toward permit programs that add a measure of security but retain some of the flexibility of riparianism.

Chapter 3
WATER DIVERSION DOCTRINES: EASTERN PERMIT SYSTEMS

About a dozen eastern states regulate consumptive uses with permit systems [8]. Eastern permit systems differ greatly: some cover groundwater and surface water; others, one or the other. In some the state itself administers the program; in others the responsibility is delegated to counties or management districts. Some programs cover the entire state; others require permits only in areas where water shortages exist [8]. It would be impossible to analyze here all the eastern permit statutes. However, it will assist the reader if he considers the National Water Commission's recommended permit statute and evaluates the recently enacted New Jersey Water Supply Management Act against this standard. He can then compare his state permit statute to the recommended NWC statute and the New Jersey act.

The National Water Commission (NWC) was a prestigious panel established by an act of Congress and appointed by the president, with a mandate to review present and anticipated national water resource problems and to report its findings and recommendations to Congress and the president. The NWC's final report, issued in 1973 and entitled *Water Policies for the Future*, recommended that all eastern states adopt legislation enabling state administrative agencies to implement permit programs wherever and whenever necessary [10]. The following list compares the NWC's suggested permit system to the New Jersey Water Supply Management Act (1981) [11].

NWC Recommendations	*New Jersey Water Supply Management Act*
1. The permit system should apply to withdrawals existing at the time the legislation is enacted as well as to future withdrawals.	Applies to both existing and future withdrawals.
2. The permit system should apply to withdrawals of groundwater as well as surface water, whether or not the supplies are interrelated.	Applies to diversions of more than 100,000 gallons per day of groundwater or surface water.
3. Any person should be eligible to receive a permit for use of water at any location. Riparian restrictions on who may use water at what locations should be abolished.	Abolishes riparian restrictions.
4. Permit applications should provide comprehensive information.	New Jersey Department of Environmental Protection (NJDEP) can set application requirements by regulation.
5. After enactment of legislation, no new withdrawal should be allowed unless a permit has been issued; existing withdrawals should be subject to termination unless a permit has been issued for them within a stated period of time.	Future diversions of more than 100,000 gallons per day are required to be permitted. Agricultural diverters require a "water usage certificate" rather than a formal diversion permit. Permits existing under prior law are automatically continued subject to NJDEP power to "limit . . . to the extent currently exercised, subject to contract, or reasonably required for demonstrated future need." Unpermitted diverters claiming "grandfather rights" (uses in effect when the statute was enacted) must renew their rights by applying for a permit or certification within six months or lose their rights.
6. Permits should be subject to cancellation for prolonged nonuse and to modification for prolonged underuse.	Permits are terminable, after a hearing, in the public interest.

NWC Recommendations	*New Jersey Water Supply Management Act*
7. State agencies should be delegated authority to set and maintain minimum flows for surface streams and minimum water levels for lakes.	NJDEP has authority to maintain minimum levels and flows. Repeals prior statute requiring flows to be maintained at the average of minimum daily flows for each of the five lowest years during the previous twenty years.
8. During periods of shortage, water should be allocated as follows: (1) postenactment users should be curtailed in inverse order of their permits (i.e., prior appropriation); (2) if the shortage remains, preenactment users should be curtailed pro rata according to rate of use (i.e., share burden of shortage); (3) preenactment permittees should be curtailed when necessary to preserve essential minimum flows.	Does not provide a scheme for allocating water during shortages. NJDEP has the power to reallocate water during a state of water emergency, but only "based on fair compensation."
9. Permits should be made transferrable subject to administrative restriction.	Permits transferrable with consent of NJDEP, but only for an identical use of water.
10. Permits should be for limited terms with automatic renewal except for water reallocated for a higher public purpose.	No fixed term for permits.

The major weakness of the New Jersey statute is its exemptions for agricultural and small (under 100,000 gallons per day) diverters. Most other eastern permit statutes contain similar exemptions. New Jersey's automatic permitting of presently used grandfather diversions is constitutionally necessary unless compensation is paid [8]. However, New Jersey's requiring compensation for reallocations of water during droughts is constitutionally gratuitous and severely inhibits the state's ability to respond to drought emergencies. It is no answer that NJDEP has the power to cancel permits in the public interest, because of constitutional and political problems involved with permit cancellations. Moreover, the absence of a statutory permit duration also diminishes state flexibility in planning for and dealing with water shortages.

Like other eastern permit states, New Jersey lacks statutory directives for allocating water during shortages. Marketplace solutions are impeded because diversion permits in New Jersey are only transferrable for identical uses with administrative approval. Thus, in New Jersey, the heavy burden of making emergency allocations falls on an administrative agency—NJDEP. In other eastern states it is the courts that must perform this function. Neither is a substitute for legislative specification of emergency priorities. It may be, as Meyers and Tarlock argue, that "Eastern permit systems function less to allocate water than to provide systematic information for state water planning" [12].

The relationships between eastern permit systems and the common law diversion rights upon which permit systems have been superimposed will undoubtedly give rise to litigation. An example is *Village of Tequesta* v. *Jupiter Inlet Corp.* [13], decided by the Florida Supreme Court in 1978.

Jupiter owned property near Tequesta on which it planned to build a 120-unit condominium project. This property was located approximately 1,200 feet from Tequesta's well field. Tequesta's wells, 75—90 feet deep, pumped in excess of a million gallons of water a day from the shallow aquifer to supply Tequesta residents with water. As a result of Tequesta's withdrawals, salt water intruded into the shallow aquifer. Jupiter was forced to drill a well to the Floridian aquifer located 1,200 feet below the surface. Of course, Jupiter's drilling and pumping costs were much greater than they would have been had Tequesta's pumping not caused contamination of the shallow aquifer.

Jupiter sued Tequesta for taking its property without just compensation. The Florida Supreme Court decided in favor of Tequesta, holding that Jupiter had no legal right to use the water beneath its land; that is, Jupiter possessed no property that Tequesta could have taken. According to the court, the Florida Water Resources Act [13], requiring diversion permits, replaced the system of common law rights that preceded it. The act provided that a common law water right would terminate unless converted into a permit water right within two years after its passage. Tequesta had perfected its water right by acquiring a permit in timely fashion, while Jupiter had lost its unexercised common law right by not filing for a permit in time. Thus, Jupiter had no water rights as against Tequesta, a permittee.

The *Tequesta* case also illustrates the problems that perfected grandfather rights may cause in eastern permit states. Tequesta was granted a permit for its current diversions even though overpumping was endangering the shallow aquifer. Like most eastern diversion permit statutes, the Florida act does not adequately address the interactions between water quantity and quality.

Chapter 4

WATER DIVERSION DOCTRINES: PRIOR APPROPRIATION

The appropriation doctrine is a water allocation system that developed as an adaptation to conditions in the western United States. In the west, the first major users of water were the gold and silver miners on federal land who quickly recognized that there was not enough water for all potential users [14]. Unaware of other legal approaches, they applied the same principle to their water as they did to their mines, that the person who first discovered a mine was protected against all later claimants [14]. This became the cornerstone of the appropriation doctrine under the proverb, "First in time is first in right."

However, the abandonment of riparian rights in favor of the appropriation doctrine was not uniform throughout the west. Riparian theories of diversion and distribution were ignored entirely in the eight more arid states (Colorado, Arizona, Idaho, Montana, Nevada, New Mexico, Utah, and Wyoming). These are generally referred to as "Colorado doctrine" states [15]. In these states, the appropriation doctrine has always been recognized as the exclusive means by which the right to divert may be acquired. However, in the generally less arid states east and west of the Colorado doctrine bloc (California, Kansas, Nebraska, North Dakota, Oklahoma, Oregon, South Dakota, Texas, and Washington), the riparian doctrine was recognized in greater or lesser degree along with prior appropriation [15].

Over the years, these California doctrine states have tended to limit unused riparian rights and integrate remaining riparians into their permit systems [16]. New diversion rights can only be obtained by appropriation and permit. Alaska qualifies as a Colorado doctrine state; Hawaii possesses a unique system based on local customary law.

The general principles of appropriationism apply in both Colorado and California doctrine states. After the principle of priority in time, the second major principle of the appropriation doctrine is that "beneficial use shall be the basis, measure, and limit to the use of water" [17]. The interplay of these two principles explains the four major differences between appropriationism and riparianism.

First, since appropriation rights are based on priority of beneficial use, not on ownership of riparian land, anyone can acquire an appropriative right for use at any location. Realistically, appropriative rights are limited only by the economics of applying water from a particular source for use in a particular place.

Second, an appropriative right exists for a definite amount of water [14] and is not correlative with other diversion rights. If an appropriator can make beneficial use of all unappropriated water in a watercourse, he can lawfully appropriate the entire quantity unless the state imposes a "minimum flow" restriction. When a water shortage occurs the burden falls on "junior appropriators" (later diverters): they are closed down completely in inverse order of priority, i.e., the latest allocation granted is the first to be closed [14]. There is no sharing the burden of shortage as in riparianism, nor do appropriative rights exist unless they are exercised. The "senior appropriators" are never closed down unless the watercourse virtually dries up. The term "senior appropriator" refers to order of temporal priority, not to location; it is possible to be either an "upstream senior" or a "downstream senior." A senior appropriator may take water needed by a junior appropriator below him, while the junior appropriator must permit the water to flow past his headgate if needed by a downstream senior.

Third, an appropriative diversion right, being separate from land ownership, is in almost all western states transferrable to a different holder, a different place, and to a new or different use [17]. Moreover, the present holder is legally entitled to change the nature of use, place of use, point of diversion, or method of diversion [17]. However, state administrative agencies will not allow transfers or changes unless junior water rights in return flow are protected [17]. An example of this point is provided by Meyers and Tarlock [12]:

> Suppose A Canal Co. obtained an appropriative right on Clear River in 1867 to divert 20 second feet of water during a growing season of 120 days. . . . Thereafter, B Canal Co., knowing these facts, obtains a right for its down-

stream ditch to 10 second feet. Though B does not know it, 10 second feet returns to the stream from A's diversion, and this return flow enters the stream above B's headgate. A proposes to sell his water right to Central City, which plans to move the point of diversion to an intake below B's canal. If A can move all 20 second feet, B will have no water supply when the flow of the river at A's old point of diversion is just 20 second feet. Central City could require the 20 second feet to by-pass B's headgate, thus depriving B of the return flow from the old diversion. Such a transfer is not permitted; only A's consumptive use of 10 c.f.s. may be transferred, leaving 10 second feet to substitute for the return flow.

Transfers of western water rights are also limited by inadequate records and restrictions on transfer of water from federal reclamation projects (roughly half the water in the west).

Finally, an appropriative water right is of indefinite duration as long as it is used in accordance with the law [14]. However, unlike a riparian right, an appropriative right can be lost through nonuse because its legal existence was created by actual use only [17]. An appropriative right can be lost by abandonment, forfeiture, or prescription. Should a rightholder not use his right, or part of it, for a statutory period of time, and intend not to use it, his water right may be lost by abandonment in a proceeding brought by the state or a junior appropriator. Intent is the key to abandonment [18]. Forfeiture is a statutory remedy for nonuse and only requires a showing of nonuse for a specific period, usually three to five years [18]. No intent need be proved apart from actual nonuse. Both riparian and appropriative rights may be lost by prescription. Prescription depends more on an adverse use than on nonuse by the rightholder. But prescription is as disfavored in western water law as it is in the east [18]. Condemnation of water diversion rights is permitted by statute in appropriation as well as riparian states.

Appropriative rights depend on beneficial use, but what is a beneficial use? Although state statutes and court decisions identify some beneficial uses, the term is operational and must be tested in each case [17]. In the past there has been a marked economic element to beneficial use; domestic, municipal, irrigation, stockwatering, power generation, mining, and milling uses have been paramount. But in recent years recreation, scenic beauty, and ecological protection have been recognized as beneficial uses [17]. For example, in 1974 the Idaho legislature directed the Department of Parks to appropriate certain unappropriated waters of Malod Canyon to maintain instream flows, declaring that "the preservation of the water for scenic beauty and recreation uses is a beneficial use of water." The Idaho Supreme Court upheld the statute against a claim that it was unconstitutional to appropriate water without an actual physical diversion [20]. Generally, actual diversion and application to a beneficial use is necessary to perfect an appropriative

right. Storage of water for future uses has long been considered a beneficial use, although storage and delayed use cannot impair the rights of
other appropriators [17].

In theory, no appropriative right attaches to water in excess of the
quantity used benefically. But waste of water is a significant problem in the
west, especially where irrigation is concerned [21]. Hutchins quotes a reclamation engineer of many years experience to the effect that "padding" and
"pyramiding" water rights—creating records of rights in excess of actual
beneficial use and filing and maintaining in good standing applications to
appropriate more water than is required for a particular purpose—have been
commonplace in appropriation states [19]. Padding and pyramiding have
been tolerated, in part, because the criterion for beneficial use has been
inefficient local irrigation practices. Moreover, in some western states salvage water is subject to appropriation by the public [19]; it cannot be reused
by the one who conserves it. Combined with the possibility of forfeiting
unused water and the requirement that downstream appropriators of irrigation return flow must be protected, the rule against use of salvage water by
the conserver has done little to discourage waste. Why invest capital to save
water that will benefit others?

States have refined the concept of beneficial use to combat waste. One
of the earliest of these attempts was the "duty of water" statutes [17]. "Duty
of water" is defined as the quantity of water essential to the irrigation of any
given tract of land. Many western states enacted statutes prescribing
maximum quantities per acre that may be appropriated for irrigation purposes, expressed in cubic feet per second for direct use and acre-feet for
storage and subsequent use [17]. Duties of water, based on local custom,
have been set at inordinately high levels. Moreover, some appropriators
who did not need the maximum quantity have been awarded it anyway,
while others who actually required more than the maximum have been
precluded from obtaining it. Some western states are moving toward more
flexible duties of water. New Mexico, for example, defines it as an amount
"diverted at a rate consistent with good agricultural practices and which will
result in the most effective use of available water to prevent waste" [22].

More important in preventing waste is the concept of "reasonable
beneficial use." The California Constitution makes reasonable beneficial use
the limit of every stream water right, and reasonableness of use is playing an
increasingly important role in other appropriation states [18]. The element
of reasonableness in western water law does not connote, as it does in
riparian states, a correlative and therefore uncertain right to use water.
Reasonableness in the west means, in the words of a Texas statute defining
beneficial use, "the use of such a quantity of water, when reasonable
intelligence and reasonable diligence are exercised in its application for a
lawful purpose, as is economically necessary for the use" [23]. The arbiters of

reasonableness in the west are generally state administrators who possess broad discretion to grant, deny, or condition new diversion permits in the public interest [19]. Negotiations aimed at eliminating waste are becoming an integral part of the permitting process. Results may include permitting diversions of different amounts at different times of year. Rarely do courts become involved. Even when they do, a fundamental principle of administrative law is that an administrative decision will not be overturned unless it is a violation of statute, a deprivation of constitutional rights, or "arbitrary and capricious" (clearly irrational or based on an inadequate record). A court will ordinarily not substitute its judgments for those of an administrator, especially where a legislature has delegated discretionary judgments to administrators based on their presumed expertise [24].

"Preferred uses" are pronounced by statutes and state constitutions to be more beneficial than other uses. One effect of a water right being preferred is that in times of shortage a preferred use may condemn a nonpreferred use in order to supply water for the higher use, regardless of temporal priority of diversion. When a preference is exercised, all or part of a nonpreferred right may be taken temporarily or permanently [18]. However, compensation must be paid for taking a water right. Another function of legislatively established preferences is that they serve as criteria for the allocating agency when rival applicants are competing for the same unappropriated water for different uses [18]. This legislative system of setting social priorities is, as has been seen, missing in eastern permit states.

The order of preference may vary among states, but normally the ranking is (1) domestic use; (2) agricultural use; (3) industrial and power use; (4) fish, wildlife, and recreation uses [18]. There is an obvious bias in favor of domestic and economic uses as against ecological and recreational uses. This emphasizes the need for state minimum flow legislation.

Many western states have adopted comprehensive "water codes" setting up procedures for (1) approving appropriations of water; (2) determining or adjudicating water rights among conflicting claimants; and (3) administering water rights and distributing water [19]. "Not all states that have administrative systems include all three functions" [19].

The first step in obtaining an appropriative water right is to file an application with the state water official, normally the state engineer [19]. In several states there are steps that can be taken in advance of filing the application, e.g., "notice of intention" in New Mexico, designed to give a prospective applicant time to make investigations, while holding priority of filing, before finalizing the application. If a supply of unappropriated water is available, the state engineer publishes a public notice to provide an opportunity for protestors to be heard [17]. Protest proceedings may be especially complicated in the California doctrine states of California and Texas where riparian rights are still of major significance [16]. Where the

proposed use is in conflict with prior diversion rights, a menace to public
welfare, or against the public interest, the state engineer may reject the
application [17]. Wasteful uses may be rejected at this stage.

If protests are resolved favorably to the applicant, and the use is
reasonable and beneficial, the applicant will then receive a permit to proceed
with the project [19]. Colorado is the only western state, apart from Hawaii,
where a permit is not necessary for a diversion. In Colorado, the required
filing of maps and construction plans is merely informational [17]. Every-
where else the permit specifies the approved project and stipulates that
construction must proceed with reasonable diligence and be completed
within a reasonable time, generally five years unless circumstances justify
an extension [17]. In most western states a permittee is granted the power of
eminent domain to take private land for his right of way for ditches [25].
Except for instream uses, the appropriation is incomplete until water has
actually been diverted and applied to a beneficial use [17]. When the permitted diversion is finished, the water right, in the form of a document called a
"license," "certificate of appropriation," or "water right certificate," is issued [19]. This document "relates back," for purposes of priority, to the date
of application or notice of intention [17]. In summary, statutory permit
systems for appropriating water exist throughout the west except for Colorado. They are the exclusive means of acquiring new diversion rights in
these states [19].

Statutes of all nineteen western states contain some kind of special
procedure for adjudicating water rights [19]. Adjudication is the formal
process of settling, describing, and recording diversion rights. An adjudication results in a decree specifying the amounts and priorities of diversions
on a watercourse. These procedures are not uniform among the states, but
three general models can be identified [17].

1. Private litigation between two or more water rights claimants or
    users. No participation by state officials is contemplated.
2. Proceedings under statutes designed to permit or encourage offi-
    cial participation in private actions. The purpose of these statutes
    is to adjudicate as many rights as possible in fewer lawsuits. A
    court may be permitted to convert a private suit among a few
    individuals into a complete adjudication of a watercourse, using
    the expertise of state officials.
3. Proceedings under comprehensive legislation authorizing either
    state action or petition of water rightholders to adjudicate an entire
    watercourse.

Courts and administrative agencies play different roles in these proceedings
depending upon the state. In Colorado the proceeding is purely judicial,
with a separate judicial apparatus (water judges, water clerks, special engi-

neers, and referees) to deal with water rights conflicts [19]. Wyoming is at the opposite pole: administrative determination is final, subject to limited judicial review [19]. Other western states utilize their own combinations and variations of these approaches. In California doctrine states differences exist with respect to the adjudication of unused riparian rights. Where a watercourse has not been adjudicated, water rights administration is subject to confusion and contention.

Once a watercourse has been adjudicated, how are the complicated determinations to be enforced? Statutory procedures for administration of water rights are in effect throughout the west [19]. In some states supervision by administrative officials goes beyond adjudicated rights and extends to unadjudicated rights evidenced by permits, licenses, or certificates of appropriation [19]. State water officials are also called upon to enforce rotation plans imposed by contract or court decree [25]. Rotation is a means of enhancing the efficiency of irrigation by giving an irrigator a large quantity of water over a short period of time rather than a lesser amount, to which he holds a right, for a longer time. Under a rotation schedule, each user is entitled to divert the entire flow of the stream for a period computed by the ratio which his appropriative right bears to all rights involved in the schedule [25]. Although an apparent departure from strict appropriative allocation, rotation is approved by legislation in many western states [25].

Some western states create water-supervision divisions or districts and provide for enforcement agencies [19]. Others authorize the state engineer to create districts where necessary. Methods of selecting watermasters, commissioners, or patrolmen, as they are variously termed, and of allocating costs of supervision, vary among states [19]. Watermasters regulate diversions from a watercourse, opening and closing headgates according to detailed schedules of priority [19]. They also have power to make arrests for tampering with legally controlled headgates [19].

Early constitutional and statutory provisions in the west declared that all unappropriated flows of surface water in watercourses were subject to appropriation [16]. A strict interpretation of this language explains why some western states do not permit percolating groundwater to be appropriated. Diffused surface water is not available for appropriation before it reaches a watercourse. Diversion rights to spring water have been as troublesome in the west as in the east, and a number of western states have enacted statutes dealing with spring water [16]. In California, where riparian rights are valuable, the law excludes from appropriation water which is "reasonably needed for useful and beneficial purposes on lands riparian thereto" [26].

It has been pointed out that where irrigation return flows are concerned, junior appropriators have legal rights in the continuation of stream conditions that existed at the time of their respective appropriations; they may later resist all proposed sales of rights and changes in points of diversion and uses of water by upstream irrigators that would injure them. Once again, in many western states salvage water is immediately subject to appropriation, and the salvagor cannot reuse it. Wastewater and return flows from foreign and developed water are treated quite differently. The "generator" of these waters may use, reuse, use for a different purpose, or dispose of the waters until he abandons them without intent to recapture. Once these waters pass from the generator's land or reach a natural watercourse they are presumed to be abandoned and become subject to appropriation. States differ as to whether these flows are governed by the existing priority system, constitute "new water" belonging to the first appropriator, or must be allocated among all users. However, in contrast to irrigation return flows, downstream appropriators have no rights to the continuation of waste discharges or return flows from foreign or developed water, and the generator can discontinue these flows at any time.

The reader can be no more confused by these categories of water than judges and attorneys are. There is much harm and little good in distinctions between irrigation return flow and irrigation seepage, and between salvage water and wastewater.

In order to promote water conservation and prevent flooding, legislatures and courts both east and west encourage impoundment of high flows. Riparian rights ordinarily extend only to normal stream flows; impounders retain control of increased stream volumes and may charge downstream riparians for them [27]. In the west, storage of water for a beneficial use is itself a beneficial use.

Western states handle the appropriation of storage water in different ways [25]. One method makes no distinction between direct flow and storage rights, integrating them as steps in the acquisition of a single appropriative right. In these states the procedures of diverting, impounding, distributing, and applying the water to beneficial use are simply phases of one complete administrative procedure. Another method deals with diversion for storage and distribution of stored water as separate segments of an overall plan and provides separate but complementary procedures in the form of "primary" and "secondary" permits. The final certificate of appropriation, however, applies to the entire project. In a few states entirely different appropriations are involved. Whatever the administrative system for appropriating storage water, it is true throughout the west that priorities on a stream system are determined on the basis of temporal priority of appropriation, regardless of whether appropriations are direct flow, storage, or both [25]. Nor is there a preference for on-channel or off-channel storage. A number of western states also make provision for storing water in natural lakes and underground, as long as the rights of prior appropriators of water from these sources are protected [25].

Although impoundment is a reasonable, beneficial use, impounders must be careful or risk liability to others. For example, an impounder cannot reduce downstream flows so as to damage downstream senior appropriators or riparians. During drought periods, even junior appropriators are sometimes protected by decrees ordering the release of upstream stored water. Liability of an impounder for damage caused by increasing the volume or velocity of flow is discussed in Chapter 8.

Chapter 5
GROUNDWATER DOCTRINES AND PROBLEMS

Five legal doctrines govern conflicts in different states among competing consumers of groundwater: (1) the rule of absolute ownership; (2) the reasonable use rule; (3) the correlative rights rule; (4) prior appropriation; and (5) the restatement of torts rule.

ABSOLUTE OWNERSHIP

This rule creates an absolute right in each landowner to pump groundwater under his land for use at any location without bearing any responsibility to neighboring owners [28]. Where there is competition for diminishing ground-water reserves, "the biggest pump wins." The doctrine of absolute owner-ship is based on an outdated assumption—the movement of groundwater is unknowable and unpredictable; thus a landowner, who is legally entitled to everything below the surface of his property, may use this property as he wishes because the law does not impose responsibility for unforeseeable consequences [28]. Waste is not prohibited under the absolute ownership rule. Absolute ownership of groundwater is the law in approximately ten states, all in the east except for Texas. Each of these states applies a different legal rule to surface water diversions.

REASONABLE USE

To compound the confusion, the reasonable use rule as applied to ground-water is not the same as the reasonable use rule as applied to surface water. Under the rubric of reasonable use, courts deciding surface water disputes announce a theory of comparative reasonableness (less reasonable uses may be cut back during shortages) but in fact impose proportional sharing with a preference for prior users. In groundwater, law courts also talk about comparative reasonableness, but in practice reasonable use of groundwater is the same as absolute ownership with two exceptions: (1) waste is prohibited, and (2) water must be used on overlying land unless it can be used (e.g., sold) elsewhere without injuring other overlying owners [28]. A groundwater pumper, in a reasonable use state, may use all the water he can pump as long as it is used on overlying land without waste. There is no proportional sharing among overlying owners as there is among riparian owners on surface watercourses. Nor does there appear to be a practical preference for prior users under the reasonable use doctrine of groundwater law. Once again, in most instances the biggest pump wins. Although the reasonable use rule discriminates against water transporters, water purveyors can purchase or condemn groundwater rights for off-site use [29]. About a dozen states, all eastern states except for Arizona, adhere to the reasonable use rule in groundwater allocation.

CORRELATIVE RIGHTS

The correlative rights rule originated in California, which has followed a mixture of riparian and appropriation surface water law. In adjudicating the rights of groundwater users, the California Supreme Court determined that in times of shortage: (1) overlying owners are entitled to no more than their "fair and just proportion" for on-site uses; (2) as between transporters out of the basin, first in time is first in right; and (3) overlying users have priority over transporters [30]. The correlative rights rule departs sharply from absolute ownership and reasonable use because it prorates water among overlying owner-users. Correlative rights is a rule of comparative reasonableness. The reasonableness of each overlying use is determined by comparing the requirements of competing overlying users and deciding whose use is more beneficial and in what degree [28]. Correlative rights are not absolute but are rights to divert water subject to the reasonable needs of others and the availability of supply. What is an overlying owner-user's "fair and just proportion" must be determined in light of the facts of each case. In a 1949 California case, *Pasadena* v. *Alhambra*, the California Supreme Court ascertained "safe annual yield" of an aquifer and apportioned it among all users—both overlying users and transporters—in proportion to their uses for five preceding years [31]. This result modifies the correlative rights rule (indeed the case was decided on a different legal theory) by treating on-site and off-site users alike and by presuming that all prior uses are equally reasonable. The California Supreme Court has since restricted the *Pasadena* rule to situations where municipalities are not involved.

A number of eastern states, including Florida and New Jersey, are correlative rights groundwater states [28]. In these states the rights of overlying owners are determined under a comparative reasonableness standard. Groundwater will be prorated based on need, custom, social utility, safe yield, and other "reasonableness" factors. It is not clear how eastern correlative rights states will settle disputes between overlying users and transporters, or among transporters themselves.

PRIOR APPROPRIATION

The original western statutes making all waters of the state subject to appropriation either ignored groundwater, specifically excluded it from coverage, or referred only to surface water and water in subterranean channels [4]. Thus, some western states did, and some still do, follow the absolute ownership rule (Texas), reasonable use rule (Arizona), and correlative rights rule (California) with regard to groundwater. But there is a clear trend in the west toward including groundwater within permit systems based on prior appropriation [4]. Western states have either applied appropriation-permit rules to all groundwaters in the state or else to particular sources or controlled areas. California controls underground streams and underflow but not percolating waters; Arizona imposes controls on critical areas [4]. Only Texas and Nebraska do not apply prior appropriation to any groundwater in the state. Groundwater rights administration in the majority of western states is by state agency, even where only critical or designated areas are included within regulations. In several states, however, local districts or boards have regulatory authority [4]. Western groundwater permit systems are either included within, or are very similar to, surface water appropriation statutes.

RESTATEMENT OF TORTS RULE

"Restatements" of legal fields are formulations by legal scholars of what the law should be. They are influential in areas, such as groundwater diversion rights, where the law is in flux.

Section 858 of the *Restatement (Second Edition) of Torts* is entitled "Liability for Use of Groundwater." This section articulates a rule which is similar to the correlative rights rule in that a landowner's right to withdraw groundwater is only limited when his use unreasonably interferes with the legitimate use of another overlying owner. The restatement rule is, like the correlative rights rule, one of comparative reasonableness.

However, the restatement rule differs from the correlative rights rule in two respects. First, the restatement rule contains no preference for on-site users over transporters. "All users, whether pumping for on-site or off-site purposes, have equal rights to the groundwater" [29]. Second, the restatement sets out three criteria for determining unreasonable interference with a neighbor's use of groundwater: (1) well interference; (2) pumping in excess of one's "fair share"; and (3) interference with stream and lake levels that are dependent on groundwater.

Whether interference with nearby wells has been unreasonable and whether a pumper has exceeded his "fair share" are determined by the same tests that have evolved for evaluating the reasonableness of surface water diversions. If a court finds a particular groundwater diversion to be unreasonable, it could require the pumper to pay for deepening a neighbor's well or providing alternative water supply. Ascertaining the reasonableless of interference with stream and lake levels will entail setting minimum flows for watercourses.

According to Teresa N. Lukas [29], the restatement rule has the advantages of (1) conforming to modern hydrological principles; (2) promoting the unification of groundwater and surface water rights by "translating the riparian doctrine of reasonable use to the ground water level"; (3) making groundwater diversion rights more definite and certain; (4) protecting minimum flows in watercourses; and (5) protecting aquifers from overdrafting. These are significant advantages, although it might be argued that the preference for overlying uses should be retained in order to encourage aquifer recharge. Thus far, the restatement rule has been adopted only by Wisconsin.

WELL INTERFERENCE PROBLEMS

Well interference is becoming a significant issue throughout the United States. In policy terms, who should bear the costs of deepening wells or providing alternative water supplies, the well owner or a subsequent user who causes the water level or pressure to drop? Courts have gone both ways on this issue, with the facts of the case, not legal doctrine, generally governing the result (e.g., What are the uses involved? How much will it cost to deepen wells?). Several eastern courts have reached interesting compromise decisions: a subsequent municipal user was required to connect affected well owners to its system without cost; and a swim club was ordered to pay half of its neighbor's well-deepening costs [32]. In the west, many states have enacted statutes in this area. Montana law declares that "priority of appropriation does not include the right to prevent changes by later appropriators in the condition of water occurrence . . . or the lowering of a water table, artesian pressure or water level, if the prior appropriator can reasonably exercise his water right under the changed conditions" [33]. Other states protect reasonable groundwater levels from interference by authorizing the state engineer to deny new diversion permits that would unreasonably interfere with existing users [12].

Other kinds of statutes have also been passed to prevent well interference. In the west, well spacing or metering may be required by legislation or ordered by the courts [4]. Some western states prohibit the exportation of water from the state. (The constitutionality of these statutes is discussed in Chapter 7.) In the east, where groundwater shortages have not been as acute as in the west, well spacing and antiexportation statutes are rare. However, most eastern states require permits for development of new public water systems, licenses for well drillers, and well completion reports. Eastern states also grant state agencies extraordinary powers to restrict withdrawals during emergencies [32]. Much of the eastern legislation deals with protection of wells or aquifers from pollution by spacing of septic tanks from wells or from each other. An increasing number of eastern states have instituted statewide or areawide permit systems for groundwater withdrawals. At present these systems are informational rather than regulatory, but given increased pressure on groundwater resources, they could be used to support administrative well-spacing programs.

CONJUNCTIVE USE

Conjunctive management—the management of groundwater and surface water as a single source of supply—has been obstructed by the legal dichotomy between the two. But the law is being changed to facilitate conjunctive use. Most western states now regulate both groundwater and surface water under uniform or complementary permit systems based on prior appropriation. Moreover, the encouragement of groundwater storage of excess surface water by western water law promotes conjunctive management [21]. In the east, a few states have adopted uniform permit programs, and other states are considering such a step. With increasing knowledge about the interrelationships and interconnections between groundwater and surface water, it is inevitable that conjunctive use problems will be more prevalent in state legislatures and state courts. Lawsuits between groundwater and surface water diverters will almost certainly proliferate. Indeed, conjunctive management will be one of the most active water law fields for the rest of this century.

COMPREHENSIVE MANAGEMENT

If water resources management in the United States is to be rationalized, comprehensive management of water quantity and quality, where possible through unitary water-use permits, must become the rule rather than the exception. For both groundwater and surface water, comprehensive management of all water uses is seriously impaired by obsolete legal and administrative distinctions between quantity and quality. Water quality control is achieved through statutory federal and state discharge permit systems that take little cognizance of water quantity issues. Cooling towers, for example, evaporate large quantities of water that would be invaluable to downstream water users or instream flow maintenance. Water diversion is governed by courts applying common law principles or state administrative agencies applying state diversion permit systems. Both these modes of water allocation treat water quality impacts as secondary at best. For example, state diversion permits in areas of abundant groundwater have led to the migration of pollutants between aquifers due to the perforation of impermeable strata by wells. In most states an industrial user of process and cooling water will require two permits—one for diversion and another for discharge—that are issued by different administrative units without adequate coordination.

Chapter 6
FEDERAL AND FEDERAL-STATE DIVERSION LAW

Most water diversion law is state law. Nevertheless, several aspects of diversion law are governed by federal law or a combination of federal and state law. These areas are discussed in this and the next chapter, as well as in Part II.

FEDERAL RESERVED RIGHTS

The U.S. Supreme Court has decided that where the United States has withdrawn public land from settlement or disposal and reserved it for a specific public purpose such as an Indian reservation, national park, national forest, or the like, the federal government is presumed to have reserved enough unappropriated water to accomplish the purposes of the reservation [12]. This implied federal reservation of water rights applies both to surface water and groundwater. It takes effect on the date of the land reservation and exempts reserved waters from appropriation under state law. It is unnecessary for the federal government to perfect its reserved right by applying for a state diversion permit.

Devil's Hole, a deep cavern on federal land in Nevada containing an underground pool inhabited by a unique species of desert fish, was reserved as a national monument by presidential proclamation in 1952. In 1968 nearby ranchers, holding state appropriation permits, began pumping groundwater from the same source as Devil's Hole, reducing the water level in the underground pool and endangering its fish. The U.S. Supreme Court granted the federal government an injunction limiting pumping by the ranchers because in 1952 sufficient water had implicitly been reserved to maintain the level of the underground pool [34].

Courts have had difficulty quantifying the amounts of water included in the federal reserved rights, especially the massive amounts of water for irrigation on Indian reservations. Under the so-called McCarran Amendment [35] the federal government has consented to its reserved rights being adjudicated in state administrative or judicial proceedings that apply to entire watercourses [12]. In addition, western politicians frequently argue the need for congressional quantification of federal reserved rights in order to remove the uncertainty in western water law caused by these nebulous federal rights. Although federal reserved rights have not been a problem in the east, water shortages may cause litigation regarding federal reserved rights for military bases and national forests.

INTERSTATE WATERWAYS

Under our federal system of government each state exercises "jurisdiction" (legal control) within its borders but not outside them. Every state administers a separate system of diversion rights governing the use of water within its boundaries. But state boundary lines have been set with only partial regard to hydrology. "Much of the water used in the United States comes from sources shared by more than one State" [36]. Whenever this situation occurs, a potential interstate problem exists. For example, what are the rights of a senior appropriator in one state against an appropriator—junior in time to him—located in an upstream state? Can an upstream state divert water for municipal supply without regard for the needs of downstream states? What are the rights of neighboring states to waters of a river or lake that forms the common boundary between them?

In the late nineteenth and early twentieth centuries, interstate water rights disputes were settled by state and federal courts in the context of lawsuits between individual diverters in different states [36]. This approach was too cumbersome, both legally and administratively, to survive into an era of increasing demands on water and increasing state involvement in water resources projects. Today, the rights of individual claimants are subsumed under the rights of their states; the contending parties are states, and the results bind all citizens of those states [37]. The three methods of resolving interstate water rights controversies are: (1) litigation between states in the U.S. Supreme Court; (2) interstate compacts; and (3) congressional allocation.

Equitable Apportionment

The U.S. Supreme Court ordinarily possesses only "appellate jurisdiction": it can only decide cases on appeal from lower federal courts; but where states sue one another the Supreme Court has "original jurisdiction." Thus, the Supreme Court is the forum for judicial settlement of disputes between and among states over the apportionment of the waters of interstate streams and bodies of water. In this capacity the Supreme Court has refused to impose doctrinaire water law rules, but instead has borrowed a principle of international water law called "equitable apportionment" [36]. The Supreme Court will apportion the waters of an interstate waterway as fairly as possible under the circumstances.

Equitable apportionment is not an entirely ad hoc process of balancing the equities in particular cases. When appropriation states sue each other, equitable apportionment begins with priority of appropriation without regard to state lines [36]. But the Supreme Court will not go as far as to fix the respective priorities of the various individual users on an interstate waterway. It will award a "mass allocation" to each state, allowing the state to allot priorities to its share [36]. The Supreme Court has also deviated from strict temporal priority in protecting a viable economy based on junior appropriations in one state against underutilized senior appropriations in another state. Prior appropriation is only a guide to equitable apportionment among appropriation states [36]. It can be varied by considering facts such as climate, nature of uses, return flows, availability of storage, degree of waste and instream losses, and comparative damage to different states. Similarly, between riparian states the Supreme Court will disregard riparian law in order to make an equitable apportionment [36].

Interstate Compacts

The U.S. Supreme Court has equitably apportioned the waters of some important interstate rivers (Laramie, North Platte, and Delaware), but it has discouraged many more lawsuits for apportionment between states. The Court feels uncomfortable making legislative-type judgments based on a vague concept such as equitable apportionment. Moreover, the High Court lacks the technical resources to cope with the complicated hydrologic, economic, and sociological questions involved. There is a far better way to settle interstate diversion rights conflicts—interstate compacts.

Article I, Section 10, Clause 3 of the U.S. Constitution provides that "No State shall . . . without the consent of Congress . . . enter into any agreement or compact with another State or with a foreign power." Early in our nation's history the interstate compact with congressional consent was used to settle disputes over navigation, boundaries, and fishing rights [37]. Compacts allocating the consumptive use of interstate waters and providing for their management, including water quality, are a twentieth century phenomenon [38]. Over thirty interstate compacts dealing with various water resources problems have followed the Colorado River Compact of 1822. These interstate compacts can be categorized as (1) water allocation compacts; (2) pollution control compacts; (3) planning and flood control compacts; and (4) multipurpose regulatory compacts [38]. Only (1) and (4) are of interest to us in this chapter.

Most water allocation compacts are found in the west. All contiguous western states have entered into at least one interstate stream agreement [37]. The earliest of these simply allocated the waters of interstate river systems among the signatory states. More recent compacts both allocate water and create independent commissions to plan and monitor [38]. Some few, like the Upper Colorado River Basin Compact, give the compact commission the power to curtail use in times of shortage [37]. Multipurpose regulatory compacts, e.g., the Delaware and Susquehanna River compacts, are rare. They grant broad powers to their compact commissions in all aspects of water resources management, including the authority to allocate water among the states, to regulate withdrawals of water, and to construct projects [38]. Interstate water resources compacts vary widely with respect to compact purposes, membership and voting provisions, kinds and scope of powers conferred, funding support, and duration [38]. A number of compacts provide for nonvoting federal representation on compact commissions, while some, the so-called federal-interstate compacts, give the federal representative equal status with the state members [38]. Like equitable apportionment by Supreme Court decree, apportionment by interstate compact supersedes private diversion rights in the signatory states [37]. As on the Delaware, an interstate compact can grow out of an equitable apportionment decree.

Congressional Apportionment

This has occurred only once, with Congress apportioning the Colorado River among the three states of the Lower Colorado River Basin—Arizona, California, and Nevada—after an interstate compact had divided the river into an upper and lower basin. Optimum use of Colorado River waters is beset by legal problems, most of which are discussed by Meyers and Tarlock in their case study of the issue [12].

It is important to notice that these three methods of resolving interstate diversion rights disputes—judicial equitable apportionment, interstate compact, and congressional apportionment—have been applied almost exclusively to surface water conflicts. Only a few interstate compacts deal with groundwater at all, and these only in peripheral ways [37]. With increased dependence on groundwater and heightened danger of groundwater overdrafts and pollution, the courts, states, and Congress will be increasingly called upon to reconcile interstate claims to groundwater resources.

INTERNATIONAL WATERWAYS

International water law governing relationships between the United States and its contiguous neighbors, Canada and Mexico, consists of treaties and the "customary international law" used to interpret these treaties [39]. The federal government has the constitutional power to enter into treaties with foreign nations; the states cannot negotiate treaties [40]. Treaties into which the United States enters with other nations take precedence over state law where the two conflict [40]. Thus, where treaties apportion the waters of international and transboundary streams, states are limited in their abilities to create diversion rights. Only uses fitting within the national share of water, and within the hierarchy of uses if set by treaty, may be effectively established by states.

The power of states to create diversion rights is primarily limited, with regard to Canada, by the Boundary Waters Treaty of 1909 and the Columbia River Treaty of 1961, and with regard to Mexico, by the Rio Grande Irrigation Convention of 1906 and the Rio Grande, Colorado and Tijuana Treaty of 1944 [40]. These treaties were negotiated under the principle of equitable apportionment of international drainage basins—the cornerstone of international water law. Important institutions established by these treaties are the International Joint Commission, which regulates the use of U.S.-Canadian boundary waters, and the International Boundary and Water Commission, which supervises the allocation of Rio Grande and Colorado River water between the United States and Mexico [40].

Chapter 7
INTERBASIN AND INTERSTATE TRANSFERS

This chapter examines two legal problems that affect the allocation of diversion rights in the United States: (1) the legality of major interbasin transfers; and (2) the constitutionality of state "antiexportation" statutes.

MAJOR INTERBASIN TRANSFERS

The large interbasin transfers that have already been constructed in the United States are almost exclusively intrastate (e.g., Colorado River Aqueduct and New York City diversions from the Delaware) [41]. This reflects the tremendous impact that political boundaries have had on water resources planning and development [41]. There are, of course, legal and political problems with large intrastate diversions. For example, the "area of origin" may demand protective legislation, state laws may inhibit financing, and a state legislature may prohibit particular interbasin transfers. However, these difficulties are relatively insignificant compared to those confronting proposed interstate diversions of any magnitude.

Professor Johnson defines "major interbasin transfers" as transfers that would carry water over one or more state lines for use in a state that either (1) lies entirely outside the basin of origin, or (2) lies partly within the basin of origin but which would import substantially more water than it contributes to the basin of origin [41]. This definition covers the following proposed diversions: (1) from the Columbia River Basin to the southwest for use in

California and Arizona; (2) from the Missouri River Basin for use in Kansas, Colorado, Oklahoma, Texas, and New Mexico; (3) from the Mississippi Basin for use in West Texas and New Mexico; and (4) those diversions in the northeast, e.g., Hudson River diversion to Northern New Jersey, proposed by the U.S. Army Corps of Engineers [41]. An out-of-basin state probably lacks standing to sue in the U.S. Supreme Court for apportionment of the waters of a river lying entirely beyond its borders; thus, major interstate diversions would have to be accomplished by interstate compact or congressional allocation [41].

As a political matter, neither Congress nor the states would act affirmatively unless the area of origin consented to the transfer [41]. Since the areas of origin are in different regions of the country from the import areas, problems of protecting areas of origin are compounded. Some area-of-origin protection statutes that have worked within states might serve as models for interregional approaches [41]. One California area-of-origin statute prohibits the release of any state-appropriated water "necessary for the development of" a county of origin. Another statute gives the watershed of origin a prior right to "all the water reasonably required to adequately supply the beneficial needs of the watershed." This is known as a "right to recapture." Colorado has a statute requiring contemporaneous construction of compensatory storage dams in the area of origin so that it will be no worse off because of the diversion. Texas prohibits diversions needed to supply the reasonable future needs of the basin of origin for the next fifty years. An Oklahoma statute instructs the State Water Resources Board to reserve to the area of origin sufficient water to take care of its present and reasonable future needs.

Because of the "watershed limitation" of eastern riparian law, areas of origin in the east might be able to obtain even greater protection than their western counterparts. In 1905 when New York City sought to obtain water from the Catskill mountain area, it was forced by the state legislature to compensate the areas of origin for every conceivable claim that might arise from these projects. The city paid not only for the value of the property, buildings, and equipment actually taken, but also for business and wage losses both to riparians whose property was taken and to nonriparians in nearby areas who were adversely affected by the projects [41]. Since under riparian law diversion rights are inherent in land ownership, the proponent of a major interbasin diversion in the east would have to (1) convince the legislature in the state of origin to modify traditional watershed limitations; and (2) compensate at least the riparian owners on source rivers for their often inchoate and unrecorded riparian rights. Especially in eastern non-permit states, these barriers to major interbasin transfers would probably prove insurmountable.

STATE ANTIEXPORTATION STATUTES

These statutes form another obstacle to major interbasin transfers. At least sixteen states and the District of Columbia have statutes directly prohibiting or regulating the export of state water; other states indirectly regulate export by narrow definitions of beneficial use [42]. Some antiexportation statutes prohibit any exportation of water; others bar exportation for certain purposes. Still others allow exportation only if the recipient state allows reciprocal transfers. Until recently, the constitutionality of these statutes was doubtful. Under Article I, Section 8, the Commerce Clause of the U.S. Constitution, the federal government has the power to regulate interstate commerce and prevent a state from imposing an "undue burden" on commerce. Prior U.S. Supreme Court decisions had struck down as "economic isolationism" state prohibitions or restrictions on exportation of natural resources, e.g., minnows and minerals. Is water an "article of commerce" like these? Are antiexportation statutes inherently illegal?

These questions were answered in a 1982 Supreme Court decision concerning a Nebraska statute forbidding the export of any state water, including groundwater, unless the recipient state allowed export of its water to Nebraska [43]. First, groundwater is indeed an article of commerce subject to federal regulation and Commerce Clause analysis. The Court then went on to consider the constitutionality of the Nebraska antiexportation statute. In the first place, although antiexportation statutes are inherently illegal where other natural resources are concerned, water antiexportation statutes are not inherently illegal because of the importance of water to public health, basically a state concern, and the traditional federal deference to state water law. Because of the preferred status of state water regulation, water antiexportation statutes will be upheld if reasonable and "narrowly drawn," i.e., no broader than necessary to accomplish the purpose of the statute. For example, a Nebraska-type statute might be upheld "if it could be shown that the State as a whole suffers a water shortage, that the interstate transportation of water from areas of abundance to areas of shortage is feasible regardless of distance, and that the importation of water from adjoining States would roughly compensate for any exportation to those States." Even an absolute ban on water exportation could be upheld where "a demonstrably arid State [is] able to marshall evidence to establish a close means-end relationship between . . . a total ban on the exportation of water and a purpose to conserve water."[43]

The Nebraska statute, however, was struck down because it was too loosely drawn. Despite Nebraska's strict regulation of intrastate transfers of groundwater from critical aquifers, the Nebraska statute burdened interstate commerce because "even though the supply of water in a particular well may be abundant, or perhaps even excessive, and even though the most beneficial use of that water may be in another State, such water may not be shipped into a neighboring State that does not permit its water to be used in Nebraska" [43]. Consequently, in order to pass constitutional muster Nebraska can either redraft its statute or restrict the exportation of groundwater through its normal allocation process. Where water is concerned, a state "may favor its own citizens in times of shortage" [43].

The decision in this case will make it difficult for coal slurry pipelines and oil shale development to proceed without express federal legislation "preempting" (invalidating) state antiexportation statutes [4].

Chapter 8
DRAINAGE LAW

Drainage law consists of those principles which govern a landowner's rights to repel water at the boundaries of his land and expel it once it has entered. Consistent with the legal distinction between diffused surface water and water in watercourses, drainage law applies different rules to drainage of diffused surface water and drainage of overflow from watercourses. As previously pointed out, state courts frequently disagree about whether floodwater, springs, and swamps are diffused surface water or watercourses. Thus, a court's classification of waters will strongly affect its decision about drainage rights as well as rights to divert water for beneficial purposes. Drainage law also distinguishes between drainage of surface water and groundwater.

DRAINAGE OF DIFFUSED SURFACE WATER

Three different rules exist as far as drainage of diffused surface water is concerned: (1) the common enemy rule; (2) the natural flow rule; and (3) the reasonable use rule [44].

In common enemy rule states, a landowner is allowed to do whatever is necessary to repel or expel diffused surface water regardless of damage to his neighbor's land. However, the potential harshness of the common enemy rule is tempered by exceptions which qualify the rule in most common enemy states: (1) a landowner may not dispose of water by an artificial channel (e.g., drain, culvert, ditch) if his neighbor is injured; and (2) a landowner may not drain into a natural watercourse so as to obstruct its flow or overtax its capacity to another's injury [44]. Courts in common enemy states have also infused elements of "reasonableness" into drainage cases. Nevertheless, a number of states which once followed the common enemy rule have abandoned it in favor of the reasonable use rule [44].

The natural flow rule is the opposite of the common enemy rule: a landowner may not obstruct or divert the natural flow of diffused surface water if his neighbor is injured. In its pure form the natural flow rule is as extreme as the common enemy rule; thus natural flow states have made exceptions for agricultural drainage and drainage into natural watercourses where capacities are not exceeded. Some natural flow states also apply "reasonableness" standards to drainage cases [44].

Under the reasonable use rule, a landowner is privileged to make reasonable use of his land even though the flow of diffused surface water is altered and a neighbor is damaged. Only when harm to a neighbor becomes unreasonable is the landowner liable for damage occasioned by his drainage project. Professor Beck has listed some of the questions bearing on reasonableness: Is there a reasonable need for the land development? Has due care been taken to prevent injury? Has the natural drainage pattern been followed as much as possible? Is the artificial drainage system reasonably feasible? Do the benefits of the project outweigh its harm [44]? Once again, the chief advantage of the reasonable use rule is its flexibility; its major disadvantage is its unpredictability.

Nowadays, major drainage projects are constructed by public drainage enterprises such as drainage districts or municipalities. All drainage districts and municipalities depend on state statutes for their existence and powers. As a result, there is a great deal of variation in public drainage law from state to state [44]. In many states there are several different types of entities involved with drainage, e.g., drainage districts, reclamation districts, flood control districts, irrigation districts, soil and water conservation districts, water management districts, levee districts, and sewerage authorities [44]. One of the factors accounting for this diversity in public districts is a trend from single-purpose to multipurpose districts without abolishing the old districts [44]. Moreover, the powers of state agencies as to drainage vary among states. Some state engineers have authority over drainage; others do not. Some state environmental protection agencies have power to control urban stormwater runoff; others do not. All in all, it is difficult to generalize about the formation, powers, financing, and dissolution of public bodies dealing with drainage [44].

However, there are two aspects of public drainage law which deserve special mention. Essentially all states give public entities doing drainage the power of eminent domain to condemn land and water rights for drainage purposes [44]. Second, public drainage institutions are given "sovereign immunity" [44]. This means that drainage districts or municipalities or their officials cannot be sued for their "torts" (wrongs), when acting in their official capacities, without the consent of the state legislature or state courts. In most states suits against public officials are sharply restricted either by state tort claims laws or common law rules of governmental immunity. For example, in New Jersey a suit cannot be brought against a public drainage body unless its action has been "palpably unreasonable"—a much higher standard than ordinary unreasonableness. Thus, in lawsuits against public drainage institutions the three surface water drainage rules are replaced by the generally stricter provisions of tort claims laws and court decrees [45]. This emphasizes the need for effective public regulation of drainage districts.

GROUNDWATER DRAINAGE

These cases are of two kinds: (1) where a landowner seeks to block the flow of groundwater from coming onto his premises; and (2) where a landowner's reduction of the water table for dry development causes dewatering or subsidence of neighboring land [44]. In the first category of cases courts generally apply the same rule that applies to drainage of diffused surface water [44]. The second class of cases has proved more difficult for courts.

Most of the dewatering and subsidence cases involve mining, although there are also a number of sewer construction cases [46]. In states that follow the "absolute ownership" of groundwater rule, there is generally no recovery of damages for dewatering or subsidence. Courts in reasonable use states will come to the same conclusion if the drainage of groundwater is not wasteful (negligent) and the drainage water is not transported away from the overlying land. In states following the "correlative rights" rule, where owners of adjacent land have a common and coequal right to percolating water, the injured neighbor usually wins, even if the mine drainage is reasonable and necessary and the mine is much more valuable than the plaintiff's property [46]. This is more of a fair share test based on proportional ownership than one of comparative reasonableness. In those western states where groundwater is subject to appropriation, the landowner cannot intercept a source of supply to streams, springs, or groundwater used by prior appropriators. The miner's only alternative is to prove that the mining activity has developed new water not tributary to any fully appropriated water source [46]. New Mexico has attempted to resolve the conflict between the prior appropriation doctrine and the needs of the mining industry by enacting a Mine Dewatering Act, which allows miners to replace water previously appropriated, e.g., to furnish a substitute water supply, to drill a deeper well for the affected user or compensate him for increased lift costs [47].

In subsidence cases there is a further complication. Adjoining land-owners owe each other absolute obligations of support, both lateral support and subsurface support. A landowner must not use his land so as to cause his neighbor's land to subside, either at or below the surface. If dewatering leading to subsidence of neighboring land is a breach of the obligation to support neighboring land, then plaintiffs will recover in all cases. Most courts faced with the problem have limited the "support" theory to situations involving removal of solid materials or water mixed with solid material [12], but other decisions refer only to dewatering. Some states, notably Texas, have enacted statutes covering subsidences caused by mining [12].

DRAINAGE OF WATERCOURSE OVERFLOW (CHANNEL MODIFICATIONS)

No one has the right to obstruct or divert the flow of a natural watercourse, or to divert the water from its natural channel into another channel, if the stream modifications cause new and injurious overflows [25]. This rule applies to impoundments, both on-channel and off-channel, dikes, embankments, levees, and other artificial channel modifications [25]. The diffused surface water rule in a given state may be the antithesis of this. In a common enemy state a landowner will not be liable for flooding caused by his construction of a dike to deflect diffused surface water, while in the same state he would be liable for downstream flooding caused by diking a stream bank to deflect high streamflows.

Like the common enemy rule, the rule imposing liability for harmful obstructions or diversions of flow is often qualified by concepts of reasonableness. For example, temporarily accelerated flows for the purpose of generating hydroelectric power may not give rise to liability if the releases, even though harmful, are as innocuous as possible [27]. A dam operator may be liable for downstream flood damage if he should have anticipated the flood conditions and released water in advance so as to have room in the reservoir for storage of flood flows [27]. An embankment builder may not be liable for damage caused by extraordinary—as opposed to merely ordinary—floods [27]. Or, a dam owner might not be liable for backflooding of land upstream of the dam if the damage is so unusual that it could not have reasonably been foreseen [27]. However, where dams break or collapse, strict liability, liability without fault, is often imposed if the break causes damage that would not have occurred otherwise [1]. Because common law liability rules for dam owners are vague, states are increasingly imposing dam safety requirements, including periodic inspection and repair or reconstruction where necessary.

Many states attempt to forestall flood damage problems by requiring permits for dam construction, stream encroachments, and floodplain construction. Regulation of channel and bank modifications is especially important because these projects are often undertaken by governmental entities (municipalities or special-purpose districts), which are exempt from liability most of the time. On the other hand, a casually granted permit can effectively insulate a defendant from liability. Although the general rule is that possession of a permit is no defense to a common law action, judges treat permits as bearing on the reasonableness of a defendant's conduct. Moreover, governmental entities are exempt from liability for negligently issued permits.

However, because constitutions are "fundamental law," governmental entities cannot escape liability where their channel modifications cause "takings" of property for which just compensation must be paid under the U.S. Constitution and most state constitutions [48]. Some states grant a considerably broader right to their citizens to sue for compensation when their property is merely damaged and not completely "taken" [45]. When channel modifications lead to permanent overflows of land above ordinary high-water mark, compensation for a taking is necessary [48]. The "navigation servitude," which enables the United States to take without compensation riparian rights within the banks of navigable watercourses, is discussed in Part II. Where the overflows are periodic, a governmental entity is liable for the value of a "flowage easement" (right to inundate part but not all of a piece of property) without having to condemn the entire parcel [48]. Temporary flooding that is relatively minor in effect is not compensable [48]. There is generally no liability where diversion of water from a channel washes away property by erosion, but when erosion results directly from flooding, rather than from a change in the direction of streamflow, a compensable taking occurs [48].

Chapter 9
WATER DISTRIBUTION ORGANIZATIONS

The major water distribution organizations in the United States are active in providing water for irrigation and municipal supply.

IRRIGATION ORGANIZATIONS

Both private and public organizations furnish water for irrigation in the west [49]. The private organizations range from associations of relatively few farmers to large nonprofit corporations and commercial irrigation companies. The public organizations are usually irrigation districts. Irrigation organizations "acquire, hold, and exercise appropriative rights in order to provide water for land which they were organized to serve" [25].

    The most popular type of private irrigation organization is the mutual water company, "a non-profit corporation that owns diversion or storage works and delivers water at cost to users who own its stock, and that derives its operating funds from assessments levied against the stockholders" [50]. Stock is divided among the stockholders based on proportionate shares of irrigable acreage. Ownership of stock in a mutual company may impair the ordinarily unlimited transferrability of appropriative water rights. Articles of incorporation frequently prohibit transfers apart from the irrigated land or without the consent of the corporation [50]. State statutes and court decisions may also limit transfers of stock apart from the land. One of the reasons for restrictions on the permanent and temporary (e.g., leasing, pledging) transfers of mutual company stock is to preclude regulation of a mutual company as a public utility.

All seventeen western states have irrigation district laws, although some are called water conservation, water improvement, or reclamation districts [50]. These state statutes differ greatly as to methods of forming irrigation districts [50]. Once formed, irrigation districts have the authority to issue bonds to fund construction of irrigation works. Bonds are financed by assessments on land within the district; assessments are based either on value of irrigation benefits received or some ad valorem formula based on land area or property tax [50]. Courts will look carefully at ad valorem assessments to determine whether they bear some relationship to benefits. Irrigation districts also raise revenues by tolls or charges for water delivered [49]. The close relationship of some irrigation districts to U.S. Bureau of Reclamation development projects is examined in Part II.

MUNICIPAL WATER SUPPLY ORGANIZATIONS

Municipal water supply organizations are favored in water law. Riparian states exempt these entities from watershed limitations and grant them condemnation powers. Appropriation states give them first preference both to unappropriated water and to condemn currently existing diversion rights. Moreover, western states have found ways to allow municipal water supply organizations to appropriate water for *future* beneficial use without the current use required of all other appropriators [25].

The number and variety of municipal water supply organizations is dizzying.

> In California nine different types of public agencies distribute water for cities and towns. These do not include municipal water departments or municipal utility districts which are subject to legislation governing municipal corporations generally. Moreover, fifty special acts have created public districts which to some extent provide urban areas with water. Added to these state agencies are the growing number of federal reclamation projects which were formerly engaged primarily in the development of water for irrigation but now deal largely with urban water [49].

Water for municipal supply in New Jersey is provided by small, developer-operated private water companies, large investor-owned private companies, water supply districts, municipal water departments, municipal utilities authorities, county utilities authorities, water commissions, and the state itself which constructs reservoirs and pipelines in order to augment the supplies of these other water supply organizations. As an example of water supply fragmentation within a major American city, the Chicago metropolitan area has 349 separate water supply systems [10].

Each institutional arrangement supplying water for municipal purposes operates in a different legal climate. The National Water Commission has recommended consolidation not only of water supply organizations but also of all organizations performing the three basic water services in metropolitan areas—water supply, waste water collection and treatment, and storm water management [10].

REFERENCES FOR PART I

1. Clark, R. E. "Classes of Water and Character of Water Rights," in *Waters and Water Rights*, R. E. Clark, ed. (7 vols.; Indianapolis, IN: Allen Smith Co., 1967−1978), I, p. 300. The seven-volume treatise is hereafter referred to as "Clark."
2. Davis, C. "The Right to Use Water in the Eastern States," in Clark, VII, p. 154.
3. Davis, C. "Introduction to Water Law of the Eastern States," in Clark, VII, p. 6.
4. Clark, R. E. "Western Ground-Water Law," in Clark, V, p. 419.
5. Corker, C. E. "Groundwater Law, Management and Administration," National Water Commission, NTIS PB205 527 (1971), pp. 56−59.
6. Champion, W. M. "Ground Water Rights," in *Water Rights in the Nineteen Western States*, W. A. Hutchins (completed by H. H. Ellis and J. P. DeBraal) (3 vols.; Washington, D.C.: U.S. Government Printing Office, 1971−1977), II, p. 639. The three-volume treatise is hereafter referred to as "Hutchins."
7. *The Random House Dictionary of the English Language* (New York, 1967).
8. Ausness, R. C. "Water Use Permits in a Riparian State: Problems and Proposals," *Kentucky Law Journal* 66:191−265 (1977), p. 197.
9. Trelease, F. J. "A Model Groundwater Code for the Northeast," in *Proceedings of a Conference on Groundwater Use Management in the Northeastern States* (Ithaca, NY: Cornell University Center for Environmental Research, 1981), p. 18.
10. "Water Policies for the Future," National Water Commission, U.S. Government Printing Office (1973), pp. 280−294.
11. N.J.S.A. 58:1A-1 et seq.
12. Meyers, C. J., and A. D. Tarlock. *Water Resources Management*, 2nd ed. (Mineola, NY: The Foundation Press, 1980), p. 197.
13. 371 So. 2d 663, *rehearing den.* (1979), *cert. den.* 444 U.S. 965 (1979). The Florida Water Resources Act can be found at § 373.016 Fla. Stat. et seq.
14. Trelease, F. J. "Federal-State Relations in Water Law," National Water Commission, NTIS PB 203 600 (1971), p. 21.
15. Clark, R. E. "Introduction to Water Law of the Western States," in Clark, V, pp. 7−8.
16. Clark, R. E. "The California Doctrine," in Clark, V, pp. 234−235.
17. Clark, R. E. "The Colorado Doctrine," in Clark, V, p. 66.
18. Radosevich, G. E., and D. R. Daines. "Water Law and Administration in the United States of America," in *Proceedings of the International Conference on Global Water Law Systems* (Fort Collins: Colorado State University, 1976), p.25.
19. Hutchins, W. A. "Background and Modern Developments in State Water Rights Law," in Clark, I, pp. 88−91.
20. *State Dept. of Parks* v. *Idaho Dept. of Water Administration*, 96 Idaho 440, 530 P. 2d 924 (1974).
21. Aiken, J. D. "The National Water Policy Review and Western Water Rights Law Reform: An Overview," *Nebraska Law Review* 59:327−344 (1980), pp. 328, 330.
22. N. Mex. Stat. Ann. § 75−5−17.

23. Tex. Rev. Civ. Stat., Art. 7476.
24. Reigel, S. A., and J. Owens. *Administrative Law* (Ann Arbor, MI: Ann Arbor Science Publishers, 1982), pp. 96−108.
25. Hutchins, I, p. 277.
26. Cal. Const., Art. XIV, § 3.
27. Davis, C. "Impoundment and Artificial Development of Waters in the East," in Clark, VII, pp. 198−199.
28. Huffmire, M. E. "Ground Water Allocation in the Northeast," in *Proceedings of a Conference on Groundwater Use Management in the Northeastern States* (Ithaca, NY: Cornell University Center for Environmental Research, 1981), pp. 138−139.
29. Lukas, T. N. "When the Well Runs Dry," *Boston College Environmental Affairs Law Review* 10(2):445−502 (1982), p. 484.
30. Hanks, E. H., and J. L. Hanks. "The Law of Water in New Jersey: Groundwater," *Rutgers Law Review* 24:621−671 (1970), pp. 638−639.
31. 33 Cal. 2d 908, 207 P. 2d 17 (1949).
32. Nash, R. A. "A Review of the Common Law and Statutory Law of Groundwater Use Management in the Northeastern United States," in *Proceedings of a Conference on Groundwater Use Management in the Northeastern States* (Ithaca, NY: Cornell University Center for Environmental Research, 1981), pp. 57−66.
33. Mont. Rev. Codes 1947, § 89−891(1).
34. *Cappaert* v. *United States,* 426 U.S. 128 (1976).
35. 43 USC § 666.
36. Corker, C. E. "Water Rights in Interstate Streams," in Clark, II, p. 294.
37. Ellis, H. H., and J. P. DeBraal. "Interstate Dimensions of Water Rights," in Hutchins, III, p. 71.
38. Muys, J. C. "Interstate Water Compacts," National Water Commission, NTIS PB 202 998 (1971), p. S-1.
39. Utton, A. E. "International Streams and Lakes," in Clark, II, pp. 404−411.
40. Waite, G. G. "International Law Affecting Water Rights," in Hutchins, III, p. 119.
41. Johnson, R. W. "Major Interbasin Transfers: Legal Aspects," National Water Commission, NTIS PB 202 619 (1971), pp. 15−16.
42. Goldfarb, W. "Litigation and Legislation," *Water Resources Bulletin* 18:899−900 (1982).
43. *Sporhase* v. *Nebraska,* 102 s. ct. 3456, 73 L.Ed. 2d 1254.
44. Beck, R. E. "The Law of Drainage," in Clark, V, pp. 477−518.
45. Goldfarb, W., and B. King. "Urban Stormwater Runoff: The Legal Remedies," *Real Estate Law Journal* 11:3−46 (1982), p. 40.
46. Clyde, E. W. "Mining and Land-Development Interference with Ground Water," in Clark, V, pp. 460−474.
47. Comment: "New Mexico's Mine Dewatering Act: The Search for Rehoboth," *Natural Resources Journal* 20:653−680 (1980).
48. Harnsberger, R. E. "Eminent Domain and Water," in Clark, IV, p. 153.
49. Swensen, R. W. "Local and Private Water Distribution Agencies," in Clark, IV, p. 368.
50. Trelease, F. J. *Cases and Materials on Water Law,* 2d ed. (St. Paul, MN: West Publishing Co., 1974), p. 612.

PART II
Water Resources Development and Protection

The law of water diversion and distribution is primarily state law. However, because the federal government is the major developer of water resources in the United States, and because of the traditional federal guardianship over navigable waters, the law regarding development of water resources and protection of them against unwise development is predominantly federal law. States can and do utilize their taxing and bonding powers to finance water resources development, and important state environmental protection statutes apply to these projects. But state laws vary to such an extent that this part focuses almost exclusively on federal law.

The federal government exercises powers delegated to it by the states and enumerated in the U.S. Constitution. "The Constitution does not contain the word water, yet the founding fathers provided for a strong nation, and the powers they gave to the central government have enabled it to engage in many water related activities and to undertake the most extensive program of water resources development in the world" [1]. The most important source of federal power over water resources is Article I, Section 8 of the U.S. Constitution, giving Congress the power to "regulate Commerce . . . among the several States." By 1865, the U.S. Supreme Court, interpreter of the Constitution, had held that "commerce" includes "transportation," which in turn includes "navigation," and that the power to regulate navigation includes the control of navigable waters for the purposes of navigation.

> The power to control navigation and navigable waters includes the power to construct obstructions that destroy the navigable capacity of the waters and prevent navigation. It also includes the power to protect navigable capacity by preventing diversions of the river and even its nonnavigable tributaries, or by preventing obstructions by bridges or dams and the power to construct flood control structures on the navigable waters, their nonnavigable tributaries or even on the watersheds. Powers to prevent obstruction in turn lead to powers to license obstructions. The power to obstruct leads to the power to generate electric energy from the dammed water [1].

The federal "navigation power" has become a broad authority for federal water resources project development and licensing. In recent years it has also become the foundation for a wide range of federal environmental protection statutes that can be utilized to protect water resources against insensitive federal development or licensing of private development.

Liberal judicial definitions of "navigability" have further widened the federal navigation power. For these purposes, a navigable waterbody is one which has been in the past, is now, or could with reasonable improvements be used as part of a continuous interstate waterway for commercial purposes, for example, floating sawlogs. Nonnavigable portions of navigable waterbodies and nonnavigable tributaries that affect the navigable capacity of navigable waters are within the scope of the navigation power. "Theoretically, therefore, few waters in the United States are immune from the navigation power" [2]. Moreover, the U.S. Supreme Court has upheld the Federal Energy Regulatory Commission's authority to require a federal license for a pumped storage project on a nonnavigable stream which did not affect downstream navigation but which generated power to be transmitted in interstate commerce [2].

Far-reaching as congressional authority over water resources development may be under the navigation power, it must be kept in mind that Congress is not required to exercise this authority. Congress does not have to authorize particular dams or require licenses for particular projects. Specific water resources development statutes are a function of the political process. The virtually unlimited navigation power simply means that if Congress chooses to legislate in the water resources development area it probably cannot be stopped by arguments that it lacks the constitutional authority to do so.

The federal navigation power is often confused with the federal "navigation servitude." The latter is "a shorthand expression for the rule that in the exercise of the navigation power certain private property rights may be taken without compensation" [2].

> Any private property right whose exercise or value depends on the use or presence of navigable waters is burdened with the "navigation servitude."

This means that if it is taken, destroyed or impaired by the federal government's exercise of powers over navigable waters, the government is not constitutionally required to pay its value or the damages, although it would have paid full compensation if it had taken or destroyed the right by the exercise of any other power. The theory is that government takes nothing; the title to the property always contained this defect or limitation by which it might be terminated [1].

The navigation servitude is synonymous with this "no compensation rule."

In riparian rule states landowners abutting waterbodies have the following rights: to (1) use the water for domestic purposes; (2) build wharves and piers; (3) have access to the water; and (4) use the water for other reasonable purposes [3]. These rights can be defeated by the navigation servitude, which extends to the ordinary high-water mark of navigable waterbodies. Nonnavigable tributaries are generally excluded from the navigation servitude. Landowners are not entitled to compensation for damage to submerged lands (e.g., destruction of oyster beds by dredging); loss of access to water; destruction of wharves and bridges; or loss of water use (e.g., loss of hydropower head) [3]. When lands above the high-water mark ("fast lands") are taken in the exercise of the navigation power, just compensation must be paid. The fair market value of fast lands is based on "all uses to which such real property may reasonably be put, including its highest and best use, any of which uses may be dependent upon access to or utilization of such navigable waters" [4]. This statute has not been tested in the courts, but if taken at face value it means that fast land values may include factors that would be noncompensable if the land were located below the high-water mark.

This part deals with the federal government as project developer and project licensor, the federal law of water resources planning, and the federal environmental protection statutes that limit water resources development.

Chapter 10

THE FEDERAL GOVERNMENT AS PROJECT DEVELOPER

BUREAU OF RECLAMATION

The Bureau, located within the Interior Department, operates in the seventeen western states and Hawaii.

> Historically, the primary function of the Bureau was to facilitate the settlement and development of Western lands through the provision of irrigation water. Today most projects are multipurpose and some do not have an irrigation component at all. However, irrigation remains the primary purpose and, in 1969 Bureau projects served approximately 8.6 million acres, slightly more than a fifth of all the irrigated land in the United States in that year [5].

The Bureau also has planning responsibilities regarding water from the Colorado River, as well as control of various loan and grant programs.

Reclamation law is a complex system of statutes, administrative actions, and court cases, based on the Reclamation Act of 1902. In late 1982, Congress made profound changes in reclamation law when it passed the Reclamation Reform Act of 1982 [6]. These changes can be better understood if certain aspects of earlier reclamation law are explained.

"The basic principle of the 1902 Reclamation Act was that the United States would build irrigation works from the proceeds of public-land sales in the . . . arid western states" [7]. Irrigators were required to repay current maintenance costs each year, and the costs of construction in full within ten years, but received a governmental subsidy in that no interest accrued on the construction costs. These repayments were intended to establish a revolving fund to finance future reclamation projects. But the reclamation fund has never been self-supporting:

> Substantial construction moneys are appropriated from the general treasury; the ten-year interest-free time for repayment by irrigation users has in practice been extended to fifty years; and irrigation users — who pay only what they are deemed able to afford — are subsidized in large part by power and municipal users [7].

Thus, the 1902 act's irrigation subsidy has been enhanced by the Bureau's forbearance and increasing sales of project water to power, municipal, commercial, and industrial users. Moreover, recreation, fish and wildlife, flood control, and navigation costs of a reclamation project are either partially or fully exempt from repayment because these aspects are viewed as national benefits. This decreases the amount of project costs that irrigators are called upon to repay. The repayment obligation is included in a contract between the Bureau and an irrigation district. Irrigation districts operate the distribution systems, furnish water to irrigators, and tax lands within the district to repay construction costs and maintenance expenses.

The congressional supporters of the 1902 Reclamation Act intended its subsidies to promote family farming in the west. In order to discourage monopolization, the act provided that water could not be sold for use on more than 160 acres, expanded by Bureau practice to 320 acres for a husband and wife, in any individual private ownership, and that the user had to be a resident or occupant of the land. An exception was made to the acreage limitations to facilitate the breakup of large farms. Project water at subsidized rates, i.e., no interest demanded and ability to pay considered, could be used to irrigate land in excess of the limits if the owner agreed in a recordable contract with the Bureau to sell the "excess lands" within ten years for their appraised value excluding prospective irrigation by project water. To discourage speculation, "even if the excess-land owner does not apply for project water for his excess land, if, before repayment is half completed, he sells those lands at a price exceeding that satisfactory to the Bureau (its value without enhancement by reason of the presence of the project. . . .), the purchaser cannot receive project water for the land" [7].

These intended antimonopoly safeguards of the act were generally ineffective. The Bureau virtually ignored the perhaps unenforceable residency requirement. Acreage limitations were circumvented by legal subterfuges, statutory exemptions, and liberal administrative interpretations. There was a growing realization within Congress that the Reclamation Act of 1902 was obsolete, but reform languished until a federal circuit court forced the issue by ordering the Bureau to enforce the Reclamation Act as written.

The 1982 amendments abolish the residency requirement. In addition, the acreage limitations have been loosened. Project irrigation water cannot be delivered to a "qualified recipient" (an individual or "any legal entity established under State or Federal law which benefits twenty-five natural persons or less") for use in the irrigation of land in excess of 960 acres "of Class I lands or the equivalent thereof . . . whether situated in one or more districts." Larger organizations, called "limited recipients," have an acreage limitation of 640 acres of Class I land or their equivalent. However, subsidized rates for the irrigation of excess lands have been eliminated, and for new recordable contracts the period during which excess lands may receive project water has been reduced to a maximum of five years. For these five years, full cost, including interest, must be paid by qualified recipients for irrigating with project water landholdings in excess of 960 acres of Class I land or their equivalent, and by limited recipients for over 320 acres or their equivalent. The ownership and full-cost pricing limitations do not apply where: (1) districts have fully repaid construction costs, including prepayment, where allowed, by existing contract with the Bureau; (2) the irrigator is temporarily provided with unmanageable oversupplies of water; (3) the land is acquired involuntarily, e.g., by foreclosure or inheritance; and (4) the excess lands are "isolated tracts found . . . to be economically farmable only if they are included in a larger farming operation but which may . . . cause it to exceed such ownership limitations." Finally, lands receiving project water may be leased, but only by written lease for terms less than ten years (twenty-five years for perennial crops).

Up to a point, a district can chose whether or not to be covered by the new acreage and full-cost limitations. The 1982 amendments apply only to new and amended contracts between districts and the Bureau. Existing contracts are covered by prior law. Should a district amend its contract to conform to the new law? The advantages of amendment would be increased acreage limitations and application of the new "equivalency principle"; the major disadvantage would be the loss of ten years delivery of subsidized water for excess lands under recordable contract. All other things being equal, an irrigation district, including very large farms, might choose to remain under the old law. But there is an additional penalty for refusing to amend a contract. Beginning four and a half years from the date of enactment, large farming operations leasing over 160 acres of land in nonamending districts will lose the subsidy rates attached to the additional leased lands. But whatever a district chooses to do, any owner or lessee within that district may individually elect to be covered by the new amendments and make additional payments directly to the Bureau.

Even though most reclamation law disputes are governed by the federal Reclamation Act or the Bureau-district or district-user contracts, difficult questions of federal-state relations remain unanswered by the 1982 amendments. For example, the U.S. Supreme Court has held that the

Bureau, in appropriating water for reclamation projects, must comply with state law just as any other appropriator; and that the state can impose reasonable conditions on the Bureau, e.g., protection of local water users or instream flow maintenance [8]. In its opinion, the Court suggested that federal condemnation of existing water rights is also controlled by state law. What if state law prohibits the Bureau from condemning water rights for a project? Moreover, the High Court declared that, where the Reclamation Act is silent, "once the waters [are] released from the dam, their distribution to individual landowners would again be controlled by state law."[8] To what extent is a right to receive project water salable if water rights are salable under state law? Questions like these, along with ambiguities in the Reclamation Act amendments, will dictate the future course of reclamation law.

ARMY CORPS OF ENGINEERS

The Corps of Engineers of the Department of the Army is the oldest of the federal agencies with water resource programs. "Corps functions include the investigation, design, construction, operation, and maintenance of works for navigation, flood control, beach erosion control, hydroelectric power generation, municipal and industrial water supply, water quality control, recreation, fish and wildlife conservation, and hurricane protection" [9]. These functions were conferred on the Corps at different times and by different statutes ("enabling acts"), most of which set out what the Corps must do in order to procure congressional authorizations and appropriations for particular public works projects. Although the details of this authorization-appropriation process differ with the specific statutes involved, they are sufficiently similar that a composite procedure can be presented [9]:

Step 1. *Congressional Authorization of a Survey Report.* The House and Senate Public Works Committees report an omnibus bill authorizing various surveys. Congressional approval may not be required for small or emergency projects.

Step 2. *Congressional Appropriation for Survey.* Appropriations for authorized surveys are usually made in a lump sum, from which the Chief of Engineers allocates the funds to specific surveys.

Step 3. *Survey Preparation.* The District Engineer (the Corps is organized into eleven divisions and thirty-seven districts) performs a preliminary examination, formulates a proposed plan, does an environmental assessment, consults with affected states, holds public meetings, and then prepares a survey report and a preliminary draft environmental impact statement. The Corps, along with other federal water project agencies planning flood control projects, must consider non-structural alternatives, including floodproofing, land use regulation, land acquisition, and population relocation. The federal government is authorized to pay 80 percent of the cost of nonstructural control measures.

Step 4.   *Division Engineer's Consideration.*   The Division Engineer reviews the report, preliminary impact statement, and public comments. He then makes his own project report to the Board of Engineers for Rivers and Harbors, composed of seven engineer officers of the Corps. The project report must consider other proposed projects on the waterway, hydrologic data, potential for erosion, local benefits and recommended local contributions, costs and benefits of the project, and all possible uses of the site as well as environmental impacts.

Step 5.   *Board of Engineers Review.*   The Board reviews the project report and preliminary draft statement. A site inspection may be made. The Board prepares its report and recommendations to the Chief of Engineers.

Step 6.   *Final Project Report Submission.*   The Chief of Engineers then prepares a Draft Environmental Impact Statement (DEIS), or a Finding of No Significant Impact (FONSI), which is circulated to affected states and relevant federal agencies. The DEIS or FONSI is also available to the public. After a comment period, a final EIS, if necessary, with public comments and the project report, is submitted to the Office of Management and Budget (OMB). After an OMB review, the Secretary of the Army files the EIS with the Council on Environmental Quality and sends it, the project report, and his own comments to Congress.

Step 7.   *Congressional Authorization of Project.*   Congress may authorize (1) an individual project at an estimated cost; (2) a comprehensive plan of improvement and specific component parts, leaving other portions of the plan to be authorized later; or (3) a comprehensive plan and sums for plan implementation, leaving it to the Corps to choose which projects should be constructed first. No project may be authorized by Congress if more than five years has elapsed from the time the initial survey report was submitted. If the proposal is controversial, the public works committees may hold extensive hearings. After the hearings, Congress may authorize a number of projects in a single omnibus bill.

Step 8. *Assurances of Local Cooperation* [10].   Construction of projects
requiring local contribution may not begin until the state and
local governments have agreed in writing to cooperate [9].
By statute, with respect to all flood control works except
dams and reservoirs, state and local governments must pay
for all lands and rights-of-way necessary for the project,
must pay for all damages caused by Corps construction, and
must maintain and operate the works in accordance with
Corps instructions. Nonfederal public bodies must pay 50
percent of the costs of recreation and fish and wildlife enhancement areas at Corps projects, except for minimum facilities and access points. State and local governments must
also agree to manage these areas. On the other hand, the
Corps may pay for "mitigation lands" to compensate for
inundated recreation and habitat areas. Additionally, state
and local governments must repay the Corps, over a fifty-
year period with interest accruing only during construction,
for the costs of at least 50 percent of municipal or industrial
water supply storage capacity in a Corps project. However,
no more than 30 percent of project costs may be allocated to
storage for future water supply. Finally, private and municipal shorefront property owners are required to share the
costs of Corps shore protection projects. According to the
prestigious National Water Commission, "A primary weakness of the federal water resources development projects is
that they have been heavily subsidized by the Federal Government; that is, by all the taxpayers of the Nation, to provide benefits for a few" [11]. Both the Carter and Reagan
administrations have advocated state and local cost sharing
for all federal water resources development projects. Increased cost sharing will probably be a conspicuous feature
of federal water resources development law in future years.

Step 9. *Congressional Appropriation of Funds for Project.*   "Authorization does not guarantee the funding and construction of
projects. Congress presently has a very substantial backlog
of authorized but unconstructed projects from which the
Administration may select in considering which should be
funded in any year. . . . Some of these projects will die. . . .
Thirty years, or more, may pass before the first appropriation for the project" [5]. On the other hand, Congress can
vote to "deauthorize" a project.

Step 10. *Final Planning and Construction.*   Advanced engineering and
design work may require up to five years. During this time the

local sponsors sign formal contribution agreements. Upon completion of detailed plans and specifications, the construction project is let out for bids, and construction contracts are awarded.

Step 11.   (?) Lawsuits.   Courts generally refuse to review (1) whether a project complies with its authorization-appropriation legislation, or (2) the sufficiency of the Corps' cost-benefit analysis. However, there has been a good deal of litigation against the Corps as project developer based on environmental protection statutes applicable to federal construction projects. For example, even though courts decline to review cost-benefit analyses directly, limited review of the Corps' balancing of costs and benefits in an EIS is available under the National Environmental Policy Act (NEPA) [12]. And if the Corps, during actual construction, deviates substantially from the project report on which authorizations and appropriations were based, a court might order the Corps to produce a supplemental EIS before the project may continue. The environmental protection statutes that limit federal water resources development are discussed in Chapter 13.

SOIL CONSERVATION SERVICE

The Soil Conservation Service (SCS) is an agency within the U.S. Department of Agriculture with a variety of responsibilities for soil and water conservation [5]. For our purposes, SCS administers the "small watersheds" program under the Watershed Protection and Flood Prevention Act of 1954, frequently referred to as Public Law 566 [13]. This program integrates nonstructural and structural approaches to the facilitation of drainage and prevention of flooding and soil erosion. "These projects combine soil and water conservation on the land with control and use of runoff by means of upstream dams and other structures. Land treatment to increase vegetation, improve soil condition, and retard surface runoff precedes structural work on the streams" [14]. The goal of the small watersheds program is watershed protection, "the protection and development of upstream drainage areas of small tributaries, as contrasted with major projects for flood control on main streams of the type undertaken by the Army Corps of Engineers" [14].

Unlike the Corps construction programs, the SCS does not itself carry out small watersheds projects. Local organizations such as soil conservation districts, flood control districts, irrigation districts, counties, and municipalities sponsor the projects, arrange for their activation, and supervise their operation and maintenance. The link between SCS and local sponsoring organizations is the "state conservationist," an SCS employee who works directly with state and local governments and special-purpose districts. "Thus, federal, state, and district personnel cooperate in an unusual though apparently workable arrangement" [15]. These contacts are especially important because SCS encourages the multipurpose projects that are generally favored by states. States "must be provided an opportunity to review and approve or disapprove applications by local organizations, recommend priorities for assistance within the State, review and comment on work plans, . . . and assist in financing costs assigned to local organizations for installing and maintaining works of improvement" [14].

SCS provides three kinds of assistance to local organizations in planning and carrying out the structural components of small watershed projects: "(1) technical assistance for planning, installing, operating, and maintaining works of improvement; (2) financial assistance to defray all of the cost for structural measures for flood prevention and part of the cost for irrigation and drainage and for fish and wildlife development and recreation . . . ; and (3) long-term credit to help local interests finance their share of the [structural] costs, including the full cost of municipal or industrial water supply" [14].

In contrast to the Corps programs, SCS stresses land treatment and management practices in smaller watersheds. Land treatment measures are generally applied by private landowners with technical and financial assistance provided by the local organization and SCS. The small watersheds program, like the Corps programs, requires a favorable cost-benefit ratio for projects; but financial and technical assistance cannot be provided if the primary monetary benefits inure to the landowners by way of additional production without significant public benefits. In order to qualify for SCS watershed protection assistance, land treatment measures must appreciably reduce erosion and sedimentation, decrease flooding, or produce drainage benefits in combination with structural techniques. If SCS is requested to finance a structure with storage capacity, over 50 percent of the relevant landowners in the drainage area must agree to implement recommended soil conservation measures [14].

By statute, small watershed projects are limited in size [14]. The watershed area, including subwatersheds, may not exceed 250,000 acres. No structure may be larger than 25,000 acre-feet total capacity, nor may any structure have a floodwater detention capacity exceeding 12,500 acre-feet. Plans involving an estimated federal contribution to construction costs of more than $250,000, or including any single structure providing more than 2,500 acre-feet total capacity, must be approved by the Public Works Committees of both the Senate and House of Representatives. Smaller projects may be administratively approved. Where there is overlap between the statutory authority of SCS and the Corps, the terms of a cooperative agreement determine which agency will prevail. In general, the Corps will provide flood protection for downstream agricultural floodplains and for urban areas with major flood problems [14]. There has been rivalry between the agencies because the SCS contends that upstream watershed protection will partially obviate large flood retention dams downstream.

SCS has not been the object of as many environmental lawsuits as the Corps. "Until the last few years of the [1960s], relationships between SCS and the organized conservation movement were excellent. The big dams, long aqueducts, and canals of the Corps and the Bureau of Reclamation were under heavy environmentalist attack, but the land treatment measures and small impoundments of P.L. 566 projects were not" [16]. But beginning in about 1968, SCS "channelization" policies came under heavy environmentalist attack. Channelization is the modification of a stream to increase its carrying capacity for flood prevention or drainage. It generally involves "excavating larger areas to deepen, widen, and straighten the stream and clear vegetation from its banks" [16]. Stream channelization has been the focus of a number of important NEPA lawsuits since 1970.

TENNESSEE VALLEY AUTHORITY

The Tennessee Valley Authority (TVA), a wholly owned federal government corporation, was created by the Tennessee Valley Authority Act of 1933 [9]. Its affairs are managed by a three-member board, appointed by the president with the advice and consent of the Senate for staggered nine-year terms. Originally created to improve navigation on the Tennessee River and to control floods in the Tennessee and Mississippi river basins, Congress has authorized TVA to become a multipurpose regional development agency.

TVA has the authority to construct and license dams and other water resources development projects throughout the Tennessee River basin.

> A series of nine multipurpose dams on the Tennessee River, with 24 other major dams on the tributaries, serve to provide a stairway of navigable lakes from the mouth of the river to Knoxville, Tenn., provide flood control on the river and downstream on the Ohio and Mississippi Rivers, and provide hydroelectric power, water supply and recreation for the entire region. Six of these dams are privately owned and water releases are directed by TVA as part of the regional system. The Corps operates the locks associated with the dams [9].

Each major TVA dam has a hydroelectric power component; in fact, with its fossil fuel and nuclear power plants, TVA is the sole supplier of electric energy in an 800,000-square-mile region [9].

TVA receives authorizations and appropriations from Congress for dam construction [5]. It also issues and sells bonds for the construction of facilities for generating and transmitting electric power. A portion of the proceeds from the sale of power is kept by the board to defray expenses of operating dams and reservoirs.

TVA has been a prime target of environmentalist lawsuits, including the notorious Tellico Dam ("snail darter") litigation that it lost in the U.S. Supreme Court. This case is discussed in Chapter 13 under the federal Endangered Species Act.

Chapter 11
THE FEDERAL GOVERNMENT AS PROJECT LICENSOR

This chapter analyzes the federal government's role, under the Commerce Clause, in controlling the use of water by nonfederal development entities. Emphasis is placed on the licensing activities of the Nuclear Regulatory Commission, the Federal Energy Regulatory Commission, and the Army Corps of Engineers as they affect water resources development. Federal grant programs for construction of waste treatment plants and sewers, as well as federal Clean Water Act permitting, are covered in Part IV.

NUCLEAR REGULATORY COMMISSION

The Nuclear Regulatory Commission (NRC) was created as an independent agency in 1974. It was delegated responsibilities formerly carried out by the Atomic Energy Commission under the Atomic Energy Act of 1954. NRC's major importance in the field of water resources development stems from its authority to license the construction and operation of nuclear power plants. Nuclear plants must be sited on watercourses or saltwater environments because of their extensive need for cooling water. Although the NRC exclusively regulates the safety related aspects of nuclear plant construction and operation, states control the determinations of power plant need, type, and siting [17]. Another area of NRC authority that can affect water resources is its search for appropriate sites in which to store highly radioactive spent fuel from nuclear reactors.

Neither the Environmental Protection Agency (EPA) nor a state is empowered to regulate radioactive discharges from nuclear plants. States and EPA can, however, set effluent limitations and water quality standards for the thermal component of nuclear plant discharges. But if these regulations on heat discharges significantly disrupt a plant's operation, the state or EPA will probably be compelled to defer to NRC. Because of NRC preemption of safety factors in plant operation and the close relationship between a plant's operation and its thermal effluent, courts generally deny recovery on traditional legal theories (e.g., nuisance, negligence) to neighboring riparian landowners or states, suing as public trustees of wildlife, that suffer injury from NRC-approved thermal discharges of nuclear power plants. However, since power companies possess the right of eminent domain, local property owners may be able to win condemnation awards if the damage has been severe enough.

Many landmark environmental lawsuits have been brought against the NRC and its predecessor, the AEC. Licenses for individual nuclear plants, research programs (e.g, the breeder reactor program), and NRC regulations have been successfully challenged on National Environmental Policy Act and other grounds.

FEDERAL ENERGY REGULATORY COMMISSION

The Federal Energy Regulatory Commission (FERC) was created in 1977 within the U.S. Department of Energy. Many of the functions previously performed by the Federal Power Commission (FPC), now defunct, have been assumed by FERC. The FERC programs that affect water resources development are its authority to license nonfederal hydroelectric projects and its responsibility to approve the location of natural gas pipelines. The FERC licensing process applies to a wide variety of developers including investor-owned utilities, private entrepreneurs, industries, municipalities, state power authorities, irrigation districts, and electrical cooperatives [18]. Federal project development agencies do not require FERC licenses or permits. FERC is authorized to issue preliminary permits for site study, minor project licenses, major project licenses at existing sites, major project licenses at new sites, and small hydroelectric power exemptions.

Prior to 1920, Congress granted the right to construct, operate, and maintain hydroelectric projects by legislative action in particular cases [9]. This separate, piecemeal water resources development was considered by conservationists to be inefficient and dangerous to resource conservation. "The Federal Water Power Act of 1920, part I of the present Federal Power Act, was seen as a great step toward the regulated and comprehensive devel-

opment of the Nation's water resources and enjoyed the support of the conservationist movement" [5]. This brief historical introduction may be helpful
in refuting the popular misconception that FERC is a single-purpose agency.

> Although the title of the Federal Water Power Act indicated that its primary
> thrust was the control and development of hydroelectric power, it is clear that
> the act required that such control and development be part of a comprehensive
> plan. The purpose of the act would be attained only if the Commission
> considered the impact of the project in the full spectrum of the public interests,
> rather than considering only some limited or partial aspect of commerce and
> the public interests [18].

Thus, the Federal Power Act (FPA) provides that licenses be issued on
condition that the project "be best adapted to a comprehensive plan for
improving or developing a waterway or waterways for the use or benefit of
interstate or foreign commerce, for the improvement and utilization of
waterpower development, and for other beneficial public uses, including
recreational purposes" [19].

One of the most famous of all water resources-related environmental
cases examined the FPC's duty to evaluate a project comprehensively,
including the alternatives to it and its adverse environmental effects. The
project involved in *Scenic Hudson Preservation Conference* v. *Federal Power
Comm.* [20] was Consolidated Edison's proposed pumped storage Cornwall
Project at Storm King Mountain on the Hudson River. The FPC issued a
license, but the second circuit overturned the agency's decision because the
FPC had not actively sought out information on power alternatives and
environmental impacts:

> In this case, as in many others, the Commission has claimed to be the represen-
> tative of the public interest. This role does not permit it to act as an umpire
> blandly calling balls and strikes for adversaries appearing before it: the right of
> the public must receive active and affirmative protection at the hands of
> the Commission [20].

Scenic Hudson is important not only in itself but also, having been decided in
1965, because its interpretation of the FPA and the FPC's responsibilities
under it served as a model for NEPA. As far as FERC is concerned, *Scenic
Hudson* and other cases make it clear that FERC, after balancing all the public
equities, may deny a license where power benefits are outweighed by
recreational and ecological losses.

The Commission's power to license nonfederal hydroelectric projects
extends to three areas: (1) the licensing of dams, conduits, powerhouses,
transmission lines, and other project works for the development or transmission of power, whether the works be across, along, or in any waterbody
which Congress may be capable of regulating under the Commerce Clause
(i.e., any waterbody used for hydroelectric purposes); (2) the licensing of

hydroelectric facilities on public lands, except national parks and monuments; and (3) the licensing of hydroelectric projects using surplus water or water power from any government dam. Where nonnavigable waterbodies are concerned, FERC has discretion to exempt the project from federal licensing and allow it to proceed under applicable state law. But where FERC accepts jurisdiction, although conflicting state statutes and regulations can legally be superseded, FERC normally requires the applicant to satisfy all provisions of state law before a license may be granted [21].

FERC, however, does not have exclusive jurisdiction over the hydroelectric projects which it licenses. Some courts have held that the applicant must obtain a Corps permit for structures or activities which affect navigation [22]. At the very least, Corps approval of plans is necessary. The Corps also regulates the operation of navigation facilities at hydroelectric projects. Moreover, under section 401 of the Clean Water Act no federal agency may license a project unless the relevant state or states certify that the proposed project will not violate state water quality standards.

FERC does not have the authority to construct hydroelectric facilities. But, it may deny a license if it decides that the development should be undertaken by the United States. Congress would then have a reasonable opportunity to study the FERC recommendations and determine whether to authorize a federal project. FERC may condition the license upon the applicant's installation of navigation devices, e.g., locks, booms, sluices, or fish ladders. Minimum flows or releases may be required. If public lands are involved, FERC may impose conditions to protect them. Each applicant must submit a "recreation plan" maximizing public recreation at the site. Licensees are expected to acquire, and include within the project boundary, enough land to assure optimum development of recreational facilities, to develop suitable recreation on project lands and waters, and to encourage public access [18]. Licensees may include these costs in their reimbursable rate bases or charge admission fees.

FPA protects FERC from becoming embroiled in the competition between public and private power interests. Section 7(a) of the act gives a preference to public applicants, all other things being equal. Furthermore, licenses may be issued for no more than fifty years. At the end of that time the project may be relicensed or the federal government may take over the project and pay severance damages to the former licensee. Permit and license applicants need not have property interests in the site. Should they be awarded a license, the FPA allows them to use the federal power of eminent domain to acquire the site [21].

Congress has recently passed a number of statutes encouraging the development of low-head hydroelectric power. Under the Public Utility Regulatory Policies Act of 1978, as amended by the Energy Security Act of 1980 [23], FERC may exempt the following from the licensing requirements of FPA: (1) facilities of 15 megawatts or less that are located on nonfederal lands and that utilize a man-made conduit operated primarily for non-hydroelectric purposes; and (2) projects that utilize an existing dam or natural water feature (rather than a conduit) and that have a capacity of 5 megawatts or less [24]. However, neither statute insulates FERC from the impact evaluation and resource protection requirements of federal laws such as NEPA. Low-interest federal loans, tax incentives, and guaranteed purchase of output are also spurs to the development of small hydroelectric power [21].

ARMY CORPS OF ENGINEERS

The Corps has authority under various statutes to regulate water resource development in tidal and nontidal waters. Most of this authority arose from "the Rivers and Harbors Acts passed by Congress for the last one-hundred-odd years. These provisions have been loosely codified in Title 33 of the *United States Code*. They are characterized by imprecision, inconsistency, and incongruity" [25]. Thus, there has been a good deal of litigation in this area. Fortunately, authoritative judicial interpretations of Corps enabling acts are incorporated into current Corps regulations [26]. These regulations are the best source of guidance as to Corps regulatory policies and practices. However, administrative regulations are not sacrosanct. Courts can over-turn them for any number of reasons—for example, exceeding statutory authority, being "arbitrary and capricious," or violating procedural or con-stitutional safeguards.

Section 9 of the River and Harbor Act of 1899 prohibits the construction of any dike or dam that completely spans a navigable waterway without congressional consent and Corps approval of plans. Where the navigable portions of the waterbody lie wholly within the limits of a single state, the dam or dike may be built under authority of the legislature of the state if the location and plans are approved by the Corps. Corps approval for these projects is in the form of a permit. Bridges and causeways are regulated by the U.S. Department of Transportation (Coast Guard), not the Corps.

Section 10 of the River and Harbor Act of 1899 prohibits the un-authorized construction in or alteration of any navigable water of the United States. It requires a Corps permit for "the construction of any structure in or over any navigable water . . . , the excavation from or depositing of materi-al . . . , or the accomplishment of any other work affecting the course, location, condition or capacity of [navigable] waters" [26]. The Corps also has jurisdiction over artificial islands, installations, and other devices located on the outer continental shelf, generally beyond the three-mile limit.

Central to understanding the legal impact of section 10 and other Corps programs is the Corps' definition of "navigable waters of the United States." This concept limits the Corps' jurisdiction and designates the area of federal navigation servitude, where the Corps is not required to pay compensation if its activities, e.g., construction projects or permit denials, significantly reduce land values. Corps regulations define navigable waters as

> those waters that are subject to the ebb and flow of the tide and/or are presently used, or have been used in the past, or may be susceptible for use to transport interstate or foreign commerce. A determination of navigability, once made, applies laterally over the entire surface of the waterbody, and is not extinguished by later actions or events which impede or destroy navigable capacity [26].

Tidal waters are presumed to be navigable. The navigability of nontidal waters depends on their suitability for commerce. "Commerce" may be shown by historical use of canoes for commercial purposes, regardless of portages around obstructions, or by commercial transportation of logs. Where a waterbody is located entirely within a state, it is considered navigable "when it physically connects with a generally acknowledged avenue of interstate commerce, such as the ocean or one of the Great Lakes" [26]. As for interstate waterbodies, "Where a waterbody extends through one or more states, but substantial portions, which are capable of bearing interstate commerce, are located in only one of the states, the entirety of the waterway up to the head (upper limit) of navigation is subject to Federal jurisdiction" [26]. To review, a navigable water of the United States must (1) be, or have been; (2) used or susceptible of use; (3) in the customary modes of trade and travel by water; (4) as a highway for interstate commerce.

Artificial channels (canals) are navigable waters if they are used, or are capable of being used, for commerce. This is true even if the canal has been privately developed or passes through private property. "Unplugged canals," open on one or both ends to navigable waters or tide-flowed, are generally navigable, while "plugged" canals are frequently not. Susceptibility for use in commerce depends upon feasibility of commerce after the construction of reasonable improvements. "The improvements need not exist, be planned or even authorized; it is enough that potentially they could be made" [26]. Once a waterbody has been navigable, or could have been navigable, it is legally navigable forever, despite its inability to presently be used for navigation. Thus, an unplugged canal which has been plugged remains navigable in a legal sense.

Federal jurisdiction and the navigation servitude over rivers and lakes include all lands and waters below the ordinary high-water mark of navigable waters. Ocean and coastal waters are presumed to be navigable up to "the line on the shore reached by the plane of the mean (average) high water." This boundary is referred to as the "ebb and flow" line, and divides "section 10 waters" from "fast" land or land above the mean high-water mark. "Where precise determination of the actual location of the line becomes necessary, it must be established by survey with reference to the available tidal datum, preferably averaged over a period of 18.6 years" [26]. Coastal marshlands are legally navigable only if subject to inundation by mean high waters.

Now that it is understood what the Corps means by "navigable waters," it is possible to appreciate the importance and controversial nature of section 404 of the Clean Water Act, which requires a Corps permit for discharge of dredged or fill material into "waters of the United States." Except for dredging unaccompanied by filling, section 404 covers the same activities as section 10. But the scope of section 404 is much broader than "navigable waters." Courts have given "waters of the United States" the broadest possible interpretation consistent with the U.S. Constitution; intrastate streams, freshwater wetlands, drainage ditches, mosquito canals, and intermittent streams are within the reach of section 404. But the Corps, which considers itself a navigation enhancement and downstream flood protection agency, has resisted any extension of its regulatory authority beyond traditionally navigable waters. There has been a continuing battle between environmentalists, on the one hand, who desire the Corps to regulate filling over a wide geographical spectrum, and the Corps, which feels uncomfortable regulating anything but navigable waters. Section 404 and another Corps regulatory provision, section 103 of the Marine Protection Research and Sanctuaries Act of 1972 that governs Corps permits for ocean dumping of dredged spoil, is described more thoroughly in Parts III and IV.

Where navigability has been established, the Corps is more receptive to considering factors in addition to navigation. As a result of several federal statutes and court decisions, the Corps conducts a "public interest review" as part of its section 10 permitting process. This is a general balancing of project benefits and detriments, including impacts on "conservation, economics, aesthetics, general environmental concerns, wetlands, cultural values, fish and wildlife values, flood hazards, flood plain values, land use, navigation, shore erosion and accretion, recreation, water supply and conservation, water quality, energy needs, safety, food and fiber production, [and] mineral needs" [26]. Understandably, the emphasis is on navigation, but the Corps has denied section 10 permits "in the public interest" on solely ecological grounds [27].

Corps permits are of two kinds, individual and general. A general permit may be either regional or nationwide. No separate application or authorization is required for a general permit. It is an authorization on a regional or national basis for a category of activities when "those activities are substantially similar in nature and cause only minimal individual and cumulative environmental impacts" [26]. For example, general section 10 permits may be issued for: (1) structures in previously authorized artificial canals "within principally residential developments"; (2) repair or replacement of previously authorized, "currently serviceable" structures; (3) small bank stabilization projects; and (4) dredging of less than 10 cubic yards. General permits last for five years subject to renewal and incorporate certain conditions, such as protection of public water supply intakes, protection of fish and wildlife, and the application of certain management practices. Division Engineers have the discretion to override general permits and require individual permits. Or, general permits may require case-by-case reporting and acknowledgment systems. Despite strong environmentalist objections, general permits have been upheld by courts and sanctioned by Congress.

The Corps has a number of enforcement options where work has been done without a section 10 permit or where an existing permit has been violated. If the violation is innocuous, the Division Engineer may accept an application for an "after-the-fact" permit. If the unauthorized activity is unacceptable, he may issue a "stop work order," a "restoration order," or both. In issuing a restoration order, the Division Engineer must consider the degree and kind of environmental disturbance caused by the violation as well as the practicality of restoration. Existing permits may be revoked or modified for failure to obey permit conditions. In serious cases, the Division Engineer may refer the matter to the local U.S. attorney for civil or criminal action. Only the Corps may sue to enforce section 10; an individual citizen or citizens' group has no standing under this statute.

Chapter 12

COMPREHENSIVE WATER RESOURCES PLANNING AND RESEARCH

Water resources planning takes place whenever a decision is made about water resources development or protection:

> Water resources planning is carried out at every level of government as well as by private industry. Planning is not decisionmaking but is the prelude to informed decisionmaking. A considerable portion of the Nation's water planning is done in urban areas by city water and sewer departments, sanitary districts, and drainage and flood control districts. In rural areas, local water planning is being done by such agencies as soil conservation districts, watershed districts, and irrigation associations. Some States now have statewide water plans. In many States there are intrastate basin planning organizations, taking many forms, from irrigation districts to river basin authorities [11].

Interstate agencies and the federal government also perform water resources planning. At the federal level, planning evolved as a preliminary to water resources development activities by federal agencies [11].

The major deficiency of American water resources planning has been its fragmentation: water planning has not been adequately integrated with land use planning; planning for river basins has neglected the water-related needs of metropolitan areas; environmental planning, or water quality planning, has been separated from water resources development planning; and federal agency plans have been project-specific, mission-specific, and uncoordinated with water resources plans of other federal agencies and nonfederal organizations [11]. Consequently, comprehensive water resources planning has become the goal of many water resources professionals. Comprehensive water resources planning has two major aspects: (1) "better coordination of the different types and levels of planning, both among Federal agencies and between Federal and non-Federal planners" [11] (i.e., regional or river basin planning); and (2) broadening the traditionally narrow developmental objectives of federal water resources planning to include multiobjective planning.

The Water Resources Planning Act (WRPA) of 1965 [28] was enacted in order to promote comprehensive water resources planning. In 1981, President Reagan nullified the WRPA's effectiveness by dissolving the Water Resources Council and the river basin commissions. However, familiarity with the WRPA's provisions is essential for three reasons: (1) Congress has not repudiated the WRPA, and its institutional system could be reinstated by a more sympathetic administration; (2) there is a clear need for comprehensive water resources planning, and (3) the WRPA experience will serve as valuable data for future institutional development.

In the WRPA, Congress attempted to "encourage the conservation, development, and utilization of water and related land resources . . . on a comprehensive and coordinated basis by the Federal Government, States, localities, and private enterprise."[28] The act established a Water Resources Council, composed of the secretaries of interior, agriculture, army, commerce, and housing and urban development, the administrator of the Environmental Protection Agency, and the chairman of the Federal Energy Regulatory Commission. The council's chairman, as designated by the president, was the secretary of the interior.

The role of the Water Resources Council was fivefold: (1) preparing the national assessment of water supply and demand; (2) developing principles, standards, and procedures for project formulation and evaluation; (3) establishing and maintaining liaison with river basin commissions, and formulating principles and standards for the preparation of comprehensive regional or river basin plans; (4) making grants to states for water planning; and (5) reviewing river basin plans. The Water Resources Council was not given a project review function by the WRPA. But the "principles and standards" for project evaluation were recognized as potentially having a crucial hortatory effect on federal development agencies.

The principles and standards were developed from the Flood Control Act of 1936 that approved federal investment and participation by the Corps in flood control projects "if the benefits to whomsoever they may accrue are in excess of the estimated costs, and if the lives and social security of people are otherwise adversely affected." This "benefit-cost analysis" was extended to other federal development agencies, making project justification depend upon a favorable ratio of benefits to costs. The principles and standards were intended to clarify and rationalize this benefit-cost analysis, and to resolve such contentious issues as the objectives of federal water resources development, the discount rate for future benefits, and the treatment of project alternatives [11].

After years of controversy, the principles and standards were issued in 1973. They defined the objectives of water and land resource planning as national economic development and environmental quality, with regional development and social well-being as secondary objectives [29]. The principles and standards established a detailed planning process, with instructions for the formulation of alternative plans and analysis of trade-offs among alternatives, including nonstructural alternatives. In practice, these principles and standards had little effect on agency planning, partly because the Water Resources Council could not enforce them through project reviews [29]. When President Carter announced his water resources policy, it included reform of the Water Resources Council and its principles and standards. Carter ordered the Council to revise the principles and standards to emphasize water conservation and nonstructural alternatives. Then, he issued an executive order requiring an independent water project review by the Water Resources Council. However, the Water Resources Council was unable to implement this order because of congressional opposition [29]. President Reagan revoked the executive order, rescinded the principles and standards, and finally abolished the Water Resources Council. New "principles and guidelines" were released on March 10, 1983, and became effective on July 8, 1983. They are not legally binding on government planners.

Under the WRPA, one of the pivotal responsibilities of the Water Resources Council was to supervise the work of the new river basin commissions and make recommendations to the president for integrating river basin plans with federal water resources development. These river basin commissions were to be established by presidential executive order on request of the Water Resources Council or a state. The Council and at least one-half the basin states were required to consent to a commission's establishment. River basin commissions were to perform planning and coordination functions:

> Each commission is to serve as the principal agency for the coordination of Federal, State, interstate, local, and private water development plans for the basin; to prepare and keep up-to-date a comprehensive coordinated joint plan, including an evaluation of all reasonable alternatives and recommendations for individual projects; to establish priorities for the collection of basic data, for planning and for construction of projects; and to undertake studies necessary for preparing the plan [11].

River basin commissions possessed no regulatory or construction authority. They were intended as consensus-building and advisory entities. Seven river basin commissions were formed under the WRPA and six survived. However, the so-called Comprehensive Coordinated Joint Plans were uneven in quality.

The structure of river basin commissions inhibited their activities. The chairman of the commission was appointed by the president, but could not be a member of a federal agency. Except for the chairman, all commission members represented, and were paid by, other organizations. Each federal agency with a substantial interest in the river basin, each state in the basin, and each appropriate interstate or international agency was entitled to membership. Nothing could be accomplished without consensus of all members [11].

As for financing of river basin commissions,

> They operate administratively on small budget. Neither Congress nor the member States appropriate money to the river basin commission for planning. Instead, Congress appropriates money directly to the member Federal agencies, and the States appropriate planning moneys to the member State agencies. The financial control over the river basin commission planning effort thus resides in the member agencies [11].

Is it, therefore, any wonder that "member Federal agencies, States, and interstate agencies often pursued their water goals without using the river basin commission" [11]? On the other hand, there is evidence that the river basin commissions served as valuable forums for bargaining and dispute resolution. At any rate, President Reagan must have felt that their costs outweighed their benefits because he discontinued them.

Many federal agencies either perform water resources research or make contracts or grants for its performance. These include the development agencies, the "protection agencies" (e.g., EPA, Coast Guard, National Park Service), and the U.S. Geological Survey in the Department of the Interior. Congress made an attempt to coordinate this governmental research with state and university water resources research in the Water Resources Research Act of 1964, and its successor the Water Research and Development Act of 1978 (WRDA) [30]. Like the Water Resources Planning Act, WRDA established a central coordinating entity, called the Office of Water Research and Technology (OWRT) in the Department of the Interior, and regional coordinating bodies, the water resources research institutes located at state land grant universities. It was the OWRT's function "to promote research and development, demonstration, and technology transfer," and "to promote the training of scientists, engineers, and other skilled personnel" by making grants and contracts for multidisciplinary water resources research, and by maintaining "a national center for the acquisition, processing, and dissemination of information dealing with all areas of water resources research, technology development, and demonstration" [30]. The state institutes were to plan and conduct research, screen proposals, coordinate with state officials, and disseminate research results. Early in his administration, President Reagan abolished the OWRT and announced his intention to cut off funding for grants to state water resources research institutes. However, President Reagan's veto of funding for the program was overridden by Congress in March 1984. The U.S. Geological Survey is now carrying out the functions once performed by the OWRT.

Chapter 13
LIMITATIONS ON FEDERAL DEVELOPMENT AND LICENSING

NATIONAL ENVIRONMENTAL POLICY ACT

The National Environmental Policy Act (NEPA) revolutionized federal water resources development, licensing, planning, and research. It requires that environmental impacts of a proposed action and its alternatives be identified early in the planning process, and that these factors be brought to the attention of concerned citizens, interested governmental officials, and if necessary the courts. Since 1970 when NEPA was signed into law, literally hundreds of water resources projects have been withdrawn or modified because they could not stand the light of NEPA's day.

Section 102(c) of NEPA requires each federal agency that proposes a major action having a significant effect on the human environment to prepare and circulate, in draft and final form, an environmental impact statement (EIS) disclosing the environmental impacts of the proposed action, reasonable alternatives and their impacts, long- and short-term effects, cumulative effects, irretrievable commitments of resources, and the agency's balance among environmental protection and economic development, national security, or other factors. Even where the proposing agency believes that a proposed action will not have a significant environmental impact, it must nevertheless prepare and circulate a mini-EIS, called an "environmental assessment," accompanied by a finding of no significant

75

impact (FONSI). Federal actions covered by NEPA are not only construction projects but also licenses, leases, contracts, permits, loans, and research projects which may have significant effects on the environment. An EIS may be programmatic, regional, or site-specific; various levels of EISs may be "tiered." When an agency does not comply with NEPA's requirements, a court may, if it serves the public interest, enjoin the proposed action until an adequate EIS has been completed and disseminated.

NEPA does not mandate particular results: it does not compel a federal agency to adopt the least environmentally damaging alternative, although the agency must explain why it was not chosen. Courts frequently refer to NEPA as an "environmental full disclosure law," obliging an agency to take a "hard look" at the environmental consequences of its actions. A complete EIS, subject, of course, to NEPA's "rule of reason," is conclusive evidence that the proposing agency has given "good faith consideration" to the environment. Once the EIS is complete, i.e., the agency makes full disclosure, the political process, not the courts, determines the outcome, unless the proposal is so outrageous that it is "arbitrary and capricious." In most instances, NEPA does guarantee that other federal agencies having expertise in the area, state and local officials, and the general public will have an opportunity to formally comment on a proposed federal action before it is undertaken, and that Congress will have access to relevant information on which to make authorizations and appropriations.

Where federal agencies have taken their NEPA responsibilities seriously, traditional agency missions have been expanded to include environmental protection. However, all too often the EIS becomes a massive, unreadably technical rationalization of an action chosen on political grounds. The Council on Environmental Quality (CEQ), also established by NEPA, has issued regulations to curtail this superabundance of NEPA riches [32]. These regulations are binding on federal agencies and enforceable in court. They are also the lay person's most reliable source of information on current NEPA law.

OTHER FEDERAL LIMITING STATUTES AND ORDERS

These are generally incorporated within the NEPA process. The Fish and Wildlife Coordination Act [33], originally enacted in 1934, requires federal agencies proposing to construct or license water resource development projects to consult with the Fish and Wildlife Service (FWS), Department of the Interior, with a view toward conserving fish and wildlife resources. The report of the FWS under the act must include proposed measures for mitigating or compensating for damage to wildlife resources resulting from the project. The proposing agency is only required to fully consider the FWS report. In contrast to the Fish and Wildlife Coordination Act, the Endangered Species Act (ESA) of 1973 [34] imposes enforceable substantive requirements on federal officials. This statute can be utilized to permanently block a water resources project if its construction or operation is inconsistent with the preservation of endangered or threatened species.

The first step in the ESA process is the listing of an endangered or threatened species and its critical habitat. Once a species and its habitat has been listed, all federal agencies "shall seek to conserve the endangered species." The act defines "conserve" as meaning "to use all methods and procedures which are necessary" to rescue a listed species from endangerment.

Most of the litigation under ESA has arisen under section 7, which requires each federal agency to "insure that any action authorized, funded, or carried out by [it] is not likely to jeopardize the continued existence of the endangered or threatened species or result in the destruction or adverse modification of [critical] habitat." When a significant adverse impact on endangered or threatened species is likely, a federal agency proposing to construct or license a water resource project must initiate a formal consultation process with the federal agency having expertise in the area. Until this "biological opinion" has been received, no action may be taken on the project. If its consultation process results in a finding that a proposed project jeopardizes the continued existence of the species or its critical habitat, the project must be dropped or modified to mitigate the potential adverse impacts.

In *TVA* v. *Hill* [35], the famous snail darter case, the U.S. Supreme Court enjoined the completion of the nearly finished Tellico Dam because the impoundment would have resulted in total destruction of the snail darter's habitat. The Court saw an "irreconcilable conflict" between section 7 and the dam's existence. Finally, Congress, as it has done in a number of NEPA cases, declared the Tellico Dam to be in compliance with ESA, allowing the impoundment to be closed.

After the *Hill* case, Congress amended ESA to create an exemption from the previously absolute bar of section 7. If an irreconcilable conflict still persists after analysis of alternatives and mitigation planning, an Endangered Species Committee may grant an exemption from section 7. Composed of federal officials and a representative of the affected state, the committee can only grant an exemption if (1) there is no "reasonable and prudent" alternative to the agency action; (2) the benefits "clearly outweigh" the benefits of conservation alternatives; and (3) the agency action is of regional or national significance. No exemption has yet been granted. Most section 7 disputes are settled by mitigation agreed upon during the consultation stage.

The National Historic Preservation Act of 1966 [36] established the National Register of Historic Places. It also requires federal agencies to consult with the Advisory Council on Historic Preservation whenever federal projects could have adverse impacts on these historic or archeological sites. In 1976 the act was amended to extend its protection to properties eligible for listing on the National Register of Historic Places. By regulation, the proposing federal agency must consult a state historic preservation officer (SHPO) when determining how its activities will affect historic or archaeological sites. The procedures also require that the SHPO, along with the advisory council and the proposing agency, reach written agreement in certain cases on how to mitigate adverse effects expected from a federal project. Before a dam is constructed or licensed, the council must be given an opportunity to collect and preserve archeological data.

The Wild and Scenic Rivers Act [37] was originally enacted in 1968, and has been subsequently amended several times. The statute is administered by the secretary of the interior, through the National Park Service, and when national forests are involved, by the secretary of agriculture through the Forest Service. The act establishes a national Wild and Scenic Rivers System and defines criteria for eligibility under each of the three classifications of the law: wild, scenic, and recreational rivers. This process is examined in detail in Part III. The act provides that "no department or agency of the United States shall assist by loan, grant, license, or otherwise in the construction of any water resources project that would have a direct and adverse effect on the values for which such river was established, as determined by the Secretary charged with its administration." As with the ESA, this prohibition is preceded by mandatory consultation between the proposing agency and the appropriate federal resource protection agency.

The Coastal Zone Management Act [38] provides for federal financial assistance to coastal state governments for the development and implementation of coastal zone management plans. These plans have as their primary function land use management for the coastal zone to assure the orderly and environmentally sound development of these ecologically sensitive areas. Under the act, a federal or federally assisted or licensed project is required to be, "to the maximum extent practicable," consistent with an approved coastal zone management plan. At the federal level, the Coastal Zone Management Program is administered by the Office of Coastal Zone Management of the National Oceanic and Atmospheric Administration of the Department of Commerce. The Commerce Department finally determines the "consistency" of a proposed project with a state plan.

Two executive orders issued by former President Carter have become part of the federal coordination process intended to prevent environmental damage from federal actions. Executive Order 11988, issued on May 24, 1977, and entitled "Floodplain Management," directs each federal agency to "reduce the risk of flood loss, . . . minimize the impact of floods on human safety, health and welfare, and . . . restore and preserve the natural and beneficial values served by floodplains." Agencies are to incorporate floodplain planning into their decision making and ensure that federal structures and facilities are consistent with federal flood insurance and floodplain management programs. The National Flood Insurance Act of 1968 [39] attempts to shift the federal focus from construction of dams and other facilities to sound land use planning within floodplain areas. The National Flood Insurance Program authorizes subsidized flood insurance for communities that participate in local land use planning in flood-prone areas. This statute is analyzed in Part III.

Executive Order 11990, issued on the same date as Executive Order 11988, is entitled "Protection of Wetlands." Each federal agency must "minimize the destruction, loss or degradation of wetlands, and preserve and enhance the natural and beneficial values of wetlands." In addition to doing wetlands planning, federal agencies must avoid undertaking or licensing construction in wetlands unless "there is no practicable alternative," and then all "practicable measures to minimize harm" must be taken.

There is no absolute prohibition on water resources projects in national parks, monuments, and wildlife refuges. However, there are specific statutes which deal with the protection of particular areas [5]. In wilderness areas established under the National Wilderness Act of 1964 [40], the president may approve a water resources project if he determines that it "will better serve the interests of the United States . . . than will its denial."

In addition to the section 404 program, several provisions of federal water pollution control law might place limitations on federal water resources development, assistance to private developers, and licensing. The Safe Drinking Water Act [41] prohibits federal financial assistance for any project that may, through a recharge zone, contaminate an aquifer designated by the Environmental Protection Agency as a sole or principal source of drinking water for an area. Examples of proscribed federal financial assistance are grants, contracts, loans, and loan guarantees.

Section 401 of the Clean Water Act [42] requires an applicant for a federal license or permit for any activity that may result in water pollution to obtain a certification from the state where the discharge originates that the discharge will comply with applicable effluent limitations and water quality standards. In contrast to the Coastal Zone Management Act, where a "consistency" determination is up to the federal agency, a state's denial of 401 certification or its conditional certification is binding on federal officials. This effectively gives states a veto over federal permits such as Corps 404 permits. Moreover, even though a federal project may be exempt from the requirement of obtaining a 404 permit, a state can control the discharge of dredged or fill material by federal agencies into navigable waters within the state unless the Corps claims interference with its navigation power, i.e., navigation cannot be maintained if the state conditions are met [43].

Under section 102(b) of the Clean Water Act, any federal agency planning the construction or financing of a reservoir shall consider the inclusion of storage for regulation of streamflow, but "storage and water releases shall not be provided as a substitute for adequate treatment or other methods of controlling waste at the source." The EPA administrator's comments on "the need for, the value of, and the impact of, storage for water quality control" must be a part of the project report submitted to Congress. The economic value of storage for regulation of streamflow is taken into account as a project benefit, but this value must not constitute a disproportionate share of project benefits. Costs of streamflow regulation features are reimbursable or nonreimbursable depending on whether beneficiaries can be identified. Where hydroelectric projects are concerned there is a quantitative limit to the inclusion of storage for regulation of streamflow for water quality control.

Finally, where federal-aid highways are concerned, section 4(f) of the Department of Transportation Act [44] prohibits the secretary of transportation from approving a project that requires the use of any publicly owned land from a public park, recreation area, or wildlife or waterfowl refuge or any land from an historic site unless (1) there is no feasible and prudent alternative to the use of such land, and (2) all possible planning has been done to minimize environmental harm. The term "use" means not only direct interference with public land but also indirect impacts such as noise or loss of access. Under section 4(f) parkland is given paramount importance, and the secretary of transportation "cannot approve the destruction of parkland unless he finds that alternative routes present unique difficulties" [45].

REFERENCES FOR PART II

1. Trelease, F. J. "Federal-State Relations in Water Law," National Water Commission, NTIS PB 203 600 (1971), p. 39.
2. Morreale, E. H. "Federal-State Rights and Relations," in *Waters and Water Rights*, R. E. Clark, ed. (7 vols., Indianapolis, IN: Allen Smith Co., 1967–1978), II, p. 9. The seven-volume treatise is hereafter referred to as "Clark."
3. Harnsberger, R. S. "Eminent Domain and Water," in Clark, IV, p. 114.
4. The Rivers and Harbors Act of 1970, P.L. 91–611, § 111, 84 Stat. 1818 (1970).
5. Hillhouse, W. A. "The Federal Law of Water Resources Development," in *Federal Environmental Law*, E. L. Dolgin and T. G. P. Guilbert, eds. (St. Paul, MN: West Publishing Co., 1974), p. 848.
6. P.L. 97–293, 96 Stat. 1263.
7. Sax, J. L. "Federal Reclamation Law," in Clark, II, p. 121. The following discussion is based on Professor Sax's exhaustive treatise.
8. *California* v. *United States*, 438 U.S. 645 (1978).
9. DeWeerdt, J. L., and P. M. Glick, eds. "A Summary-Digest of the Federal Water Laws and Programs," National Water Commission, U.S. Government Printing Office (1973), p. 73.
10. Castleberry, J. N. "Federal Flood Control Activities," in Clark, IV, p. 222.
11. "Water Policies for the Future," National Water Commission, U.S. Government Printing Office (1973), p. 128.
12. 42 U.S.C. § 4321, et seq.
13. 16 U.S.C. § 1001, et seq.
14. Castleberry, J. N. "Watershed Protection," in Clark, IV, p. 243.
15. Goldfarb, W., and J. Heenehan. "Legal Control of Soil Erosion and Sedimentation in New Jersey," *Rutgers Camden Law Journal* 11(3):379–422 (1980), p. 402.
16. Holmes, B. H. "History of Federal Water Resources Programs and Policies, 1961–1970," U.S. Department of Agriculture, U.S. Government Printing Office (1979), p. 71.
17. *Pacific Gas & Electric Co.* v. *State Energy Resources Conservation and Development Commission*, 18 ERC 1991 (United States Supreme Court, 1983).
18. Castleberry, J. N. "The Federal Power Commission and Water Power Licenses," in Clark, IV, p. 301.
19. 16 U.S.C. § 803(a).
20. 354 F. 2d 608 (2nd Cir., 1965), *cert. den.* 384 U.S. 941.
21. Energy Law Institute, Franklin Pierce Law Center. "National Hydroelectric Power Resources Study: Legal and Institutional Aspects of Hydroelectric Power Development and Operation," Corps Report IWR-82-H-5 (1981), p. VII.

22. Goldfarb, W. "Litigation and Legislation," *Water Resources Bulletin* 17(3):522–523 (1981).
23. 16 U.S.C. § 823, et seq.
24. Burke, S. H. "Small Scale Hydroelectric Development and Federal Environmental Law: A Guide for the Private Developer," *Boston College Environmental Affairs Law Review* 9(4):815–861 (1981), p. 845.
25. Power, G. "The Federal Role in Coastal Development," in *Federal Environmental Law*, note 5 above, p. 813.
26. 33 CFR pt. 320 et seq.
27. *Zabel* v. *Tabb*, 430 F. 2d 199 (5th Cir. 1970), *cert. den.* 401 U.S. 910 (1971).
28. 42 U.S.C. § 1962 et seq.
29. Jaffe, A. B. "Benefit-Cost Analysis and Multi-Objective Evaluation of Federal Water Projects," *Harvard Environmental Law Review* 4(1):58–85 (1980), p. 70.
30. 42 U.S.C. § 7801 et seq.
31. 42 U.S.C. § 4321 et seq.
32. 40 CFR pt. 1500 et seq.
33. 16 U.S.C. § 661 et seq.
34. 16 U.S.C. § 1531 et seq.
35. 437 U.S. 153 (1978).
36. 16 U.S.C. § 470 et seq.
37. 16 U.S.C. § 1271 et seq.
38. 16 U.S.C. § 1415 et seq.
39. 42 U.S.C. § 4001 et seq.
40. 16 U.S.C. § 1131 et seq.
41. 42 U.S.C. § 300h-3(e).
42. 33 U.S.C. § 1341.
43. 33 U.S.C. § 1344(t).
44. 49 U.S.C. § 1653(f).
45. *Citizens to Preserve Overton Park* v. *Volpe*, 401 U.S. 402 (1971).

PART III
Nontransformational Uses

Law is an institutionalized means of resolving conflicts in socially acceptable ways. Thus, as conflicts in a particular sphere of social interaction increase so does legal activity. The burgeoning demand for nontransformational uses of water resources in recent years has intensified disputes among nontransformational users, e.g., competition for Colorado River rafting permits, and between nontransformational and transformational users, e.g., trout fishermen against dam builders. Heightened legal activity in these areas can be expected to continue.

Three categories of nontransformational use are discussed in this part: (1) recreational, aesthetic, and ecological uses of rivers, lakes, and shorelands; (2) floodplains and wetlands protection; and (3) water resource enhancement without additional water treatment.

Chapter 14
USE OF RIVERS AND STREAMS

PUBLIC USE: OWNERSHIP OF BEDS AND BANKS

To a great extent, public use of rivers and streams for fishing, boating, and swimming, and public use of riverbanks for hiking, camping, and similar activities depends on whether the riverbed and immediate banks are owned by a state or by private riparian owners. Where a state owns the beds and banks, a river is said to be "public"—capable of public in-place use up to the limit of state ownership, the high-water mark. These public rights are qualified in two major ways: (1) public users must legally gain access to the river corridor; and (2) public users must comply with state and local regulations regarding fish and game, noise, littering, etc.

In almost all states, beds and banks of tidelands and navigable rivers are owned by the state. Even in those few states where beds and banks of nontidal navigable rivers are owned by riparians, the result is the same because the riparian owner holds the beds and banks subject to public rights of navigation and in-place use [1]. The concept of "navigability" is one of the most meaningful and difficult elements of water law. As shown in Part II, the limits of federal jurisdiction over waters based on the Commerce Clause, i.e., federal regulation and the navigation servitude, are determined under a federal navigability test: Is the waterway tidal or suitable for interstate commerce? "Navigability" also governs ownership of beds and banks, and this second navigability test is also a matter of federal law; but there are significant differences between this "title test" and the "jurisdiction test" discussed in Part II. In the first place, the "title test" involves navigability at the time of the formation of the Union in the original states or the admission to statehood of those formed later, not whether the waterway can be made navigable by artificial improvements [2]. Second, under the title test navigability in *intrastate* commerce is all that is required, not usability in *interstate* commerce [2]. The first difference is more important where rivers are concerned: potential navigability after dredging or channelization will not satisfy the title test, although it will satisfy the jurisdiction test. The second difference is more important where lakes are concerned: large, isolated, intrastate lakes might satisfy the title test but not the jurisdiction test. Both tests liberally interpret "commerce" in terms of fur traders' canoes or commercial log floating. In summary, tidal waters and all nontidal waters that are reasonably capable of supporting intrastate commerce by commercial water craft, in the manner and mode that was customary at the date of a state's admission to the Union, are deemed navigable waters, and the beds and banks are owned by a state [3].

In some states the state itself also holds title to beds and banks of waters that are not navigable under the federal title test. But the overwhelming majority rule is that riparian owners on rivers that are nonnavigable under the federal title test own up to the "thread" (center line of the main channel) of the river. The derivation of this rule is as follows:

> Historically, public rights attained to navigable waters because of the public need to use such waters. Since the basic public use was navigation, it was assumed that waters not susceptible to navigation were not required for public use. As a consequence, there were no public rights in non-navigable waters, their beds, or banks [3].

Thus, the classic legal position was that the public had no rights to use waterways nonnavigable under the federal title test.

The strict classic rule has been modified or abolished in every state except Colorado, where a landowner can prohibit floaters from using a stream overlying his riverbed even though no contact with bed or banks is made [4]. Some states bar wading and fishing from a boat but allow floating on the theory that water cannot be privately owned, but is owned by the state in trust for the general public. Other states prohibit wading but allow fishing from a boat because fish are also held in trust by the state. Still other states bar wading but allow contact with the streambed for pushing or pulling a boat. In many states, particular nonnavigable rivers have become public because of long-term public use ("prescriptive easement") [4].

But the most interesting development toward loosening the classic restrictions on public use of nonnavigable rivers is the tendency of states to redefine "navigability" under state law to support public uses. Courts in a number of states have decided that public rights exist in waters that are "navigable in fact," "floatable," or usable by boats. In other states, legislatures have defined "navigability" as the capacity to "float logs," or, more generally, in terms of suitability for pleasure craft [4]. We have here a third definition of "navigability," this time under state law, which emphasizes recreational navigation and other appropriate public uses. And where the river or stream itself has become public, the public will also be able to make reasonable recreational use of the banks below the high-water mark. According to Professor Stone, the trend is toward opening for public use all waters suitable for public use [1]. The states of California, Florida, Massachusetts, Michigan, Missouri, New York, Ohio, and Wisconsin, among others, have already moved in this direction, and we can expect legal activity in other states pointed toward making erstwhile private streams public.

PUBLIC ACCESS

Although a river, the beds and banks of which are privately owned, may still be usable by the public, this designation will be academic unless there is public access. It is true that state and local governments can prosecute crimes and abate nuisances which take place on private property. But governments cannot simply declare public rights of use on private property above the high-water mark without opening themselves up to takings claims. "For example, it is clear that a privately-owned farm will not be subject to public use for pheasant hunting, against the wishes of the owner, . . . even though, if hunting is conducted thereon, State regulations will control as to seasons, licensing and bag limits" [3]. Access to public waterways through private property must in most cases be purchased, leased, or acquired by eminent domain from the landowner. And in these days of depleted government coffers, this may be tantamount to no public access at all.

Fortunately, there are many instances where access to public waters may be procured without governmental outlay. The river may be reached from a public right of way for a road or railroad; once there, a user can walk or wade below the high-water mark. Canoeists may gain access at upstream public property and float down through private property, beaching their canoes and using the immediate banks for picnicking and camping. In addition, there are state legal doctrines mitigating the general rule that the public has no right to cross private land to reach public waters. New England Great Ponds are not only public waters but the public is given rights to cross certain private lands in order to reach them. Access may also be simplified in states once covered by the Northwest Ordinance [1].

Prescriptive easements and implied dedication may also be relied upon to establish public access. An "easement" is a legal right to use another's land, most often for passage. Where the public generally has used a pathway continuously, openly, and adversely to the landowner for the prescriptive period, the public may acquire an easement to continue that use. Commonly, a landowner's defense to the claim of a public prescriptive easement is to assert that the public use was permissive, not adverse [1]. But permissive use may give rise to an implied dedication of access to the public:

> Dedication is the donation of land, or of rights in land, to the public for the use of the public. It requires only an intent on the part of the landowner . . . to dedicate and an acceptance on the part of the public. Unlike prescription, no minimum period of public use is required, . . . And since an essential element is the intent that the public have the use of the land, dedication is necessarily permissive in character; the critical question is likely to be whether by his acquiescence the landowner intended a permanent dedication or only a temporary, revocable license [1].

Actual public use is the key to proving an implied dedication, but it is also helpful if public funds have been used to maintain the disputed right of way, or if the landowner has fenced the area off from his other lands.

INSTREAM FLOW PROTECTION

Assurances of public usability and public access are futile if the streamflow is inadequate for public recreational use. Consequently, legal protection of minimum instream flows has expanded commensurate with increased recreational demands on water resources.

In Professor Tarlock's view, "The discretion to allow public or private diversion or dedication of waters to instream use rests with the appropriate sovereign; there is no federal or state duty to dedicate water for instream uses" [5].

Eastern and western states take different approaches to instream flow protection. Once a western state has made a political decision to preserve minimum flow, it can choose among direct and indirect methods of flow preservation.

> Direct methods of dedication include (1) public . . . appropriative rights to a specific quantity of flow for a particular period of time, (2) administrative or legislative withdrawals or reservations of specific streams or specific amounts of water in the stream from appropriation, (3) the systematic review by the permit-granting agency of new appropriation applications to determine if reservation in-place for fish and wildlife preservation, for example, constitutes a higher beneficial use, thus justifying denial or modification of an application to appropriate where unappropriated water is otherwise available, and (4) federal reserved rights for instream uses [5].

Indirect methods include limited term permits, vigorous prosecution of forfeiture and abandonment cases, and conservation.

All western states have enacted statutes recognizing recreation and fish and wildlife protection as beneficial uses. Only Washington lists aesthetics as beneficial. But there are formidable legal obstacles to implementing direct methods of flow preservation [5]. In the first place, many western rivers are already fully appropriated. Compensation would be necessary to preserve minimum flows on these waterways. Second, a few states still require an actual diversion before an appropriative right can be granted. Third, federal reserved rights to instream flows were limited by the U.S. Supreme Court in the *U.S.* v. *New Mexico* case [6], where the Court held that the Forest Service cannot claim reserved rights for instream flows where forest and watershed protection are not directly involved. Nevertheless, the effectuation of direct instream flow protection strategies has proceeded remarkably smoothly in the west when one considers that under classic appropriation law an appropriator can divert the entire streamflow for a beneficial use.

Eastern instream flow protection statutes differ widely as to intention and methodology. Some eastern states seek to protect downstream riparians from the potential adverse effects of upstream flood control impoundments. These states have typically enacted statutes requiring that historical or reasonable flows be maintained below dams. Other state legislatures intended to maintain minimum flows for fish and wildlife preservation or broad "public interest" reasons. The instream flow standards found in these eastern statutes vary considerably [7]. Some are purely descriptive ("average flow," "average minimum flow," "normal flow," "optimum flow"). Others attempt to set minimum flows more quantitatively. For example, a North Carolina statute looks to "the average minimum flow for a period of seven consecutive days that have an average of one in 10 years" [8]. Where legislature or administrative agencies in eastern states fail to set minimum flows, courts may be forced to do so in the context of private lawsuits among riparian landowners. However, public interests may not be adequately served by the sharing among private landowners that is characteristic of the riparian system.

WILD AND SCENIC RIVERS PROTECTION

In 1968 Congress passed the Wild and Scenic Rivers Act [9], declaring it to be "the policy of the United States that certain selected rivers of the Nation which, with their immediate environments, possess outstandingly remarkable scenic, recreational, geologic, fish and wildlife, historic, cultural, or other similar values, shall be preserved in free-flowing condition, and that they and their immediate environments shall be protected for the benefit and enjoyment of present and future generations." This act established the wild and scenic rivers system, which now includes approximately 2,300 miles of twenty-seven rivers. The Alaska National Interest Lands and Conservation Act of 1980 added twenty-six Alaskan rivers to the national system.

Rivers are admitted to the system in two ways. The legislature of a state through which a river flows may designate the river as wild, scenic, or recreational and request the governor to petition the secretary of the interior for inclusion in the federal system. The secretary can only consent if the river is to be permanently administered by the state "without expense to the United States other than for administration and management of federally owned lands." Land and Water Conservation Act funds are not considered as an "expense to the United States." Because states have so little to gain by this method of inclusion in the federal system, and so much to lose by foreclosing options with regard to a river, few rivers have been added to the system by state designation. Proponents of river preservation recommend that Congress establish a separate grants program to stimulate state designation of rivers.

Most rivers in the federal wild and scenic rivers system have been included by act of Congress. A number of "instant" river components were designated when the Wild and Scenic Rivers Act was passed in 1968. Nowadays, Congress must first designate a particular river or segment as a "study river." (Occasionally, Congress votes a river into the system without a formal study having been made, as in the case of the New River in North Carolina.) Then, the secretary of the interior, through the National Park Service (NPS) which administers the system, performs a study and reports to the president on the suitability of the river for inclusion in the system. Before submitting its report to the president, NPS must solicit comments from the federal water resource development agencies and the governor of each state involved. On the basis of the report and comments, the president may recommend designation to Congress, which may then pass another act admitting the river to the system. This process is so protracted and cumbersome that, for the most part, comparatively few noncontroversial rivers are designated. Ironically, congressional nomination as a study river may result in destruction of the very values that made the river worthy of potential admission to the system. Since there are no restrictions on private activities during the study period, lasting ten years in some cases, land speculation, development, and tourism — enhanced by increased publicity — exacerbate existing threats to a river's wild, scenic, and recreational resources.

In passing a river into the federal system, Congress names a federal management agency that is required to determine the boundaries of the river component, decide whether it is to be managed as a wild, scenic, or recreational river, and prepare a management plan. However, the boundaries of the river component are limited to 320 acres per mile, approximately one-fourth mile, on both sides of the river. The Wild and Scenic Rivers Act makes no attempt to protect a river from the adverse effects of private development in the watershed beyond the corridor.

Even within the corridor federal management authority is limited. The act contains no authority for federal agencies to regulate, by zoning or otherwise, private land uses within the corridor. Moreover, there are strict acreage, percentage, and other restrictions on federal condemnation of fee simple interests in the corridor. (A "fee simple interest" is the entire bundle of rights that we call land ownership.) Congress placed these restrictions on fee condemnation in order to placate local governments, which traditionally complain of a federal "land grab" when they lose property tax ratables by condemnation. Instead, Congress stressed the purchase or condemnation of "scenic easements," rights to develop river corridors, which are less than fee simple interests and accordingly leave "title" in the landowner. But scenic easements are almost as expensive as fee interests, and funds for the acquisition of easements are scarce. Because the threat of federal condemnation is frequently hollow, a wild or scenic river is inadequately protected against private development that jeopardizes its integrity. Local governments are generally more interested in development than preservation.

In contrast, a federal wild, scenic, or recreational river is protected against incompatible *federal* activities by section 7(a) of the act:

> The Federal Power Commission [now the Federal Energy Regulatory Commission in the Department of Energy] shall not license the construction of any dam, conduit, reservoir, powerhouse, transmission line, or other project or works . . . , on or directly affecting any river which is designated . . . as a component of the national wild and scenic rivers system or which is hereafter designated for inclusion in that system, and no department or agency of the United States shall assist by loan, grant, license, or otherwise in the construction of any water resources project that would have a direct and adverse effect on the values for which such river was established, as determined by the Secretary charged with its administration. Nothing contained in the foregoing sentence, however, shall preclude licensing of, or assistance to, developments below or above a wild, scenic or recreational river area or on any stream tributary thereto which will not invade the area or unreasonably diminish the scenic, recreational, and fish and wildlife values present in the area.

Study rivers are afforded the same protection during the first six years of the study period. Federal lands within or adjacent to the corridor must be managed in accordance with the management plan developed by the managing federal agency.

Because of its lack of authority for federal control of private activities inside and outside river corridors, the federal Wild and Scenic Rivers Act has been more successful in preserving rivers that flow through federal land. An alternative to inclusion of a river in the federal wild and scenic rivers system is utilization of a state rivers preservation program. Approximately twenty-five states have rivers protection legislation. These are variable with regard to methods of designation, land use controls, condemnation powers, and prohibitions on state activities [10,11]. Admission to a strong state program may be preferable to the vagaries of the federal process, but no state rivers statute can conclusively protect a river against federal development activities or private development under federal license. Another major advantage of the federal process is that designation of a wild, scenic, or recreational river creates an implied federal reserved right for instream flow maintenance with priority as of the designation date [5]. This is true even though states otherwise control water diversions on wild and scenic rivers.

The state of Oregon has adopted unique measures for protecting its riverine areas. First, an owner of riparian land who agrees to protect or restore streamside vegetation is eligible for a complete property tax exemption for qualifying lands. Second, Oregon law provides for a state personal income tax credit for up to 25 percent of the costs incurred in a fish habitat improvement project certified by the state.

COMPETING NONTRANSFORMATIONAL USES

Conflicts between nontransformational and transformational river users have been common for many years; e.g., disputes over instream flow protection, attempts to forestall or modify water resources development using one of the federal statutes mentioned in Part II or a state counterpart, and water pollution control efforts. But a relatively recent phenomenon is the competition among nontransformational users for river recreation. These conflicts arise both between and within use classes. For example, boat and bank fishermen may lobby for restrictions on canoeing in a particular river because the fishermen claim that canoeists are disturbing them and the fish. Within the fishing fraternity, fly-fishermen frequently seek to exclude bait and spin fishermen from a river by recommending the imposition of "fly-fishing only" or "catch-and-release" regulations. These internecine battles among nontransformational users can only intensify as recreational pressure on river resources increases.

In this context, the case of *Wilderness Public Rights Fund* v. *Kleppe* [12] was a harbinger of the future. There, the U.S. Court of Appeals for the Ninth Circuit was called upon to determine the validity of a National Park Service decision allocating user days on the Colorado River between commercial and noncommercial rafters. Access to Colorado River rafting has been limited since 1972. No raft trip may be made without an NPS permit, and river use had been frozen at the 1972 level — 92 percent allotted to commercial concessioners who lead guided trips for a fee, and 8 percent to noncommercial users who apply for permits as private groups. The plaintiff, Wilderness Public Rights Fund (WPRF), argued that its members were being unfairly treated, and advocated a lottery or first-come-first-served permit system which would allow successful permittees to choose between joining a guided party or a noncommercial party. Is it fair, asked the WPRF, that noncommercial applicants be compelled to plan their trips years in advance while these neophytes who make guided trips can contact concessioners and make arrangements at the last minute? Before the court could render its decision, NPS changed its allocation to 70 percent of user days for commercial trips and 30 percent for noncommercial trips.

Chapter 15
USE OF LAKES

Property owners located on the shores of an ocean, sea, or lake are called "littoral owners" and their water rights are referred to as "littoral rights." This chapter focuses on rights of littoral owners and the general public in recreational resources of inland lakes.

Like rivers, lakes are either public or private. Public lakes are those (1) whose beds and banks are owned by the state, (2) that are "navigable-in-fact" or suitable for public recreation under liberal state definitions of "navigability," (3) where public use has been established by prescriptive easement or dedication, and (4) that are considered public by local law, e.g., the Great Lakes, New England Great Ponds, and in some public land states lakes that were meandered (outlined) in the original government surveys. As with rivers, a lake may be public even though its bed is privately owned; and here too, legal availability for public use is unavailing without public access.

Ownership of lake beds and banks generally depends on a lake's navigability under the federal title test. As a rule, beds of large lakes are in state ownership, while beds of small lakes are in private ownership. In contrast to riverbed owners, lakebed owners hold title up to the low-water mark. In most states the beds of nonnavigable lakes belong to the littoral owners. However, in a few states, for example, some states where lakes were meandered, the state itself holds title to the lands beneath some nonnavigable lakes [1]. Interesting anomalies may occur in those minority-rule states where the state has conveyed lakebed titles to persons other than the littoral owners. In such a situation the littoral owners, who own only down to the low-water mark, may be excluded from using the lake because the rule is that where the bed is owned almost entirely by nonlittorals the littoral owners have no rights to use the lake surface.

However, the majority rule is that lakebeds of nonnavigable lakes belong to the littoral owners. Determining the boundaries of lakebed property is far more difficult than ascertaining the riverbed rights of a riverine riparian:

> Hopefully the lake may be round, in which case it can be divided as a pie; or it may be elongated with a fairly regular shoreline, in which case it can be divided down the middle, with just the ends divided as a pie. But if it is odd-shaped, with bays, inlets, promontories, and arms, and perhaps a sprinkling of privately-owned islands, the trial judge will not only have to exercise the wisdom of Solomon, but also have to execute his decree by dividing the baby [1].

Allocating ownership of a lakebed among littoral owners may be important for a number of reasons. A littoral owner may wish to extract minerals from his portion of the lakebed; or if the lake is drained it will be necessary to plot boundary lines [1]. Moreover, although it may sound absurd, in some states littoral owners have exclusive recreational rights to the lake surface overlying their lakebeds. In these states, one littoral owner can prevent others from using his piece of the pie. The more modern and increasingly popular rule is that littoral owners share in common the use of the lake surface as mutual easements over one another's lakebeds. One littoral owner may use the entire lake surface as long as his use is reasonable, i.e., does not interfere with the reasonable uses of other littoral owners. Littoral owners who own the lakebed of a private lake may lawfully prohibit the general public from using the lake.

As with rivers, access to public lakes must be obtained by permission of littoral owners, purchase or lease of littoral property, governmental purchase or condemnation of easements, prescriptive easement, or dedication (express or implied). Difficult lacustrine access problems arise where littoral property is subdivided. In a Michigan case [13] analyzed by Meyers and Tarlock [2], a land development corporation purchased a littoral parcel of land which had 1,415 feet of frontage on a 2,680-acre lake which was used primarily for recreational purposes. The corporation subdivided the parcel into approximately 150 lots, only 16 of which abutted directly on the lake. The developer was to dig a canal to provide lake access for back lot owners. Before the canal had been completed, other littoral owners sued to enjoin the development for alleged violation of their littoral rights. The Michigan Supreme Court held that (1) since riparian (littoral) rights do not attach to an artificial watercourse, and the canal would be an artificial watercourse, back lot owners did not possess littoral access rights; and (2) since riparian rights are not transferrable apart from riparian land, the developer could not have legally transferred access rights to the back lot owners. The case was "remanded" (referred back) to the trial court for consideration of whether the developer could have given the back lot owners permission to use its access rights; but the Michigan Supreme Court suggested (and the trial court later held) that permission was unreasonable in light of the lake's limited carrying capacity. Since this court decision, Michigan and Wisconsin have enacted statutes requiring permits for lakeshore development which might be injurious to ecosystems or to other littoral owners [2].

Maintaining lake levels is just as important as preserving instream flows in rivers. Some riparian law states follow a "natural flow theory" with regard to littoral rights to lake-level maintenance. Littoral owners in these states can sue to prevent interference with the lake's natural level. Other riparian states adopt a "reasonable use theory," offering a remedy only where there is unreasonable interference with a legitimate use [2]. Under both rules, virtually all uses by littoral owners on a nonnavigable lake are equal. Except for domestic use, there is no automatic preference for non-transformational or transformational uses. Lake-level maintenance in appropriation law states is governed by the same doctrines applied to riverine flow preservation in those states.

Troublesome cases have arisen in eastern states where purchasers of littoral property on a lake formed by the construction of a private or state-licensed dam sue to prevent the lake from being drained. Do these landowners lack littoral rights because the lake is an artificial one? Can they assert rights based on prescriptive easement or dedication? As you might imagine, courts have gone both ways on roughly similar sets of facts [2]. A Florida statute declares it unlawful to drain any lake over two square miles in areas outside the Everglades without the written consent of all littoral owners [14]. Other eastern states prohibit lake drainage without a state permit.

So diffuse is eastern water law on the issue of lake-level maintenance that Florida and a number of midwestern states have enacted lake-level maintenance statutes.

> They are designed to perform two basic functions. First, establishment of a level through a statutory procedure quantifies the littoral owner's common law right. Second and related to this, the statutes provide some protection for littoral owners for property damage caused by dams and other structures which result in a substantial alteration of the level of a lake [2].

These statutes vary widely as to form of proceeding (administrative or judicial), waters covered (public or private), and standards for fixing lake levels ("average normal water level," "natural ordinary high water level," or "normal height and level") [2]. Once lake levels are set, these statutes provide sources to fund the construction or maintenance of dams.

Fluctuating lake levels also affect the rights of recreational users of the surface. Although a littoral owner's title runs to the low-water mark, where the level of a navigable lake fluctuates due to natural or artificial causes, the public has a right to go where the navigable waters go, even though the navigable waters lie over privately owned lands. A littoral owner cannot fill his shoreland below the high-water mark so as to conflict with the public's right of navigation.

The recent California case of *National Audubon Society* v. *Superior Court of Alpine City* [15] indicates that the public trust doctrine, discussed more extensively in the following chapter, may be relied upon to maintain lake levels.

Mono Lake, the second largest lake in California, sits at the base of the Sierra Nevada escarpment near the eastern entrance of Yosemite National Park. The lake is saline with no outlet. It contains no fish but supports large populations of brine shrimp that feed vast numbers of nesting and migratory birds. Mono Lake is also scenically and geologically important.

Historically, most of Mono Lake's water has come from snowmelt carried by five freshwater tributary streams arising in the Sierra Nevada. In 1940, however, the predecessor to the California Water Resources Board granted the city of Los Angeles a permit to appropriate virtually the entire flow of four of the five tributary streams. Since that time, Los Angeles has gradually diverted this water into the Owens Valley Aqueduct for water supply in the city.

As a result of these diversions, the level of Mono Lake has dropped, the surface area has diminished by one-third, and the lake's salinity has drastically increased. In the court's words, "The ultimate effect of continued diversions is a matter of intense dispute, but there seems little doubt that both the scenic beauty and ecological values of Mono Lake are imperiled." On the other hand, "the need of Los Angeles for water is apparent, its reliance on rights granted by the board evident, [and] the cost of curtailing diversions substantial."

How does the public trust doctrine affect this clash between the degradation of "a scenic and ecological treasure of national significance" and the genuine water needs of a large city fulfilled by a long-standing appropriation permit? Before reaching this question, the California Supreme Court had to deal with two subsidiary issues: (1) Does the public trust doctrine apply to nonnavigable tributaries of a navigable waterbody? and (2) Is the public trust doctrine subsumed in the state water rights system or does it function independently of that system?

On the first question, the court held that under California law the public trust applies to activities on nonnavigable tributaries that interfere with public interests in navigable waterbodies—the Mono Lake situation. On the second question, the court held that the public trust doctrine is neither independent of nor subsumed under the appropriative water rights system:

> We are unable to accept either position. In our opinion, both the public trust doctrine and the water rights system embody important precepts which make

the law more responsive to the diverse needs and interests involved in the planning and allocation of water resources. To embrace one system of thought and reject the other would lead to an unbalanced structure, one which would either decry as a breach of trust appropriations essential to the economic development of this state, or deny any duty to protect or even consider the values promoted by the public trust.[15]

Therefore, an "accommodation" of the two systems must be forged. The principles of this accommodation are:

- The state retains continuing supervisory control over its navigable waters and the lands beneath those waters; no vested right may be acquired to appropriate water in a manner harmful to the interests protected by the public trust.
- Nevertheless, the state has the power to grant appropriative permits that may unavoidably diminish instream uses if the state's population maintenance and economic health outweigh protection of public trust uses.
- The state has an affirmative duty to take the public trust into account in the planning and allocation of water resources, and to protect public trust uses whenever feasible.
- Once the state has approved an appropriation, the public trust imposes a duty of continuing supervision over the taking and use of appropriated water. The state is not confined by past allocation decisions which may be incorrect in light of current knowledge or inconsistent with current needs.
- The state accordingly has the power to reconsider allocation decisions even though those decisions were made after due consideration of their effect on the public trust.

Applying these principles to the Mono Lake situation, the court sent the matter back to the lower court and the California Water Resources Board to reconsider the appropriation permits to Los Angeles in light of ecological damage to Mono Lake. A key fact in this case was the Board's limited powers in 1940 when the permits were granted. At that time the Board had neither the power nor the duty, as it now has, to consider public trust interests in making allocation decisions. Temporal priority of actual appropriation for a beneficial use was the only concern in those days. Thus, with regard to the Mono Lake diversions, no responsible body "has determined that the needs of Los Angeles outweigh the needs of the Mono Basin, that the benefit gained is worth the price. Neither has any responsible body determined whether some lesser taking would better balance the diverse interests."

In California, after the Mono Lake decision, an appropriative diversion permit can always be contested as violating the public trust, even where the instream flow uses were considered in granting the permit. Will other states also allow ostensibly "vested" diversion rights to be reconsidered at any time when citizens assert public trust interests?

Chapter 16

ACCESS TO BEACHES AND MARINE FACILITIES

Under the Submerged Lands Act of 1953 [16], coastal states own the beds of the marginal seas out to three miles or, in the cases of Texas and the Gulf coast of Florida, three marine leagues, which is approximately ten and one-half miles, seaward from the ordinary low-water mark [1]. The dividing line between the landward ownership of the states and the seaward ownership of private littoral owners is generally the mean high-tide line, although Delaware, Massachusetts, Maine, New Hampshire, and Virginia use the low-water mark as a demarcation point [2]. Thus, in most coastal states the state itself owns the "foreshore," the wet sand area between the high- and low-water marks. The majority rule is consistent with the doctrine that states own the beds and banks of navigable waterways, with any area subject to tidal action presumed to be navigable.

A state's tidelands ownership is subject to a public trust for its citizens. In the words of a venerable U.S. Supreme Court decision, "It is a title held in trust for the people of the State that they may enjoy the navigation of the waters, carry on commerce over them, and have liberty of fishing therein freed from the obstruction or interference of private parties" [17]. Recent cases have made it clear that public recreation is also a valid public trust purpose. The public trust doctrine extends to the beds, banks, and water of all navigable waters, not merely tidal waters.

"Public trust" is an evolving legal doctrine that will undoubtedly generate much water rights litigation in years to come. However, it currently presents us with more questions than answers. For example, public trust waterlands can legally be transferred by a state to a private party as long as the private use is reasonably related to genuine state interests. But does the public trust survive the transfer, at least until the area is filled or becomes fast land? Can the private transferee exclude the public from the water and wet sand area? What are the limits of the common law riparian right to build wharves, docks, and piers ("wharf out")? Are the waters and fish in private waterbodies part of the public trust? And if they are, what are the implications for public use and access? Can the public trust doctrine be used to preserve instream flows and lake levels?

The public trust doctrine has been employed to gain public access to coastal beaches. New Jersey courts have declared that municipally owned as well as privately owned dry sand areas are within the public trust and must be made available to residents and nonresidents on equal terms. In other states, courts have relied on prescriptive easements, express and applied dedication, and local custom to allow access to shorelands above mean high tide. Some states have provided for public access by statute. Here again, private owners will claim "taking" in order to protect their interests. But most of these doctrines are invulnerable to taking arguments because they assume that the private owner either never possessed or else relinquished a right to exclude the public.

In *Kaiser Aetna* v. *United States* [18] the U.S. Supreme Court rejected an attempt to enhance public access by means of the public trust doctrine thinly disguised as the federal navigation servitude. Kuapa Pond on Oahu, Hawaii, was a shallow lagoon contiguous to Maunalua Bay but separated from it by a barrier beach. Ponds such as Kuapa have traditionally been considered private property under Hawaiian law. In 1961 a company called Kaiser Aetna bought the pond and surrounding lands for a subdivision development to be known as "Hawaii Kai." Kaiser Aetna dredged and filled parts of the pond, erected retaining walls, and built bridges within the development to create the Hawaii Kai Marina. Subsequently, Kaiser Aetna dredged an 8-foot-deep channel connecting Kuapa Pond to Maunalua Bay and the Pacific Ocean. The Army Corps of Engineers had been informed of Kaiser Aetna's activities, but had responded to Kaiser Aetna that no permits were necessary under section 10 of the Rivers and Harbors Act.

As a result of Kaiser Aetna's development activities, a marina-style community of approximately 22,000 persons surrounds Kuapa Pond. It includes approximately 1,500 waterfront lot lessees. The waterfront lot lessees, along with a number of nonmarina lot lessees from Hawaii Kai and some nonresident boat owners, pay fees for maintenance and security of the pond. Kaiser Aetna restricts access to the pond from the bay to boats belonging to members and their guests.

In 1972 the Corps demanded that Kaiser Aetna provide public access to the pond, claiming that as a result of improvements it had become a navigable water of the United States. When Kaiser Aetna refused to grant public access, the United States sued for an injunction in federal court. Two lower federal courts disagreed on the public access question.

The U.S. Supreme Court rejected the government's contentions. Justice Rehnquist, writing for a six-judge majority, began by differentiating between "navigability" and the "navigational servitude" with its "no compensation rule." In the Court's view, the federal navigational servitude is not applicable to all navigable waterways for all purposes. As for Kuapa Pond in particular,

> It is clear that prior to its improvement Kuapa Pond was incapable of being used as a continuous highway for the purpose of navigation in interstate commerce. Its maximum depth at high tide was a mere two feet, it was separated from the adjacent bay and ocean by a natural barrier beach, and its principal commercial value was limited to fishing. It is not the sort of "great navigable stream" that has previously been recognized as being "incapable of private ownership" . . . And, as previously noted, Kuapa Pond has always been considered to be private property under Hawaiian law. Thus, the interest of petitioners in the now dredged marina is strikingly similar to that of owners of fast land adjacent to navigable waters.

Even though Kuapa Pond is now navigable, it is not subject to the federal navigational servitude because it is an artificial waterway.

The Court then concluded that the government's elimination of Hawaii Kai's "right to exclude" the public would amount to an unlawful taking of property for which just compensation would have to be paid according to the Fifth Amendment to the U.S. Constitution. Public access would cause an "actual physical invasion of the privately owned marina" tantamount to a taking:

> Thus, if the Government wishes to make what was formerly Kuapa Pond into a public aquatic park after petitioners have proceeded as far as they have here, it may not, without invoking its eminent domain power and paying just compensation, require them to allow free access to the dredged pond while petitioners' agreement with their customers calls for an annual $72 regular fee.

The majority was obviously impressed by Hawaii Kai's large investment and the Corps' past condonation of Kaiser Aetna's water resources projects at Hawaii Kai.

In a dissenting opinion, Justice Blackmun wrote that it does not "advance analysis to suggest that we might decide to call certain waters 'navigable' for some purposes, but 'non-navigable' for purposes of the navigational servitude. . . . In my view, the power we describe by the term 'navigational servitude' extends to the limits of interstate commerce by water; accordingly I would hold that it is coextensive with the 'navigable waters of the United States'." For the three dissenters, "the developers of Kuapa Pond have acted at their own risk and are not entitled to compensation for the public access the Government now asserts."

Thus, after *Kaiser Aetna*, although the federal government can regulate private canals under the navigation power, it cannot demand access to them under the navigation servitude or, by implication, the public trust doctrine.

Chapter 17

FEDERAL OUTDOOR RECREATION PROGRAMS

Outdoor recreation has experienced phenomenal growth since the end of World War II, and roughly half of all outdoor recreation is water oriented [19]. The federal outdoor recreation program is the focal point of a national network of federal, state, county, and municipal public recreation sites, many featuring water-related outdoor activities.

The secretary of the interior is authorized to (1) inventory and evaluate the nation's outdoor recreation needs and resources, (2) prepare a nationwide outdoor recreation plan identifying problems and recommending solutions, (3) provide technical assistance to public and private interests, and (4) promote coordination of federal plans and activities relating to outdoor recreation [20]. The National Park Service has replaced the Heritage Conservation and Recreation Service and its predecessor, the Bureau of Outdoor Recreation, as the organ within the Department of the Interior that is responsible for federal outdoor recreation planning.

Budget cuts have sharply curtailed not only federal outdoor recreation planning but also implementation of plans through the Land and Water Conservation Fund [21]. The Fund is made up of congressional appropriations, admission and user fees from federal outdoor recreation areas, and certain other receipts. In general, 60 percent of the fund is available for grants to states on a 50–50 matching basis for planning, acquisition, and development of land and water areas, and 40 percent for acquisitions by the National Park Service, Forest Service, and Fish and Wildlife Service. No state may receive funds unless it has a comprehensive statewide outdoor recreation plan (SCORP) approved by the Department of the Interior. A sizable portion of a state's share is passed through to local governments. "About three-fourths of the Federal funds and two-thirds of the State and local funds have gone to water-oriented recreation" [19]. The Fund is now administered by the National Park Service.

Nearly 700 reservoirs constructed by the Army Corps of Engineers and the Bureau of Reclamation have public recreation facilities. These facilities are generally administered by the construction agency itself, but occasionally by the National Park Service, the Forest Service, or the Fish and Wildlife Service. The National Water Commission has pointed out that construction agencies do a notoriously poor job of administering recreation [19]. In light of this failure, Congress enacted the Federal Water Project Recreation Act of 1965 [22] stipulating that (1) nonfederal bodies must agree to administer recreation and pay one-half of the construction costs allocated to recreation and all the maintenance, operation, and replacement costs for recreation; (2) without an agreement the construction agency can build only minimum recreation facilities for health and safety, plus acquire potential recreation land and hold it for ten years pending negotiation of the required cost-sharing agreement; and (3) at the end of ten years if no agreement has been reached the acquired land must be sold. However, this statute has been more honored in the breach than the observance [19]. The Soil Conservation Service was also faulted by the National Water Commission for failing to arrange for public access to thousands of small watershed projects that it finances.

Since 1916 the National Park Service has managed public land for preservation and recreation, including water-based recreation [23]. NPS administers the national parks, national recreation areas, national monuments, national seashores, national lakeshores, national rivers, national wild and scenic rivers, the Boundary Waters Canoe Area in Minnesota, national gateway parks, and the Big Thicket and Big Cypress national preserves. The major legal problem confronting the NPS is whether and to what extent it can regulate activities on inholdings and adjacent lands that are inimical to the purposes of the parks without having to pay compensation. For example, can the NPS regulate logging activities on private lands outside Redwood National Park where the private logging causes siltation of the streams in the park?

Under the Wilderness Act [24], Congress has set aside some 19 million acres for preservation in the National Wilderness Preservation System. Wilderness areas are managed either by NPS or the Bureau of Land Management in the Department of the Interior, or the Forest Service in the Department of Agriculture. Water resource projects cannot be built in wilderness areas without presidential approval. However, mining in wilderness areas could impair lakes and streams. Hunting and fishing are allowed in wilderness areas, but motorboats are not [23]. It is probable that

the establishment of a wilderness area will serve as a reservation of rights
to instream flows.

The Forest Service administers the 190 million acres of the National
Forest System, and the Bureau of Land Management the 450 million acres of
public lands, under a statutory standard of "multiple use, sustained yield."
The multiple uses that must be delicately balanced by the management
agency are outdoor recreation, range, timber, watershed, fish and wildlife,
and scenic-archaeologic. Some land will be used for fewer than all of these
resources, but the potential for using each relevant resource must be preserved. The multiple use criterion is so ambiguous that it places virtually no
legal constraints on a management agency.

Finally, the Fish and Wildlife Service in the Department of the Interior
oversees over 30 million acres of the National Wildlife Refuge System.
Although managed primarily for fish and wildlife conservation, hunting,
fishing, and recreational boating are permitted as long as these activities are
consistent with fish and wildlife management [23]. In one case, a federal
district court prohibited powerboat use in a wildlife refuge. As with most
federal lands, state fish and game laws apply in national wildlife refuges.

Chapter 18

FLOODPLAINS PROTECTION

Floodplains, the areas adjacent to rivers periodically required to hold or carry flood flows, are attractive to developers.

> In addition to the obvious aesthetic, recreational, production and transport features of riverfront location, floodplain parcels are often attractively inexpensive, available in larger blocs, and strategically located near developed areas. Moreover, they do not require extensive grading and site preparation. Where governmental control works or other subsidies are available, floodplain investment can produce windfall profits for land speculators [25].

Approximately 5 percent of the United States population now lives on floodplains at a time when our society is becoming increasingly aware of the enormous economic and environmental costs of flood control structures.

There is no doubt that "extensive encroachment upon floodplain storage areas will result in significant increases in flood flows and flood hazards" [25]. However, the common law can do little to inhibit floodplain development. As pointed out in Part I, no riparian landowner has the right to obstruct the flow of a river if downstream riparians are injured. But in order to win a lawsuit against an upstream riparian, a downstream plaintiff must prove "causation," that is, the damage would not have occurred without the defendant's construction. This is especially difficult to prove in flood damage cases "where the hydrologic and economic injury effects of local obstructions co-mingle with those of myriad upstream users" [25]. Moreover, "acts of God" (extraordinary floods) and "sovereign immunity" defenses often preclude recovery. Even if the downstream riparian wins his case, other existing and prospective upstream floodplain developers remain unaffected by the judgment.

107

The major federal statutes enacted to control floodplain development are known as the National Flood Insurance Program (NFIP) [26]. Under NFIP, the federal government provides insurance protection directly and through private insurance companies in flood-prone areas where flood insurance was previously unavailable. In return, communities must adopt zoning ordinances to discourage incompatible development in floodplains and require floodproofing of allowed structures.

The federal agency in charge of NFIP, now the Federal Emergency Management Agency (FEMA), was first required to define flood hazard zones. In general, these are lands on the 100-year floodplain. FEMA then had to map ("delineate") these zones in participating communities. While the mapping was in progress, during the "emergency phase" of the program, existing properties and new construction received federally subsidized flood insurance if the community adopted quite minimal standards to restrict floodplain development. The "regular phase" of the program began with the publication of Flood Insurance Rate Maps (FIRMs) delineating zones within the floodplain which were subject to different levels of danger. These FIRMs must have been completed by 1983. After the publication of a FIRM, any new construction within the floodplain must pay full actuarial (true risk) flood insurance rates instead of subsidized rates. However, existing structures continue to receive subsidized flood insurance during the regular phase until they are damaged and require repairs greater than 50 percent of their market value. The availability of flood insurance during the regular phase is contingent on the community adopting federally approved floodplain regulations that are more stringent than those required during the emergency phase.

Ironically, NFIP has encouraged floodplain development [27]. In the first place, NFIP has made flood insurance available in high-risk areas for the first time. The subsidized rates offered during the emergency phase have not discouraged people from building in areas subject to floods. Second, a great deal of construction has been undertaken during the emergency phase because subsidized rates are retained for the existing construction once a community enters the regular phase [25]. Third, developers have begun immediate construction during the emergency phase in order to avoid the more stringent floodplain regulations required during the regular phase [27]. Finally, FEMA has not adequately monitored or enforced the obligation of local communities to police their floodplain regulations [28]. Realistically, communities must participate in NFIP or else forfeit development and tax ratables [29]. However, once enrolled in NFIP the tendency toward "slippage" (chronic nonenforcement) is strong.

How does the availability of federal disaster aid affect development in floodplains? One commentator argues that disaster aid encourages development [25]. Another believes that the federal disaster assistance program has the "potential to elicit conformity with federal floodplain use standards" because (1) disaster assistance for rehabilitating property is not available in nonparticipating communities; (2) FEMA grants for reconstructing public facilities and private nonprofit facilities are contingent on construction practices complying with federal standards that emphasize hazard mitigation; and (3) Small Business Administration long-term, low-interest disaster loans for the restoration of homes and businesses will pay for relocating and replacement if the disaster victim is prevented from rebuilding by floodplain regulations, or else will provide funds to meet the requirements of city, county, and state construction codes [29].

Partly because of NFIP, floodplain zoning ordinances have become commonplace in flood-prone communities. Moreover, a number of states, including New Jersey, have enacted statutes limiting floodplain development. The New Jersey Flood Hazard Area Control Act [30] mandates the New Jersey Department of Environmental Protection (NJDEP) to delineate "floodways" (if possible, identical to NFIP delineations) and "flood fringe areas." NJDEP is authorized to adopt rules and regulations governing land use in floodways, and to operate a permit program with provision for variances to alleviate hardship. Construction in nondelineated floodways must also receive an approval from NJDEP. Approval of floodway projects and enforcement against violators may be delegated to counties. As for flood fringe areas, NJDEP must set minimum standards for the adoption of local zoning ordinances relating to development. If the municipality does not adopt conforming ordinances, NJDEP may itself regulate flood fringe development. Municipalities are free to adopt stricter standards than NJDEP for development in floodways or flood fringe areas. However, no municipality can grant construction approval in a floodway or state-regulated flood fringe area unless NJDEP has previously approved the construction.

The major legal problem with floodplain regulations is their vulnerability to "taking" claims. The taking issue is briefly discussed in previous chapters, but its special importance in floodplains and wetlands cases dictates a more thorough examination here. At some point a regulation such as a floodplain ordinance will become a taking requiring the payment of compensation to a burdened landowner, but it is difficult to predict in abstract terms what that point will be. Each case is unique and must be decided on its own facts.

Moreover, courts apply four different tests in determining when a regulation has become a taking. The "diminution of value" test looks to the amount of economic value remaining to a landowner after the imposition of a regulation. If he is not left with substantial economic value, compensation must be paid. For example, it is not a taking for a community to prohibit sand and gravel operations as long as landowners can use their properties for residential or business purposes. Under this test a landowner is not entitled to the highest economic use of his land, but is entitled to reasonable economic uses. The second test, the "private loss-public gain" test, balances diminution of private value against societal gain from the regulation. If the diminution of value is great, the social need must be compelling for the regulation to be upheld. For example, a fire department may totally destroy a dwelling in order to prevent the spread of fire without having to consider compensating the owner. The third test may be referred to as the "public injury-public benefit" test. Here, it is never a taking when a regulation prevents a public injury, but it is a taking when government uses its regulatory power to confer gratuitous benefits on the public. It would be a taking, for example, to zone private property for use as a public park. The final and most recently formulated test is the "overriding ecological value" test. According to this test, no landowner has the right to develop an ecologically sensitive tract of land, regardless of whether he was aware of its ecological value when the property was purchased.

Floodplain regulations have been struck down under the diminution of value test on the one hand, and upheld under the private loss-public gain and public injury-public benefit tests, on the other. Thus far the overriding ecological value test has been applied only in wetlands cases. The modern trend is away from diminution of value as the sole criterion of regulatory takings. Judges have become more sympathetic to environmental regulation that is reasonably related to a strong public need, despite the effects on individual private landowners. In all likelihood, a reasonable floodplain regulation will be upheld because it is necessary to prevent a grave public danger—flooding.

Chapter 19
WETLANDS PROTECTION

Because of the profound ecological importance of wetlands and because wetlands frequently transcend municipal boundaries, many states have enacted wetlands protection legislation of one kind or another. Twelve eastern and Gulf states require permits for the alteration of coastal wetlands [2]. California, Maine, New Jersey, and Washington have comprehensive coastal zone development statutes. In Michigan, Minnesota, and Washington development in the beds of inland waterways and related shoreland development is regulated [2]. Connecticut, Massachusetts, Michigan, New Hampshire, New York, and Rhode Island require permits for the modification of inland wetlands [27]. State floodplain statutes, environmental impact statement requirements, wild and scenic river systems, and water pollution control statutes often protect wetlands indirectly. Moreover, wetlands can lie within the jurisdictions of regional agencies such as the Adirondack Park Agency in New York and the Pinelands Commission in New Jersey.

Until the early 1970s, landowner plaintiffs were generally successful in their contentions that state and local wetlands regulations as applied to them amounted to unconstitutional takings of their property [31]. But in 1972 the Wisconsin Supreme Court decided the case of *Just* v. *Marinette County* [32], firmly establishing the "overriding ecological value" test as the takings criterion in wetlands cases. In upholding the Marinette County shoreland zoning ordinance, adopted under a state enabling act, against the constitutional claims of littoral owners who purchased their property before the ordinance was passed, the court said with reference to the plaintiffs' proposed fill of shoreland wetlands:

> An owner of land has no absolute and unlimited right to change the essential natural character of his land so as to use it for a purpose for which it was unsuited in its natural state and which injures the rights of others. . . .

111

> The Justs argue their property has been severely depreciated in value. But this depreciation of value is not based on the use of the land in its natural state but on what the land would be worth if it could be filled and used for the location of a dwelling. While loss of value is to be considered in determining whether a restriction is a constructive taking, value based upon changing the character of the land at the expense of harm to public rights is not an essential factor or controlling.

In other words, the Justs could not lose what they never had; and they never had a right to develop an area of overriding ecological value. Interestingly, the Wisconsin Supreme Court relied in part on the public trust doctrine, which Wisconsin by statute has applied to navigable waters. But courts in other states have followed the *Just* v. *Marinette* reasoning without mentioning the public trust doctrine.

In Part II several provisions of federal law that might be used to limit unwise development in wetlands were identified. These include section 10 of the Rivers and Harbors Act, the National Environmental Policy Act, the Endangered Species Act, the Wild and Scenic Rivers Act, Executive Order 11990, and the sole source aquifer section of the Safe Drinking Water Act. In addition, point and nonpoint source pollution control under the Clean Water Act can preserve water quality in wetlands.

There are also federal programs that are suitable for acquisition of wetlands interests. The Wild and Scenic Rivers Act, the Coastal Zone Management Act, and the Endangered Species Act all authorize funds for land acquisition [33]. Section 73 of the Water Resources Act [34] authorizes the Army Corps of Engineers to purchase land for nonstructural flood control. The Corps can also use dredged spoils to create wetlands at federal cost [29]. The Land and Water Conservation Fund Act [21] provides federal funds on a 50–50 matching basis for state and local acquisition of land for recreation and open space. The Water Bank Act [35] establishes a program under which the Department of Agriculture may lease farmlands on a ten-year renewable basis in order to preserve wetlands. The National Estuary Protection Act [35] set up the Wetlands Inventory and provides funding for state acquisitions of estuarine areas [33]. Finally, federal wildlife laws authorizing wetlands acquisition are the Anadromous Fish Conservation Act [37], the Migratory Bird Conservation Act [38], the Federal Aid in Wildlife Restoration Act [39], and the Federal Aid in Fish Restoration Act [40].

Section 404 of the Clean Water Act [41], which makes it unlawful to discharge dredged or fill material into waters of the United States without a Corps permit, is the major federal regulatory program for protecting inland wetlands. As pointed out in Part II, section 404's geographical coverage is broader than section 10's coverage because section 404 gives the Corps jurisdiction over all "waters of the United States," an area as wide as federal regulatory powers under the Commerce Clause [42]. Thus, in its regulations

[43], the Corps defines "waters of the United States" to include "mudflats, sandflats, *wetlands*, sloughs, prairie potholes, wet meadows, playa lakes, or natural ponds" (emphasis added). The Corps regulations define a "wetland" as an area that supports "a prevalence of vegetation typically adapted for life in saturated soil conditions [including] swamps, marshes, bogs, and similar areas." However, section 404 is narrower than section 10 with regard to the scope of activities covered. Section 404 applies only to "*discharge* of dredged or fill material" (emphasis added), meaning the material must emanate from a discrete pipe, ditch, channel, or conveyance. As a result, 404 permits are unnecessary for draining, clearing, or flooding wetlands without deposits of fill material. Permits are also unnecessary for activities that alter upland drainage patterns and block runoff into wetlands [44]. On the other hand, courts have held that construction of a drainage ditch or levee in a wetland requires a 404 permit, as does the clearing of a wetland's vegetative cover with construction equipment [45].

Another major difference between section 404 and section 10 is that section 404 is jointly administered by the Corps and the Environmental Protection Agency. EPA's role in the section 404 process is to (1) promulgate jointly with the Corps "Guidelines for Specification of Disposal Sites for Dredged or Fill Materials"; (2) veto the issuance of permits if necessary to protect the environment; (3) designate geographic areas where no permits may be issued; (4) approve and oversee the delegation of 404 permitting to states; (5) take independent enforcement action against unauthorized dischargers if the Corps does not act; (6) evaluate the impacts from federal construction projects that are exempt from 404; and (7) make final wetlands determinations [44]. Thus far, however, section 404 has not been a high priority with EPA.

In 1977, Congress exempted from section 404 certain activities that it believed were more appropriately supervised by the states or other federal agencies. These exemptions are (1) normal farming, silviculture, and ranching activities, including "minor drainage"; (2) maintenance and reconstruction of flood control and transportation structures; (3) construction and maintenance of farm or stock ponds or irrigation ditches and the maintenance, excluding the construction, of drainage ditches; (4) construction of temporary sediment basins on construction sites, as long as no fill is placed in waters of the United States; (5) any activity that is being regulated by a state under section 208 of the Clean Water Act (best management practices for nonpoint sources of pollution); (6) construction or maintenance of farm roads, forest roads, or temporary mining roads, where the roads are constructed and maintained with best management practices; and (7) projects planned, financed, and constructed by a federal agency where the environmental impacts of the discharge are addressed in an environmental impact statement submitted to Congress prior to authorization or appropriation of money for the project. The first six exemptions are unavailable if the proposed activities are new water uses that would impair the flow or circulation of waters or reduce their reach. Thus, a farmer is unable to procure an exemption under the normal farming category when he is converting wetlands into dry, arable farmland.

General permits have been one of the most controversial aspects of section 404. As mentioned previously, no notification or application is required for specific activities under general permit. Under the latest Corps regulations, all discharges into the following waters are permitted generally: (1) nontidal rivers, streams, and their lakes and impoundments, including adjacent wetlands, that are located above the headwaters; and (2) nontidal waters below the headwaters that are not part of a surface tributary system to interstate or navigable waters. "Headwaters" are defined as the point on a nontidal stream above which the average annual flow is less than 5 cubic feet per second. Thus, discharges above the headwaters and discharges below the headwaters into isolated wetlands and nonnavigable lakes are automatically permitted. Moreover, the regulations also grant nationwide general permits to certain identified classes of activities such as discharges of materials for backfill for utility line crossings, materials for bank stabilization to prevent erosion, fill for minor road crossings, and replacement fill.

There are a number of safeguards against abuse of general permits. General permits for classes of identified activities must only be issued after public notice, opportunity for comment and public hearing, and public interest review. No general permit is valid if (1) the discharge is located near a public water supply intake; (2) the discharge would destroy an endangered or threatened species or adversely modify its critical habitat; (3) the discharge consists of toxic pollutants in toxic amounts; (4) the fill is not properly maintained and causes erosion; (5) the discharge occurs in a component of the National Wild and Scenic Rivers System; or (6) specified best management practices are not followed [43]. EPA can veto a general permit for inconsistency with jointly promulgated disposal site guidelines. A state can veto a general permit by denying a water quality certification under section 401 of the Clean Water Act, or refuse to certify that the activity is consistent with its coastal zone management plan. Moreover, the Corps has discretion to require individual permits for activities that are ordinarily permitted generally. Finally, general permits expire and must be reviewed after five years. However, all these potential safeguards presuppose a high degree of public vigilance. Where a general permit is concerned, the burden of coming forward to show environmental damage is on the public; there is no initial burden on the discharger to show that the environment is not being harmed. How well can the public, for the most part without expert legal or technical assistance, play this watchdog role? This question is especially important where section 404 is concerned because, unlike section 10, citizens can sue to enjoin 404 violations.

Further restrictions on the use of general permits are included in a recent agreement to settle a lawsuit brought by a number of environmental organizations against the Corps and the EPA. Under the settlement agreement, the regulations must be modified to require discharge permit applicants to notify the Corps before performing activities that will cause loss or modification of more than one acre of U.S. waters. The agreement requires the Corps to notify the applicant within twenty days of conditions to be imposed on the project; if no notice is given, the applicant may then proceed with the proposed discharge. In instances where a proposed project will affect ten acres or more of U.S. waters, the Corps must require that an individual dredge or fill permit be obtained for the project. During review of permit applications, the Corps is required to submit applications for review by EPA, the Fish and Wildlife Service, the National Marine Fisheries Service, and appropriate state natural resource agencies, according to the agreement. The agencies have the opportunity to express their views on the environmental effects of a project.

If a proposed project does not qualify for a general permit, an application for an individual permit must be filed with the District Engineer (DE). After brief initial review, the DE prepares a public notice of permit application and circulates it to federal, state, and local governments as well as members of the public who have requested notice. Comments are especially solicited from the Fish and Wildlife Service and EPA. Usually, public comments are accepted for a thirty-day period. A citizen may request a public hearing, but granting a hearing is within the DE's discretion. As a rule of thumb, a hearing is held only when there is "significant" public interest in a permit application [27]. The DE then prepares an environmental assessment of the proposed project. If significant environmental impacts are predicted, an environmental impact statement must be prepared and circulated. After this process is completed the DE either grants the permit as requested, grants it subject to conditions, or denies the permit. Only under exceptional circumstances, for example, when EPA or the Fish and Wildlife Service objects, is a permit "escalated" to the Division Engineer or to Washington [27].

Wetlands protection is an integral part of the Corps' public interest review. With an individual permit there is a presumption that a discharge of dredged or fill material is environmentally harmful unless the applicant can demonstrate otherwise. Only "water-dependent" activities will receive a 404 permit unless the proposed activity clearly benefits the public interest [43].

> Examples of water dependent activities are levees, dams, intake and outfall structures of wastewater treatment plants and fish and wildlife management. Activities which are not water dependent are apartments, hotels, parking lots, office buildings, domestic or industrial waste treatment facilities, pipelines other than those associated with oil and gas activities, and cross-country electric and other utility lines [27].

The reviewers are also supposed to consider the "cumulative effect of numerous . . . piecemeal changes" on a "complete and interrelated wetland area" [43]. In certain cases where wetlands damage is unavoidable, the Fish and Wildlife Service or the Corps may recommend that the applicant consider creating "mitigation wetlands" elsewhere as a permit condition. Lastly, the DE may not grant a 404 permit unless "the benefits of the proposed alteration outweigh the damage to the wetlands resource" [43].

A state may elect to take over the federal 404 program. If EPA finds that a state program is adequate, the state will be delegated responsibility for existing general permits and for issuing new individual and general permits for proposed discharges into nonnavigable waters. Corps jurisdiction over activities in navigable waters is not delegable. There is federal oversight even after state takeover. EPA retains its veto power, and if the state's performance proves to be unsatisfactory EPA can rescind the state program and return it to the Corps. Moreover, EPA has backup enforcement power.

Thus far, no state has received delegation of the 404 program. The major reasons for state reluctance to administer section 404 are the absence of financial incentives and the need for new state legislation [44]. However, if a state does adopt a 404 program, neither its actions nor those of EPA in supervising the program are subject to the National Environmental Policy Act. Moreover, courts have held that EPA's failure to veto a state permit is not subject to judicial review.

Section 404 has been, and continues to be, one of the most volatile areas of water law. For example, on May 12, 1983, the Corps proposed revisions to its section 404 regulations [46]. Some of the more important proposed changes are:

1. Add economics, water supply and conservation, energy needs, and property ownership as factors in the public interest review.
2. Change the statement, "No permit will be granted unless its issuance is found to be in the public interest," to, "A permit will be granted unless its issuance is found to be contrary to the public interest." In effect, this change would eliminate the presumption of environmental harm for activities conducted in wetlands.
3. Instruct the Corps to defer to decisions of state and local governments "unless there are significant issues of overriding national importance."
4. Authorize Corps approval by "letter of permission" where "the proposed work would be minor, would not have significant individual or cumulative impact on environmental values, [and] should encounter no appreciable opposition." Letters of permission would not require public comment or review by other federal agencies.

5. Add two new nationwide permits for private activities linked to Corps or non-Corps federal projects.

If these proposed revisions are finally promulgated, a new round of section 404 litigation will undoubtedly commence.

Chapter 20

WEATHER MODIFICATION

"Weather modification" is defined as "any artificially produced change in the composition, behavior, or dynamics of the atmosphere, when such change is produced with intent to alter the weather" [47]. This definition excludes inadvertent weather changes such as those potentially caused by fossil fuel burning, and it implicitly excludes "climate modification" involving relatively long-term or lasting climatic changes. Seeding clouds with silver iodide or other chemicals to increase precipitation, especially to augment winter snowpack, is the most popular weather modification technique. But attempts are also made at hail and lightning suppression, hurricane diversion, and fog dissipation [48].

As weather modification technology advances, and as intentional climate modification becomes possible, international and national regulation will be necessary because (1) the potential effects of weather modification transcend political boundaries, and (2) as a common good, the atmosphere is not amenable to individual or national ownership. However, there is presently no international law specifically applicable to weather modification, and U.S. legislation is meager. Public Law 92–502, enacted in 1971, requires individuals and nonfederal public entities to report weather modification activities to the Commerce Department's National Oceanographic and Atmospheric Administration (NOAA), which compiles and publishes these reports. The National Weather Modification Policy Act of 1976 [49] was directed toward developing "a comprehensive and coordinated national policy and a national program of weather modification research and experimentation." Under this act, NOAA is to conduct studies, report to Congress on the status of weather modification technology, and make recommendations as to necessary funding and institutional or legislative changes desir-

118

able to facilitate or control weather modification. In other words, federal activity with reference to weather modification has been "preregulatory."

Nevertheless, approximately thirty states have enacted some form of weather modification legislation [48]. These statutes typically contain one or more of the following:

1. A definition of weather modification limited to artificial nucleation of clouds.
2. Establishment of an administrative agency, board, or commission to review and approve weather modification activities.
3. Prerequisites for license and permit application approval, including qualifications for competency and financial responsibility of the applicant, and standards for the method of proposed operation.
4. A requirement that modifiers maintain records of their operations.
5. A requirement for publication of notice in the target area of modification activities.
6. A declaration of legislative intent [48].

A few states require public hearings or environmental assessments prior to license approval. Some Great Plains states have enacted legislation authorizing the formation of weather control districts by local balloting or by petition [47]. District supervisory boards can tax lands within the district and hire cloud seeders.

As is often the case with new technologies, weather modification has generated a number of lawsuits between private litigants. Thus far at least, litigants have not relied on water law doctrines such as riparianism or prior appropriation [50]. Instead, four tort theories generally pervade these cases: nuisance, trespass, negligence, and strict liability.

Nuisance is a "cause of action" (a set of facts giving rise to an enforceable claim) that allows recovery for an unreasonable interference with a landowner's use and enjoyment of his land. It has frequently been asserted in pollution cases and would be appropriate in lawsuits against weather modifiers. In nuisance cases, judges are entitled to "balance the equities," in other words, to weigh the social value of the defendant's conduct against the plaintiff's loss. Equity balancing might preclude recovery in weather modification cases. For example, in *Slutksy* v. *City of New York* [51], a resort owner asked for an injunction against cloud seeding operations near his Catskill Mountain resort by the City of New York, then in the throes of a drought. The court denied the injunction, concluding that the potential benefit of an increased water supply for the City greatly outweighed any loss of business suffered by the resort owner due to lack of sunshine.

Trespass to land is a physical invasion of a landowner's exclusive possession of his land. The trespass may be by visible pieces of matter or by fumes, odors, vibrations, or invisible particles [48]. Unnatural wind or rain caused by weather modification might constitute a trespass and support the award of an injunction and damages. In a Texas case, a cloud-seeding defendant was enjoined from "modifying or attempting to modify any clouds or weather over or in the air space over lands of the [plaintiffs]" [52].

Negligence is the least promising cause of action upon which to predicate recovery against a weather modifier. In order to establish negligence, it must be shown that the defendant violated a duty of due care to the plaintiff by failing to act in a reasonably prudent manner under the circumstances. "One major difficulty with this approach is that so little weather modification activity has been conducted and these controversies have so seldom reached the courtroom, that the establishment of a legal standard of care for a reasonably prudent weather modifier is practically impossible" [48].

Strict liability for an "abnormally dangerous activity" is a more attractive theory. Here, a defendant is liable without fault if he causes damage by using a technology which is unusual in the community and which threatens serious harm even if due care is used. For example, crop dusting is an abnormally dangerous activity in many states. But as with nuisance, courts will balance the equities to determine whether an activity is indeed abnormally dangerous.

The major stumbling block to recovery in weather modification cases, however, is the problem of causation. Under any of these theories, a plaintiff must prove by a preponderance of the evidence that a defendant's weather modification activities were the "legal cause" (direct or "but for" cause) of his damage. The following quotation from an article by Professor Weiss is valuable not only for what it tells us about weather modification lawsuits, but also as an illustration of the differences between "proof" in the legal and scientific communities:

> The most difficult problem in weather-modification litigation remains that of establishing that the weather-modification activity *caused* the damage in question. For example, plaintiff needs to establish that the increase in rainfall from cloud-seeding caused the flooding which damaged the home or business. Few scientific experts, if any, would be willing to make this statement. At best, we will be able to give a probabilistic statement as to whether or not weather modification could have caused the damage. But not all courts are willing to adjust their procedure to consider a range of statistical probabilities. Usually judges ask only whether it is more probable than not that something occurred or, in a criminal case, whether or not the evidence establishes beyond a reasonable doubt that the defendant committed the crime. Even if we accept the necessity for using probability statistics to establish cause, we will still have uncertainty as to whether or not any given cloud-seeding operation caused specific damage. For example, if cloud-seeding increased rainfall an average of 25% over a six-year period, rain could have increased 50% or none at all on any

single day. The fact that there is a high statistical probability of a 25% increase in rainfall from seeding does not by itself definitely prove that seeding increased the rain by 25% on the day the damage occurred. Even if the rainfall did increase by 25%, the injured party still has to show that this increase in rainfall caused the damage. There may also be difficult questions of how remote the damage can be from the direct impact of the rain and still be eligible for compensation [50].

Causation problems are further compounded in weather modification cases by the availability of an "act of God" defense or sovereign immunity where a governmental unit attempts to control the weather. There is a ray of hope for plaintiffs, however. In a few cases, where serious risks to public health were threatened, courts have shifted to defendants the burden of proving that their conduct would *not* endanger the public [53].

Because of these bars to recovery, and because the potential damages from weather modification are so vast that no insurance company will insure against them, one commentator predicts that as weather modification activities proliferate the federal government will have to establish an insurance-indemnity fund such as that created for the nuclear industry [47]. But Congress must be cautious lest liability limitations discourage the development and implementation of safer weather modification practices.

Private development of weather modification may also be retarded if firm water rights to the augmented water supplies are unavailable. Under various water allocation theories, water from augmentation practices might belong to the federal government, state governments, modifiers, senior appropriators, riparian owners, or landowners on whose lands the increased precipitation falls. Moreover, causation problems will also complicate legal allocation of allegedly enhanced water supplies.

Chapter 21
ACID PRECIPITATION PREVENTION

Fossil fuel combustion and weather modification are similar in that (1) both activities may cause damage in other states or nations, and (2) because of atmospheric mobility and incomplete scientific knowledge it is nearly impossible to prove that specific damage was caused by a specific source.

A rudimentary understanding of how acid precipitation is formed will aid in critically examining the effectiveness of our legal regime for controlling it.

> Sulfur and nitrogen oxides are the compounds most responsible for acid precipitation. Once released into the atmosphere, these gases are converted into sulfates and nitrates through oxidation. The sulfates and nitrates — including sulfuric and nitric acids — are returned to earth in water vapor and small particles of solid material. The presence of sulfuric and nitric acids increases the acidity of the solution and, if not neutralized by other components in the atmosphere, the precipitation falling onto the earth will be acidic. . . . sulfur and nitrogen oxides are byproducts of the burning of fossil fuels [54].

The dynamics of acid precipitation and sulfate formation are not entirely known.

Acid rain, more accurately described as acid deposition, has been implicated in the destruction of fish and plant life; the contamination of drinking water supplies through the leaching of heavy metals from soil, sediment, and plumbing; the accelerated weathering of buildings, bridges, and monuments; the aggravation of respiratory disease; and the reduction of visibility. Although they have become an issue of national concern, the ecological

122

effects of acid deposition are primarily a problem in the northeast because the region's soils and bedrock lack the capacity to neutralize increased acidity. The major sources of acid rain in the eastern United States appear to be electrical generating facilities located east of the Mississippi River.

The federal Clean Air Act [55] is the pivotal legal mechanism for controlling air pollution in the United States. This complicated piece of legislation relates to acid precipitation in many ways. But the act as presently administered by the Environmental Protection Agency is incapable of controlling interstate transport of the sulfur oxides, nitrogen oxides, and sulfates that cause acid precipitation [54].

The Clean Air Act rests on the identification and promulgation by EPA of health-based National Ambient Air Quality Standards (NAAQS) and state implementation of the national standards in Air Quality Control Regions (AQCRs) within the states through emissions limitations in State Implementation Plans (SIPs). The act does not require uniform national emissions limitations for existing sources of a pollutant if the AQCR is an "attainment area" for that pollutant. Both sulfur and nitrogen oxides are "criteria pollutants" for which NAAQS have been set, but no standard has been set for sulfates. Ironically, most AQCRs in the United States are attainment areas for sulfur and nitrogen oxides [54]. EPA has resisted tightening the NAAQs for these pollutants for the same reason that it has refused to set a sulfate standard — lack of adequate scientific proof on which to base a standard.

The Clean Air Act is oriented to *intrastate* pollution. States are responsible for attaining and maintaining NAAQS in AQCRs or portions of AQCRs within their borders. In attainment areas, states will protect their own industries by setting emissions limitations as high as possible as long as relevant NAAQS within the state are not exceeded. It is true that the act does contain mechanisms that allow a state affected by interstate pollution to attempt to force the abatement of emissions from a source in another state. However, the downwind state is burdened with the awesome task of proving the source of its acid precipitation. Proof problems restrict the act's interstate pollution provisions to disputes between contiguous states or situations where sources in other states are violating their emissions limitations [54].

State-by-state control and emissions limitations based on local air quality have not reduced acid precipitation. Recommendations for change include setting a NAAQS for sulfates and tightening those for sulfur and nitrogen oxides, as well as amending the Clean Air Act to require reasonable available control technology for existing sources in attainment areas [54]. Moreover, there is presently pending in Congress a bill which, if enacted, would require utilities in thirty-one states east of and bordering the Mississippi River to reduce sulfur dioxide emissions by 8 million tons over twelve years.

Chapter 22

CONSERVATION AND REUSE

"Conservation" is a term with a meaning for almost every occasion [56]. "At any time (and for any specific resource use issue) there is an underlying tension between development and preservation views over what constitutes conservation-oriented resource management" [57]. Properly defined, water resource conservation should include supply-side structural approaches such as storage reservoirs, in addition to demand-side conservation such as reuse. The legal aspects of transformational conservation methods are discussed in Parts I and II. This chapter concentrates on demand-side nontransformational conservation modes in the agricultural and municipal sectors. Water reuse is given special attention because of its unique public health ramifications. Industrial water conservation through pollution control is addressed in Part IV.

AGRICULTURAL WATER CONSERVATION

"Irrigated agriculture is the largest water user in the United States, accounting for 82% of all flows returned after use" [58]. Nearly 90 percent of all United States irrigation is located in the seventeen western states; in some western basins irrigated agriculture makes over 90 percent of all groundwater and surface water withdrawals [58]. Irrigation efficiency in the west is reportedly under 50 percent, and technical conservation solutions are available, but "so severe are the existing legal constraints and uncertainties over

124

rights to conserved water, and so strong are the legal protections for those relying on the return flows which would be reduced, that one federal study estimates that only 20% of the total reduction possible through conservation may actually be legally available for new uses" [58].

The prior appropriation system's historic tolerance of waste is examined in Part I. Some of Pring and Tomb's recommendations for change in western water law are [58]:

1. Strict enforcement of conservation practices before granting new diversion rights.
2. Where existing diverters are concerned, state assertion of forfeiture for waste in applications for change in point of diversion, nature of use, or place of use; and enforcement of efficiency standards in general adjudication proceedings.
3. Enforcement of water quality law with a view toward water conservation (better return flow quality is tantamount to more water available for downstream uses).
4. Rejection of "custom" as the primary standard in determining beneficial use and setting duties of water.
5. Recognition of all conserved or salvaged water as becoming the property of the conserver or salvager.
6. Modification of statutory preferences to disallow condemnation by an inefficient "higher use" of an efficient "lower use."
7. Provision of financial incentives to encourage conservation and establishment of "withdrawal charges" scaled to discourage inefficiency.
8. Reform of wasteful Bureau of Reclamation water distribution practices, e.g., increasing artificially low prices of reclamation project water.
9. Institution of "water banking" by a central agency to encourage transfer of inefficiently used water.

These themes will resound through western water law for many years to come.

The western rule that salvage water does not belong to the salvager has its riparian law counterparts in restrictions on transfers of riparian rights and prohibitions on nonriparian or trans-watershed uses of water. Why should a farmer save water when he cannot use it, or sell it for use elsewhere? However, the trend in the eastern states is away from these restrictions, especially in those eastern states that have adopted permit systems. A permit system also assists conservation by facilitating planning and implementation of state water goals.

MUNICIPAL WATER CONSERVATION

Opportunities for municipal water conservation exist in two main areas: (1) reuse of municipal wastewater; and (2) reduction of demand for water by customers of municipal water supply systems.

It is being recognized throughout the United States that municipal wastewater is an attractive source of reusable water:

> Unlike many agricultural and industrial effluents, municipal wastewater is not subject to salt buildup. The flow of municipal wastewater is relatively consistent over time, unlike highly seasonal agricultural discharges. Municipalities generate vast volumes of wastewater, and sewer systems for collecting and transporting wastewater to a central treatment point already exist in most communities. Finally, because wastewater must be treated to meet pollution control requirements, the effluent produced is already of sufficient quality for some secondary uses. With additional treatment, this effluent can be put to many other uses [59].

But this additional treatment will probably not be undertaken because most people are reluctant to accept reclaimed wastewater for drinking or hygienic purposes. Thus, reuse of municipal wastewater means, practically speaking, the use of municipal effluent treated to meet pollution control standards for irrigation, industrial applications, groundwater recharge, and noncontact recreation.

One legal obstacle to reuse of municipal wastewater may be the rights of downstream appropriators in the west to the maintenance of return flows. The trend in western judicial decisions, however, is to define municipal effluent either as wastewater, developed water, or foreign water. Consequently, western courts have upheld the right of a municipality to discontinue wastewater discharges into a waterbody despite the claims of other appropriators [2]. Furthermore, a California statute grants the owner of a wastewater treatment plant an exclusive right to the treated effluent [59].

Ironically, municipal water priorities have weakened the incentives to reuse wastewater. Municipalities in both the east and the west have top priority to divert virgin water under statutory preferences, contracts (e.g., with the Bureau of Reclamation), and common law preferences such as "pueblo rights" in California. The conservation disincentive of municipal use priority has led to recommendations that municipal preferences to virgin water be limited to uses that require virgin water [59]. Reused municipal wastewater is also at a competitive disadvantage to diversion of virgin water because the latter has been seriously underpriced, especially in the west. Because it is unlikely that the price of virgin water will ever reflect its true costs, subsidies for municipal reuse will be necessary [59]. The federal Clean Water Act authorizes preferential construction grant funding for wastewater reclamation facilities. However, "faced with limited funding and legislative mandate to abate pollution of the nation's waterways, EPA has primarily funded traditional pollution control facilities, thus deemphasizing wastewater reclamation and other innovative approaches to water quality enhancement" [59]. The state of California has actively assisted the financing of wastewater reclamation projects, but the overly stringent treatment requirements set by the California Department of Health Services have undercut these subsidies [59].

Even secondary uses of reclaimed municipal wastewater could pose risks to public health if treatment plants malfunction or pretreatment standards go unenforced. Moreover, illicit dumping of hazardous materials into sewer lines is common in some areas. The legal problems facing a municipality considering wastewater reuse are similar to those confronting a weather modifier: insufficient knowledge of potential health risks; extensive potential damage; uncertain liability; and inability to procure private insurance. Once again, if municipal wastewater reuse is to progress in the United States, public insurance-indemnity funds may have to be established to reassure municipalities and compensate victims.

Reduction of demand for water by customers of municipal water supply systems does not encounter such formidable legal hurdles. Demand reduction measures generally fall into three categories: (1) pricing policies, (2) management practices, and (3) pure conservation modes [60]. Pricing strategies include overall rate increases, summer surcharges, and conservation pricing (flat or increasing block rates) instead of decreasing block rates for large users. Leak control and metering are examples of management practices. Pure conservation modes are revised plumbing and building codes, public education, and retrofitting devices on showers and commodes. It seems clear that reasonable demand reduction techniques are well within the legal authority of most municipalities, although private water companies would generally require approvals by state public service commissions [61]. However, in some states, municipalities are prohibited from making "profits" on water sales, thus limiting their flexibility to adjust rates [60].

THE SUPREME COURT AND WATER CONSERVATION

The U.S. Supreme Court's power to equitably apportion the waters of interstate rivers among contending states is examined in Part I. For many years the Court has considered waste and potential conservation as factors in determining equitable apportionments. In a recent decision [62], the Court stated:

> Our prior cases clearly establish that equitable apportionment will protect only those rights to water that are "reasonably acquired and applied." Especially in those Western states where water is scarce, "(t)here must be no waste

of the 'treasure' of a river. . . . Only diligence and good faith will keep the privilege alive." Thus, wasteful or inefficient uses will not be protected. Similarly, concededly senior water rights will be deemed forfeited or substantially diminished where the rights have not been exercised or asserted with reasonable diligence.

We have invoked equitable apportionment not only to require the reasonably efficient use of water, but also to impose on states an affirmative duty to conserve and augment the water supply of an interstate stream. [Citations omitted.]

It is probable that the Supreme Court's lead will soon be followed by state legislatures, courts, and administrative agencies over a broad spectrum of water rights allocations.

REFERENCES FOR PART III

1. Stone, A. B. "Public Rights in Water Uses and Private Rights in Land Adjacent to Water," in *Waters and Water Rights*, R. E. Clark, ed. (7 vols.; Indianapolis, IN: Allen Smith Co., 1967–1978), I, p. 198. The seven-volume treatise is hereafter referred to as "Clark."
2. Meyers, C. J., and A. D. Tarlock. *Water Resource Management*, (2d ed.; Mineola, NY: Foundation Press, 1980), p. 1035.
3. Dewsnup, R. L. "Public Access Rights in Waters and Shorelands," National Water Commission, NTIS PB 205 247 (1971), pp. 12–13.
4. Marvel, C. C. "Public Rights of Recreational Boating, Fishing, Wading, or the Like in Inland Stream the Bed of which is Privately Owned," 6 *American Law Reports* (ALR) 4th (Rochester, NY: Lawyers Cooperative Publishing Co., 1981), pp. 1030–1053.
5. Tarlock, A. D. "The Recognition of Instream Flow Rights: 'New' Public Western Water Rights," *Rocky Mountain Mineral Law Institute* 25:24–1 to 24–64 (1979), p. 24–6.
6. 438 U.S. 696 (1978).
7. Davis, C. "The Right to Use Water in the Eastern States," in Clark, VII, pp. 87–95.
8. N. Car. Gen. Stat., § 143-215.48.
9. 16 U.S.C. § 1271 et seq.
10. Knudson, D. M. "Analysis of Implementation Barriers for State Scenic River System Formulation," *Water Resources Bulletin* 15(3):718–726 (1979).
11. *Flowing Free* (Washington, DC: River Conservation Fund, 1977), pp. 22–31.
12. 608 F. 2d 1250 (1979).
13. *Thompson* v. *Enz.* 379 Mich. 667, 154 N.W. 2d 473 (1967).
14. Fla. Stat. Ann. § 298.74.
15. 33 Cal. 3d 419, 189 Cal Rptr. 346 (1983).
16. 43 U.S.C. § 1301 et seq.
17. *Illinois Central Railroad* v. *Illinois*, 146 U.S. 387 (1892).
18. 444 U.S. 164 (1979).
19. "Water Policies for the Future," National Water Commission, U.S. Government Printing Office (1973).
20. 16 U.S.C. §§ 460l-460l-3.
21. 16 U.S.C. § 460l et seq.
22. 16 U.S.C. § 460l-12 et seq. (1965).
23. Coggins, G. C., and C. F. Wilkinson. *Federal Public Land and Resources Law* (Mineola, NY: Foundation Press, 1981), p. 125.

24. 16 U.S.C. § 1131 et seq. (1964).
25. Plater, Z. J. B. "The Takings Issue in a Natural Setting: Floodlines and the Police Power," *Texas Law Review* 52(2):201–256 (1974), p. 207.
26. 42 U.S.C. § 400 et seq.
27. Shaw, S. R. "New Jersey's Freshwater Wetlands—A Vanishing Resource in Need of Protection," Master's Thesis, Rutgers University, (1982).
28. "National Flood Insurance:—Marginal Impact on Flood Plain Development—Administrative Improvements Needed," U.S. General Accounting Office Report CED-82-105 (1982), pp. 22–23.
29. Holmes, B. H. "Federal Participation in Land Use Planning at the Water's Edge—Floodplains and Wetlands," *Natural Resources Lawyer* 13(2):351–410 (1980), p. 361.
30. N.J.S.A. 58:16A–50 et seq.
31. McCraw, S. M. "State and Local Wetlands Regulation in the Courts: Constitutional Problems on the Wane," *Harvard Environmental Law Review* 1:496–514 (1976), p. 497.
32. 56 Wis. 2d 7, 201 N.W. 2d. 761.
33. Kussy, E. V. A. "Wetlands and Floodplain Protection and the Federal-Aid Highway Program," *Environmental Law* 13(1):161–264 (1982), p. 226.
34. 33 U.S.C. § 701b et seq.
35. 16 U.S.C. § 1301 et seq.
36. 16 U.S.C. § 1221 et seq.
37. 16 U.S.C. § 757.
38. 16 U.S.C. § 715.
39. 16 U.S.C. § 669.
40. 16 U.S.C. § 777.
41. 33 U.S.C. § 1334.
42. Thompson, E. "Section 404 of the Federal Water Pollution Control Act Amendment of 1977: Hydrologic Modification, Wetlands Protection and the Physical Integrity of the Nation's Waters," *Harvard Environmental Law Review* 2:264–287 (1978), p. 272.
43. 33 CFR pts. 320–330 (1982).
44. Blumm, M. C. "The Clean Water Act's Section 404 Permit Program Enters Its Adolescence: An Institutional and Programmatic Perspective," *Ecology Law Quarterly* 8(3):409–472 (1980), p. 418.
45. *Avoyelles Sportsmen's League, Inc.* v. *Alexander*, 473 F. Supp 525 (W.D. La. 1979) rev'd on other grounds, sub. nom. *Avoyelles Sportsmen's League, Inc.* v. *Marsh*, 19 ERC 1841 (CA5, 1983).
46. 48 FR 21466.
47. Wood, L. D. "The Status of Weather Modification Activities under United States and International Law," *Natural Resources Lawyer* X (2):367–392 (1977), p. 368.
48. McKenzie, A. G. "Weather Modification: A Review of the Science and the Law," *Environmental Law* 6(2):387–430 (1976), pp. 392–397.
49. Pub. L. 94-490.
50. Weiss, E. B. "Weather Modification and the Law," in *Pollution and Water Resources, Columbia University Seminar Series*, G. J. Halasi-Kun, ed. (New York: Pergamon Press, 1981), Vol. XIII, pt. 2, p. 20.

51. 197 Misc. 730, 197 N.Y.S. 2d, 238 (1950).
52. *Southwest Weather Research, Inc.* v. *Rounsaville*, 320 S.W. 2d 211 (1958).
53. *Reserve Mining Co.* v. *E.P.A.* 514 F. 2d 492 (8th Cir. 1975).
54. Gallogly, M. R. "Acid Precipitation: Can the Clean Air Act Handle It?" *Boston College Environmental Affairs Law Review* 9(3):687–744 (1981–1982), pp. 688–690.
55. 42 U.S.C. 7401 et seq.
56. Herfindahl, O. C. "What Is Conservation?" in *Three Studies in Mineral Economics* (Washington, DC: Resources for the Future, 1961), pp. 1–12.
57. Shabman, L. "Discussion," *Water Resources Bulletin* 18(2):345–347 (1982), p. 346.
58. Pring, G. W., and K. A. Tomb. "License to Waste: Legal Barriers to Conservation and Efficient Use of Water in the West," *Rocky Mountain Mineral Law Institute* 25:25–1 to 25–67 (1979), p. 25–4.
59. Brown, E. C., and N. Weinstock. "Legal Issues in Implementing Water Reuse in California," *Ecology Law Quarterly* 9(2):243–294 (1981), p. 248.
60. Moomaw, R. L., and L. Warner. "The Adoption of Municipal Water Conservation: An Unlikely Event?" *Water Resources Bulletin* 17(6):1029–1034 (1981), p. 1030.
61. Baram, M. S. "Legal, Economic and Institutional Barriers to Water Reuse in Northern New England," U.S. Department of the Interior Report OWRT/14-34-0001-9424 (1980), pp. 87–96.
62. *Colorado* v. *New Mexico*, 51 USLW 4045 (1982).

PART IV
Water Treatment and Land Use

Water treatment and restrictions on land development are the primary approaches to protecting, restoring, and improving water quality. "Water treatment" is defined here as subjecting water to a cleansing agent or action, or segregating it from contact with other waters. This can take place at any of three points: (1) before wastewater is or would be discharged to a waterbody or groundwater; (2) in the process of removing pollutants that presently exist in waterbodies; and (3) after withdrawal for uses such as drinking water. Land development prohibitions are generally imposed only where water treatment cannot protect high-quality waters.

As the following quotation from Leonard B. Dworsky points out, water quality law has evolved independently of other aspects of water law:

> Historically, the strategy for managing water resources is to capture and store waters in order to have them available for use when and where they are needed. Lakes and simple embankments across flowing streams are centuries-old means for accomplishing this. Only within the last hundred years has a new component, based on the scientific concepts of quality arising out of the work of Pasteur and the other early bacteriologists, been added to the age-old strategy.
>
> Today the strategy is to make water available when needed, where needed, and of the right quality. For nearly three-quarters of a century, science, technology, and public policy have been moving in the direction of improving society's ability to manage this new component, quality. It has turned out to be much more difficult than the task of managing quantities of water, even flood waters, because water quality or pollution control is involved

with so many uses of water by so many people. Although the political and technical skills for dealing with this issue have been improving, further sophistication is needed before this important problem can be dealt with adequately. An important part of this problem is finding more effective ways to integrate water pollution control into the overall water resources planning and development task [1].

One goal of modern water law is to facilitate comprehensive water resources management by creating a new synthesis from disintegrated fragments of prior water law.

Chapter 23
THE CLEAN WATER ACT: INTRODUCTION

This long and complicated statute [2] combines two approaches to water pollution control, a water quality-based approach and a technology-based approach. In the context of the CWA both are "regulatory" strategies, that is, they entail administrative permitting of allowable discharges and enforcement against permit violators. Nonregulatory "market" mechanisms, such as "effluent charges" and "pollution rights" auctions, have been proposed [3], but have not been adopted by Congress.

Water quality standards are the focus of the water quality-based approach to pollution control. A "water quality standard" is a legal designation of the desired use for a given body of water and the water quality criteria appropriate for that use. "Water quality criteria" are specific levels of water quality which, if not violated, are expected to render a body of water suitable for its designated use. Criteria may be expressed as either a number, a narrative, or both. An example of a numerical criterion is a dissolved oxygen (DO) criterion, which for swimming and nontrout fishing might set a level of 5.0 milligrams of DO per liter of water as a twenty-four-hour average, with no less than 4.0 milligrams per liter at any time. For a "parameter" (aspect of water quality) such as taste and odor, the criterion might be expressed narratively: "None offensive to humans or which would produce offensive tastes and/or odors in water supplies and biota used for human consumption. None which would render the waters unfit for the designated uses." Water quality standards are measures of "ambient" (instream) water quality.

For permitting and enforcement purposes, water quality standards must be translated into water quality-based effluent limitations for particular dischargers. "Effluent limitations" are restrictions on quantities, rates, and concentrations in wastewater discharges measured at the discharger's outfall pipe. A water quality-based effluent limitation is established using a water quality model, a mathematical technique for predicting the effect of discharges on ambient water quality. Based on the model, dischargers are given "wasteload allocations" defining the total maximum daily load of pollutants (TMDL) each discharger of waste is allowed to release into a specific waterway in order to restore or maintain the applicable water quality criterion. A discharger's wasteload allocation is expressed as a water quality-based effluent limitation.

Before 1972, American water pollution control policy was based on the water quality-based approach, and it was a failure [4]. In the first place, there is not yet an adequate scientific basis for tying water quality criteria to designated uses. The following passage is taken from a U.S. General Accounting Office (GAO) report criticizing the Environmental Protection Agency's water quality criteria as being too strict, but the same argument could be used to attack other criteria as overly loose:

> DO concentrations are important in gauging water quality. In fact, DO has been called "probably the single most important water quality parameter in fisheries management." Therefore, a complete and thorough scientific basis for the recommended DO criterion would be expected, but cannot be found. Scientists disagree considerably on how much DO fish need. Most species of adult fish (including brook trout) can survive at very low DO concentrations. Minimum tolerable levels reported by some investigators are several times greater than those reported by others for the same fish species, tested at about the same temperatures. Many apparent contradictions also exist about the effects of DO levels on hatching of fish eggs and growth of many young fish [5].

Moreover, general criteria are not appropriate to all waters at all times of the year, nor are they sensitive to differences in intensity, frequency, duration, and extent of violations.

Second, assigning wasteload allocations to dischargers based on mathematical models is still an uncertain enterprise because of the relatively primitive nature of even the most advanced water quality models [5]. According to the GAO, "It is very difficult to model complex natural processes found in many water bodies because so little is known about them" [5]. Most stream models concentrate on DO, ignoring other components such as toxic substances and "nutrients" (nitrogen and phosphorus). DO models are themselves imprecise because natural processes such as stream reaeration are not fully understood, "nonpoint source" (runoff) loads are neglected, measurement errors are frequent, mistaken assumptions are used in the absence of adequate water quality data, and many models are not properly verified [5].

Modeling and wasteload allocation difficulties are compounded by the concept of "mixing zones," a traditional part of water quality standards. A mixing zone is an area around a discharge point in which a discharger is permitted to mix its wastes without liability for violating water quality standards. For example, current New Jersey regulations define the boundaries of nonthermal mixing zones as follows:

> The total area and volume of water assigned to non-thermal mixing zones shall be limited to that which will not interfere with biological communities or populations of important species to a degree which is damaging to the ecosystem or which diminishes other beneficial uses disproportionately. Furthermore, mortality of aquatic life shall not occur within the non-thermal mixing zone.

The vagueness of this concept precludes rational application, especially where there are many dischargers to a stream segment.

Third, even if waterbodies could be modeled precisely there would be thorny problems of distributional equity in attempting to allocate wasteloads [6]. Should downstream dischargers receive lower TMDLs because the water is dirtier? If a percentage allocation is utilized, should large and small firms be treated alike? Should waterbodies be zoned for wasteload allocation purposes? If so, where should zonal lines be drawn? What allowances should be made for future growth?

Distributional problems are merely one aspect of the major enforcement disadvantage of water quality-based effluent limitations—their variability. Identical dischargers located on different waterbodies or even on different segments of the same stream are allocated different TMDLs because of variations in receiving water quality. Enforcement efforts are countered by "forum shopping," discharger threats to relocate to states or areas with cleaner water. These threats gain credibility because the firm is placed at a competitive disadvantage simply by virtue of its geographical location. Pressures on pollution control officials to compromise at the expense of water quality are extreme where enforcement might lead to plant closings and consequent economic dislocation.

In 1972 Congress redirected America's water pollution control program. The CWA retained water quality standards and wasteload allocations, but only as a temporary, secondary line of defense. Its principal control mechanism is uniform national technology-based effluent limitations, progressively tightened until a "zero-discharge" goal is reached. "Such direct restrictions on discharges facilitate enforcement by making it unnecessary to work backward from an over-polluted body of water to determine which . . . sources are responsible and which must be abated" [7]. They focus on "the preventable causes of water pollution" rather than its "tolerable effects" [7]. The act's technology-based effluent limitation approach has significantly reduced or prevented water pollution in the United States [8,9]. Debate about the act now involves whether further water quality improvement is worth the cost of installing expensive control technology, and whether these more sophisticated control mechanisms are necessary to restore or maintain desired waterbody uses. There is a movement toward reinstating the water quality-based approach, including an economic component, above the uniform level of technological control already attained. In short, the tension between proponents of the water quality-based and technology-based approaches remains, and will probably continue to remain, unresolved.

The following detailed discussion of the CWA amplifies these introductory remarks. Emphasis is placed on the act's three major water pollution control modes, the construction grants program for reducing municipal discharges, the National Pollutant Discharge Elimination System (NPDES) permit program for control of point source discharges, and water quality management planning for nonpoint source control.

Chapter 24
THE CLEAN WATER ACT: POLLUTION REDEFINED

Pollution is not a fact of nature but a human value judgment. Society decides what is clean and what is polluted. Prior to 1972, American law implicitly defined "pollution" as an unacceptable transformational use. Waterbodies were thought to possess "assimilative capacities" which could be used to decompose or dilute wastes so as to maintain desired uses. Wasteload allocations represented allocations of assimilative capacities, and water quality standards represented desired uses. Pollution meant overloading a waterbody with wastes and exhausting its assimilative capacity, precluding desired uses (violating water quality standards) [10]. Before 1972, desired uses were set by individual states, which classified navigable waters in categories ranging from Class A (swimming) to Class D (agricultural and industrial use). If a state was satisfied that a particular river was esthetically tolerable and fit for navigation, the law did not afford relief unless the river stank or corroded hulls. One river, the Cuyahoga in Ohio, was not considered legally objectionable until it caught fire, because the state-designated use of that river was waste disposal. Moreover, some states established weak water quality standards in order to retain resident industries and attract new ones [4].

In summary, water pollution control law prior to 1972 gave a right to discharge until waters were polluted, meaning until state-set water quality standards were violated. The public had a right to water only as clean as the state dictated in its water quality standards. Pollution was a transformational use that was unacceptable to society, as represented by state government.

One key to understanding the CWA of 1972 is to recognize that it redefined "pollution." Section 502* of the CWA defines "pollution" as "the man-made or man-induced alteration of the chemical, physical, biological, and radiological integrity of water." Any transformational discharge into water is pollution. A right to discharge is the exception rather than the rule. The public has a right to water in its unpolluted natural state wherever attainable. Our national goal is the curtailment of all discharges in order to restore and maintain the natural character of our waterbodies. States are no longer authorized to designate waterbodies for uses below minimum standards of cleanliness. In fact, all waters of the United States must be at least suitable for fishing and swimming wherever attainable.

But like all rights, the public's right to clean water is not unqualified: Congress has created certain rights to discharge based on receiving water quality or economic factors; the right to clean water must be foregone where it is inherently unattainable; and its fulfillment must be postponed where economically reasonable technology to eliminate discharges is unavailable, as long as receiving waters are fit for fishing and swimming where these uses are attainable. But in the meantime, development of new technology will be encouraged by establishing governmental research programs. Once feasible technology has been developed, its implementation will be ensured by imposing progressively stricter technology-based effluent limitations on dischargers, limitations that will be uniform throughout the United States. Installation of improved municipal control technology will be stimulated by federal construction grants as well as municipal effluent limitations. Moreover, if compliance with technology-based effluent limitations by dischargers to a waterbody will not make it suitable for fishing or swimming, and these uses are indeed attainable, more stringent water quality-based effluent limitations will be imposed in order to force technology development, or to compel production cutbacks or plant shutdowns. Applicable effluent limitations, either based on technology or water quality, will be included in enforceable discharge permits, and except in compliance with a permit "the discharge of any pollutant by any person shall be unlawful" [11]. Finally, an active enforcement program will deter violations.

---

*All references to the Clean Water Act are to the original congressional section numbers, not those found in the *United States Code*. For example, section 101 of the act is officially listed as 33 U.S.C. section 125. Unofficial section numbers are used here because these are the numbers known by water resources professionals, partly because the copies of the act distributed by EPA were based on congressional prints, and partly because the congressional section numbers are easier to remember.

Although the technology-based effluent limitation approach remains in the ascendant, the pollution control tide may be turning again toward the advocates of a water quality-based strategy. First, Congress has recently enacted two amendments to the CWA that reflect a water quality-based approach, allowing waivers for certain municipal ocean dischargers and easing secondary treatment requirements for small communities. Second, the Reagan administration is supporting a proposed amendment to make pretreatment requirements dependent on receiving water quality. Third, federal construction grant and research funds have been seriously cut, inhibiting compliance with current technology-based effluent limitations and discouraging the development of new technology on which to base stricter effluent limitations. Last, we have learned since 1972 that much of our water pollution comes from nonpoint source runoff that is presently intractable to a technology-based approach. The continued viability of water quality thinking is illustrated by the following definition of "pollution," found in a 1980 report of Congress's investigation arm, the General Accounting Office:

> Contamination or other alteration of the physical, chemical, or biological properties of water—including changes in temperature, taste, color, or odor—or the discharge into water of any liquid, gaseous, radioactive, solid, or other substance *that may create a nuisance or render such water detrimental or injurious to public health, safety, or welfare* (emphasis added) [5].

Perhaps this echo of the past is also an augury of the future.

Chapter 25

THE CLEAN WATER ACT: GOALS AND POLICIES

With the CWA's general philosophy in mind, its goals and policies become more intelligible. Section 101 declares:

> (a) The objective of this Act is to restore and maintain the chemical, physical, and biological integrity of the Nation's waters. In order to achieve this objective it is hereby declared that, consistent with the provisions of this Act—(1) it is the national goal that the discharge of pollutants into the navigable waters be eliminated by 1985; (2) it is the national goal what wherever attainable, an interim goal of water quality which provides for the protection and propagation of fish, shellfish, and wildlife, and provides for recreation in and on the water be achieved by July 1, 1983; (3) it is the national policy that the discharge of toxic pollutants in toxic amounts be prohibited; (4) it is the national policy that Federal financial assistance be provided to construct publicly owned waste treatment works; (5) it is the national policy that areawide waste treatment management planning processes be developed and implemented to assure adequate control of sources of pollutants in each State; and (6) it is the national policy that a major research and demonstration effort be made to develop technology necessary to eliminate the discharge of pollutants into the navigable waters, waters of the contiguous zone, and the oceans.

The objective of restoring and maintaining the integrity of America's waters and the goal of zero discharge are useful for mobilizing effort and interpreting ambiguities in the act's language. They are not enforceable requirements. Nor are they as strong as the national "policy" to prohibit toxic discharges. However, "fishability-swimmability" is both a goal and a requirement, but only "wherever attainable." That these goals are not quixotic is shown by the restoration of important waterbodies to fishable-swimmable status [8] and the attainment, or prospective attainment, of zero discharge by major categories of industry. The CWA should not be condemned as a failure because the 1983 and 1985 goals are unachievable by those dates. Goals are inherently flexible, and even enforceable requirements can be modified by Congress if necessary. It has been learned since 1972 that water pollution control is more complicated and expensive than was first anticipated. Thus, it is no disgrace to postpone fulfilling some of our goals and to "fine tune" certain enforceable requirements. In fact, Congress should be proud of having enacted such a dynamic and durable statute.

What is this "chemical, physical, and biological integrity of the Nation's waters," this natural state to which we are entitled wherever attainable? The CWA does not, as some of its critics suggest, attempt to recreate a preindustrial American utopia, a dehumanized state of primeval purity. Instead, the CWA's legislative history [12] makes it clear that what Congress meant by "integrity" of a waterbody was its ecological stability, its ability to respond to change by maintaining ecological diversity. The existence of fish and wildlife in and around a waterbody and its capacity to sustain human recreation are indicators of ecological stability. Moreover, a waterbody's integrity must be viewed in the context of unalterable realities intrinsic to our highly industrialized and urbanized society.

But why is zero discharge necessary to maintain the integrity of water? Cannot some wastes be discharged without jeopardizing the ecological stability of a waterbody? Theoretically the answer is yes, but in practice the water quality-based approach has proved to be unenforceable. So we have created a presumption that any measurable discharge of any substance into a waterbody is inconsistent with the integrity of its water. Unlike some presumptions, this one is rebuttable. All discharges are presumed to be violations of the public's right to clean water wherever attainable, unless Congress allows a temporary right to discharge because of the unavailability of feasible control technology, or a more permanent discharge right based on receiving water quality or overriding economic factors.

Chapter 26

THE CLEAN WATER ACT: ANTIDEGRADATION AND ATTAINABILITY

The term "antidegradation" cannot be found in the CWA. Section 101 merely declares a policy to "restore and *maintain*" clean water. Nevertheless, antidegradation requirements have traditionally been a prominent feature of water pollution control law [13]. Our national goal is not only to clean up dirty waterbodies but also to forestall degradation of presently high-quality waters.

Federal regulations promulgated on November 8, 1983, require each state to adopt a statewide antidegradation policy and identify the methods of implementing it [14]. The state antidegradation policy and implementation methods must, at a minimum, protect and maintain existing instream water uses. Existing water uses, trout propagation for example, are the bottom line of the 1983 antidegradation regulations. High-quality waters that exceed those levels necessary to support fishing and swimming must be maintained and protected unless the state, after public participation, chooses to allow lower water quality where "necessary to accommodate important economic or social development." Additionally, no long-term degradation is allowed in high-quality waters "which constitute an outstanding National resource" such as parks, wildlife refuges "and waters of exceptional recreational and ecological significance."

The concept of "attainability" is closely related to antidegradation. It has been seen that the CWA establishes a minimum fishable-swimmable use for waterbodies "wherever attainable." But what does this important phrase mean? In the first place, a use is attainable if it is already being attained. Thus, where existing water quality standards specify designated uses less than those that are presently being attained, the state must revise its standards to reflect the uses actually being attained. Second, a use is attainable if it can be achieved by the imposition of technology-based effluent limitations for point sources "and cost-effective and reasonable best management practices for nonpoint source control" [14]. Third, a use is deemed attainable unless the state, after an "attainability analysis," can demonstrate that attaining the designated use is not feasible because:

(1) Naturally occurring pollutant concentrations prevent the attainment of the use; or (2) Natural, ephemeral, intermittent or low flow conditions or water levels prevent the attainment of the use, unless these conditions may be compensated for by the discharge of sufficient volume of effluent discharges without violating State water conservation requirements to enable uses to be met; or (3) Human caused conditions or sources of pollution prevent the attainment of the use and cannot be remedied or would cause more environmental damage to correct than to leave in place; or (4) Dams, diversions or other types of hydrologic modifications preclude the attainment of the use, and it is not feasible to restore the water body to its original condition or to operate such modification in a way that would result in the attainment of the use; or (5) Physical conditions related to the natural features of the water body, such as the lack of a proper substrate, cover, flow, depth, pools, riffles, and the like, unrelated to water quality, preclude attainment of aquatic life protection uses; or (6) Controls more stringent than [the CWA's technology-based effluent limitations] would result in substantial and widespread economic and social impact [14].

The vagueness of these criteria makes it probable that they will be, as their predecessors have been, politically and legally controversial. Serious political and economic consequences depend on how they are interpreted. For example, how much growth will be permitted at the expense of water quality? In water-short areas, what tradeoffs will be permitted between diversions and impaired quality? When is restoration of more natural water quality feasible? These questions reflect the tensions inherent in the concept of "attainability."

Chapter 27

THE CLEAN WATER ACT: INDUSTRIAL POINT SOURCE DISCHARGERS

In the CWA the term "discharge of a pollutant" means "any addition of any pollutant to navigable waters from any point source." As pointed out in Part II, "navigable waters" is generously defined by the CWA as "waters of the United States" including the territorial seas within the three-mile limit. In turn, courts have interpreted "waters of the United States" to include wetlands, drainage ditches, mosquito canals, and intermittent streams. The CWA is silent about whether "waters of the United States" includes groundwater. Different courts have held both ways on the matter. But the Environmental Protection Agency has acted as though the CWA's point source discharge requirements do not apply to groundwater discharges.

A "point source" is "any discernible, confined and discrete conveyance, including but not limited to any pipe, ditch, channel, tunnel, conduit, well, discrete fissure, container, rolling stock, concentrated animal feeding operation, or vessel or other floating craft. . . . This term does not include return flows from irrigated agriculture." [2] "Point source" is to be liberally construed, and has been held to include earth-moving equipment in a wetland and ponded mine drainage which is allowed to erode a channel to a waterbody. On the other hand, EPA has discretion to treat point sources as "nonpoint sources" (sources other than point sources) for regulatory purposes. For example, dams are point sources capable of causing diminution in downriver water quality, but EPA, with court approval, treats dams as if they were nonpoint sources.

The CWA's approach to regulating point source discharges is to impose progressively stricter technology-based effluent limitations on categories of point sources in pursuit of a zero-discharge goal. Where imposition of technology-based limitations will not produce fishable-swimmable waters where attainable, more stringent water quality-based limitations must be applied. The two major classes of point source dischargers are industries and publicly owned treatment works (POTWs). Industries are either "direct dischargers" to waterbodies or "indirect dischargers" into POTWs which then discharge to waterbodies. This chapter deals with industrial point source direct dischargers.

PHASE I

When the CWA was enacted in 1972, it contained two phases of technology-based limitations. In Phase I existing industrial point sources were required to apply the best practicable control technology currently available (BPT), as defined in EPA regulations, by July 1, 1977 [15]. During Phase II, categories of industrial point sources were to meet effluent limitations based on best available technology economically achievable (BAT), or if feasible zero discharge, by July 1, 1983. New industrial discharge sources were expected to meet strict "standards of performance," based on BAT or zero discharge, immediately [16]. However, having met the applicable new source standard of performance, the discharger could not be required to meet stricter standards for ten years or the plant's amortization period, whichever ended first [16].

In setting effluent limitations based on BPT, Congress instructed EPA to consider

> the total cost of application of technology in relation to the effluent reduction benefits to be achieved from such application, and . . . also take into account the age of equipment and facilities involved, the process employed, the engineering aspects of the application of various types of control techniques, process changes, non-water quality environmental impact (including energy requirements), and such other factors as the Administrator deems appropriate [17].

Legislative history indicates that BPT was seen primarily as available "end-of-pipe" treatment, and that EPA's definition of BPT would be acceptable as long as control costs and economic impacts were not "wholly out of proportion" to water quality benefits. In contrast, BAT was thought of primarily as in-plant process changes that had been or were capable of being achieved. Compliance costs were considered in setting BAT; no cost-benefit analysis was necessary as with BPT. Congress realized that some businesses would be forced to cut back production or even close down as a result of their inability to afford the costs of complying with these technology-based standards.

EPA's strategy in setting BPT effluent limitations was to divide industries into categories based on products manufactured and subcategories based on processes utilized. For example, the asbestos manufacturing category contained asbestos-cement sheet and asbestos paper subcategories. Based on an average of the performance of the cleanest "exemplary plants" in each subcategory, EPA promulgated regulations containing effluent limitations for relevant parameters set out in terms of maximum daily and monthly averages per unit of production. These "single number" effluent limitations were uniform for existing plants in a particular subcategory wherever located. However, a discharger that objected to inclusion within a certain subcategory was entitled to a variance if it proved that "factors relating to the equipment or facilities involved, the process applied, or other such factors . . . are fundamentally different from the factors considered in the establishment of the guidelines." Abnormal compliance costs were to be considered in determining whether a plant was "fundamentally different," although economic capability to meet compliance costs was not to be considered [18]. Nor could a plant be fundamentally different because of impurities contained in its intake water, because effluent limitations were net, not gross. The impacts of a discharge on local receiving water quality were also not to be considered. Effluent limitations for fundamentally different dischargers were to be based on best professional judgment (BPJ). Finally, EPA's first round of effluent limitation regulations also contained standards of performance for new sources in specific subcategories.

Effluent limitations based on BPT were comparatively stringent with regard to those parameters which are now called "conventional pollutants," e.g., biochemical oxygen demand, total suspended solids, fecal coliform, pH (acidity-alkalinity), and oil and grease. However, little progress was made during Phase I in controlling "toxic pollutants," defined in the CWA as pollutants or combinations of pollutants which "upon exposure, ingestion, inhalation, or assimilation into any organism, either directly from the environment or indirectly by ingestion through food chains, will . . . cause death, disease, behavioral abnormalities, cancer, genetic mutations, physiological malfunctions (including malfunctions in reproduction) or physical deformations, in such organisms or their offspring."

Nevertheless, the industrial community responded with hundreds of lawsuits challenging EPA's general BPT methodology and its application to particular subcategories. In 1977 the U.S. Supreme Court upheld EPA's approach to setting BPT effluent limitations [19]. Most industry challenges to the application of this methodology have also been resolved in EPA's favor.

By the 1977 statutory compliance date a high percentage of industrial dischargers were meeting their BPT-based effluent limitations. Where compliance facilities were under construction by dischargers who acted in good faith, Congress extended the deadline to April 1, 1979. By now, all industrial point source dischargers have presumably met Phase I effluent limitations except the two West Coast paper mills that Congress exempted from these requirements. Phase I has been markedly successful in removing conventional pollutants from America's waters and in restoring waterbodies to fishable-swimmable quality.

PHASE II

In 1977 Congress decided that the cost of moving to BAT for conventionals was too great. A modified requirement, called best conventional pollutant control technology (BCT), was to underlie the development of further technology-based effluent limitations for dischargers of conventionals, and compliance was to be achieved by July 1, 1984. BCT includes two cost tests: (1) a comparison between the costs of reducing discharges of conventionals and the resultant water quality benefits; and (2) a comparison between industrial and municipal treatment costs. Congressional supporters of BCT felt that it would most often fall between BPT and BAT.

EPA has found the BCT cost tests difficult to apply. In fact, its first BCT effluent limitations regulations were held by a federal circuit court of appeals to be in violation of the CWA. A second round of BCT regulations was proposed late in 1982. Consequently, it is likely that the 1984 BCT compliance date will be extended.

One of the reasons why there was minimal control of toxic pollutants during Phase I was the ambiguous control strategy of the CWA as originally enacted. On the one hand, dischargers of toxics were subject to phased technology-based effluent limitations for industrial categories. On the other hand, there was an alternative pollutant-by-pollutant approach requiring EPA to (1) publish a list of toxic pollutants; (2) set effluent standards for these pollutants based not on technology or water quality standards but on toxicity, persistence, degradability, and ecosystem effects; (3) set a margin of safety; (4) hold lengthy hearings; and (5) enforce compliance with effluent standards within one year of promulgation. Confused by these inconsistent mandates and preoccupied with conventional pollutants and POTW pollution, EPA virtually ignored industrial dischargers of toxics until numerous environmentalist lawsuits forced EPA into a court-approved settlement. The famous "Consent Decree" of 1976 [20] confirmed EPA's ultimate decision to regulate toxic pollutants primarily by requiring dischargers to comply with effluent limitations based on BAT. The Consent Decree also established timetables for EPA to promulgate effluent limitations for sixty-five identified priority toxic pollutants* applicable to twenty-one (now twenty-three) industrial categories. According to the Consent Decree, dischargers were to meet effluent limitations for toxics by the CWA's Phase II compliance date, July 1, 1983.

In 1977 Congress both codified and modified the Consent Decree. The CWA was amended to establish a class of toxic pollutants, consisting of the sixty-five materials that appear in the Consent Decree and additional toxics that EPA may list. Industrial dischargers of toxic pollutants must achieve BAT-based effluent limitations by July 1, 1984, for the Consent Decree toxics (a one-year postponement), or within three years of promulgation for newly listed toxics. But in emergency situations EPA can require immediate cessation of discharge or up to a one-year compliance period [21].

The Consent Decree's timetables for EPA promulgation of BAT-based effluent limitations for toxic pollutants were undisturbed by the 1977 CWA amendments. However, EPA fell seriously behind these schedules, prompting further court proceedings and an amendment of the Consent Decree to furnish EPA with more time to perform its obligations. Further promulgation delays took place when the Reagan administration unsuccessfully sued to overturn the Consent Decree. Proposed BAT-based effluent limitations for industrial dischargers of toxics began to appear toward the middle of 1982, and promulgation should be completed by June 1984. A good deal of litigation will undoubtedly greet these standards, even though in many cases BAT is identical to BPT. Obviously, the 1984 compliance date will have to be extended.

In addition to conventional pollutants and toxic pollutants, the 1977 amendments created a third class of nonconventional pollutants, defined as all pollutants, such as chlorine, phosphorus, and chemical oxygen demand, which are neither toxic nor conventional pollutants. Dischargers of nonconventional pollutants must meet BAT-based effluent limitations between 1984 and 1987. Dischargers of conventional pollutants may seek only the "fundamentally different factors" (FDF) variance. Dischargers of toxics may not seek the FDF variance, but may be awarded extensions of BAT compliance dates for adoption of innovative technology [22]. By contrast, dischargers of nonconventionals have access to two variances based on costs of compliance. First, there is a potential modification that "will represent the maximum use of technology within the economic capability of the owner or operator" and "will result in reasonable further progress toward the elimination of the discharge of pollutants." A second variance provision allows

---

*Some of these are families of compounds. There are approximately 130 items on EPA's "priority pollutants" list.

EPA, with state consent, to impose a substitute effluent limitation which will: (1) be at least as strict as one based on BPT; (2) not result in additional requirements being placed on another point source; and (3) not interfere with the attainment or maintenance of fishable-swimmable waters or endanger human health.

There has been no change in the regulation of new sources since 1972. They are still required to achieve BAT or zero discharge immediately, with an exemption from further requirements during at least their amortization period or ten years, whichever comes first.

HEAT DISCHARGERS

The CWA regulates dischargers of heat differently from other industrial dischargers. Heat discharged into water is a pollutant, and dischargers of heat must meet effluent limitations based on BAT by the established compliance date. Nevertheless, under subsection 316(a) of the CWA, a variance based on receiving water quality is available to dischargers of heat. Whenever the discharger can demonstrate

> to the satisfaction of the Administrator (or, if appropriate, the State) that any effluent limitation proposed for the control of the thermal component of any discharge from such source will require effluent limitations more stringent than necessary to assure the protection and propagation of a balanced indigenous population of shellfish, fish, and wildlife in and on the body of water into which the discharge is to be made, the Administrator (or, if appropriate, the State) may impose an effluent limitation . . . with respect to the thermal component of such discharge (taking into account the interaction of such thermal component with other pollutants), that will assure the protection and propagation of a balanced, indigenous population of shellfish, fish, and wildlife in and on the body of water.

This "balanced indigenous population" test for thermal variances has, if a pun may be excused, created more heat than light. Power companies, anxious to avoid the expense of cooling towers, have brought section 316(a) proceedings which are so complex that many remain unresolved after ten years of administrative consideration. Once again, the water quality-based approach has failed because the effects of effluents on ecosystems are poorly understood.

Subsection 316(b) requires that in effluent limitations for thermal dischargers there be provisions "that the location, design, construction and capacity of cooling water intake structures reflect the best technology available for minimizing adverse environmental impact." This clause has also produced controversy, particularly with regard to EPA's approval of intake structures for the Seabrook nuclear plant in New Hampshire. Although EPA regulates intake structures for nuclear power plants, the U.S. Supreme

Court has held that radioactive discharges are under the jurisdiction of the Nuclear Regulatory Commission [23].

WATER QUALITY-BASED EFFLUENT LIMITATIONS

It may come as a surprise that the CWA perpetuated the water quality-based approach for heat and, more importantly, for all point source dischargers on water quality-limited stretches. After all, did not the failure of this strategy lead directly to the passage of the CWA with its emphasis on uniform national effluent limitations founded upon technological availability? Indeed, the original drafters of the 1972 act, the staff of the Subcommittee on Air and Water Pollution of the Senate Public Works Committee working under the supervision of Senator Muskie, were committed to substituting the technology-based approach for the discredited water quality-based approach. As a result, the Senate bill did not provide for postenactment revision and approval of water quality standards [12]. The House, on the other hand, was not willing to forego water quality standards. Congressman Blatnik, chairman of the House Public Works Committee and one of the sponsors of the House bill, had been one of the architects of the Water Quality Act of 1965, which codified the water quality standards approach. Also, there was feeling in the House that the novel technology-based effluent limitation approach might prove unsuccessful, and therefore water quality standards should be retained "just in case." Finally, members of the House envisioned "a dual approach; . . . whichever is the stronger shall apply." Thus, the House bill contained a section substantially identical to section 303 of the CWA, which the Senate was forced to accept—against its better judgment—by way of political compromise.

Section 303 requires that water quality standards be set for all waters, establishes procedures for the periodic review and revision of standards, and outlines a continuing water quality planning process for each state. Water quality standards must

> protect the public health or welfare, enhance the quality of water and serve the purposes of [the CWA]. Such standards shall be established taking into consideration their use and value for public water supplies, propagation of fish and wildlife, recreational purposes, and agricultural, industrial and other purposes, and also taking into consideration their use and value for navigation.

For a number of years EPA administered this clause under a rule of "presumptive applicability." A state criterion for a particular parameter had to be at least as stringent as the recommended criterion contained in EPA's guidance document referred to as the "Red Book" [24], unless this state was able to justify a less stringent criterion. However, the "presumptive applicability" rule has been rescinded, and a state may now set site-specific criteria subject to EPA review.

Each state is to reconsider its existing water quality standards at least every three years, revise them where appropriate, and submit revisions to EPA for approval. EPA must review the revised standards to determine whether they protect the public health or welfare, enhance the quality of water, and serve the purposes of the CWA. If EPA determines that the revised standards meet the requirements of the act, EPA approves the standards. EPA must promulgate its own standards where it finds state revisions inadequate. EPA is authorized not only to react to those revisions submitted by states, but to issue federal standards on its own initiative where appropriate. Under a 1981 amendment to the CWA, states must adopt new or revised water quality standards by December 29, 1984. After this date, no construction grants for publicly owned treatment works shall be made in a state that has not adopted new or revised standards unless EPA approval has been unreasonably delayed.

Section 303 also establishes a procedure for the attainment of water quality standards. A state must first identify those waters within its boundaries for which technology-based effluent limitations are not stringent enough to attain water quality standards. These "water quality-limited stretches," as opposed to effluent-limited stretches, are to be ranked in order of priority, taking into account designated uses and severity of pollution. The state must then set total maximum daily load of pollutants for water quality-limited stretches. Under section 303, "Such loads shall be established at a level necessary to implement the applicable water quality standards with seasonal variations and a margin of safety which takes into account any lack of knowledge concerning the relationship between effluent limitations and water quality." Maximum daily loads must be submitted to the EPA administrator, who is authorized to set alternative loads if he finds a state's to be inadequate. Finally, maximum loads are to be converted to water quality-based effluent limitations as part of the state's continuing planning process. Under section 301(b)(1)(c) of the CWA, water quality-based effluent limitations incorporated in discharge permits must have been achieved by 1977. One would have to assume that new water quality-based effluent limitations must be met immediately.

Thus, the CWA combines the technology-based and water quality-based regulatory approaches. The problem is that this amalgam of effluent limitations contravenes one of the basic tenets of the CWA, discouraging "forum shopping" by industry through the development of uniform national effluent limitations based on available technology. Elsewhere, I have characterized this paradox as the "better than best" problem [10]. Because most water quality-limited stretches will occur in heavily industrialized states, industry will be encouraged to site new plants in relatively less polluted or even high-quality areas. In order to attract industry, industrialized states will be compelled to revise their water quality standards. This will have a debilitating effect on the drive for clean water, because water quality standards serve a psychological, hortatory function as unmet goals. Revising standards connotes "writing off" a waterbody. A future siting scenario might find an industry playing off an industrialized state's promised revision against a less industrialized state's agreement to degrade high-quality waters. Existing industries might also use interstate disparities in effluent limitations to demand revisions or enforcement concessions. These industries would justifiably argue that they are being asked to bear a disproportionate pollution control burden not only as against their counterparts in other states but also as against nonpoint sources. Although nonpoint sources contribute as much to pollutant loadings as point sources, section 303 requires that wasteload allocations be set only for point source discharges, as if nonpoint pollution were insignificant. Moreover, the CWA does not adequately control pollution from nonpoint sources. In summary, retention of water quality-based effluent limitations promotes diversity in standard setting, and thus subverts the CWA.

EPA has reacted to this inconsistency in an oddly ambivalent way. Where industrial dischargers are concerned, EPA does not write water quality-based effluent limitations into discharge permits unless the relevant state insists through its certification process. For obvious reasons, states rarely impose more stringent limitations, even though they are legally entitled to do so [25], either when they certify EPA permits or administer their own permit programs. Nor has EPA taken advantage of section 302 of the CWA, which gives it the authority to set more stringent "water quality-related limitations," independent of the states, after performing a cost-benefit analysis. Moreover, EPA does not put pressure on states to develop TMDLs and water quality-based effluent limitations for industrial dischargers; and given exigencies of conflicting demands for resources, states devote a minimum of time and money to the industrial 303 process. In other words, EPA has avoided the "better than best" problem where industrial dischargers are concerned by placing section 303 on the back burner. However, EPA has taken an opposite tack in the area of pollution from publicly owned treatment works, requiring and funding costly Advanced Waste Treatment (AWT) in order to meet water quality-based effluent limitations.

Environmentalists have also been ambivalent about water quality-based effluent limitations. The Consent Decree and its amendments treated them as an embarrassing afterthought. America has not yet dealt with the real issues: (1) How can water quality-based effluent limitations, with their potential costs and business dislocations, be set in the absence of reliable water quality models? and (2) How can destructive competition among states to degrade and revise in order to retain or attract industry be avoided?

My recommendation is that the CWA be amended to eliminate binding water quality-based effluent limitations. Water quality standards should be retained, but only for purposes of planning and evaluation, for example on antidegradation stretches. We should take this opportunity to return to the original Senate conception of the CWA. Binding water quality-based effluent limitations are not only unnecessary but counterproductive. We should rely on progressively stricter but uniform technology-based limitations to achieve cleaner water and ultimately zero discharge. Added to this should be a viable program of nonpoint source pollution control. The CWA prescribes that BAT-based limitations be reviewed at five-year intervals. These reevaluations should be used as opportunities to examine the availability of new technology and the desirability of imposing stricter technology-based standards along the road to zero discharge. Further reliance on the water quality-based approach will cause more confusion and a backlash against the water pollution control program.

NEW CONCEPTS IN INDUSTRIAL POINT SOURCE CONTROL

EPA is considering several innovations in effluent limitations and water quality standards in order to reduce compliance costs. One, already promulgated for the iron and steel category, is the "bubble" concept. A bubble approach applies effluent limitations to plant discharges as a whole, instead of focusing on individual discharge points. Otherwise excessive discharges from one process can be set off against surplus effluent reductions from another process in order to reduce total treatment costs.

> Bubbles also can be applied to groups of plants that discharge into the same waterway. Under such inter-plant bubbles, one plant can exceed its discharge limits if the excess discharge is offset by greater-than-required pollutant removal by another plant "under the bubble." This type of approach is not included in the final iron and steel rule [26].

There is some question about the legality of bubbles under the CWA.

Similar to the bubble concept is that of "trading" surplus effluent reductions. Trading would either be "fixed" or "flexible," depending on whether or not a permit modification were necessary for each trade. Trading might be facilitated by central "banking" of surplus reductions. EPA is studying not only potential trades between point source dischargers but also trades between point and nonpoint sources [26].

"Seasonal" or "variable" effluent limitations would set permit limitations to reflect periodic changes in waterbody assimilative capacities. Water quality standards might also be responsive to different desired uses at different times of the year. Legalities aside, adoption of such concepts would place an extraordinary administrative burden on states.

Chapter 28
THE CLEAN WATER ACT: MUNICIPAL EFFLUENT LIMITATIONS

Publicly owned treatment works are also subject to technology-based effluent limitations and, on water quality-limited stretches, to water quality-
based effluent limitations. The technology-based limitations for POTWs are
based on "secondary treatment," and the attainment date is July 1, 1988,
postponed by Congress from 1977 and 1983. POTWs must comply regardless of whether their owners have received federal construction grants.

"Primary treatment" involves the use of mechanical means, such as
screens, grit channels, and settling tanks, to remove large materials and
suspended solids from the largely liquid waste stream. The process removes
about 30 percent of biochemical oxygen demand from sewage. "Secondary
treatment" entails additional settling and placing the sewage in contact
with microorganisms, by way of trickling filters, activated sludge, or lagoons,
to break down the organic matter in the sewage stream. An additional
50–60 percent of BOD, most suspended solids and some toxic materials,
that enter the sewerage system mainly from indirect dischargers and
street runoff, are removed at this stage. The liquid effluent from secondary
treatment is generally chlorinated and discharged. Sludge residues of primary and secondary treatment are either incinerated, spread on land, buried in landfills, dumped in the ocean, or composted for use as a soil condi-
tioner. Advanced waste treatment, sometimes referred to as "tertiary treatment," refers to processes which remove additional pollutants from waste-

water beyond those eliminated by primary and secondary treatment. AWT processes may remove nutrients or higher percentages of BOD and suspended solids.

Section 301(h), added to the CWA in 1977, authorizes the Environmental Protection Agency, with the consent of a state, to modify the act's secondary treatment requirement for POTWs which discharge into marine waters if the applicant can show that

> (1) there is a water quality standard specific to the pollutants for which the modification is requested, and the modified discharge would not violate the standard; (2) the modified requirement will not interfere with the attainment of fishable-swimmable waters, or with the existing ecosystem; (3) a practicable monitoring system has been established to measure the impact of the modified discharge on aquatic biota; (4) the modified discharge will not place added burdens on other dischargers; (5) controls have been placed on indirect dischargers to the system; (6) nonindustrial toxics are, to the extent practicable, being denied entrance to the system; and (7) the modified effluent limitation will not be exceeded.

Section 301(h) defines "marine waters" as ocean and coastal waters as well as "saline estuarine waters where there is a strong tidal movement and other hydrological and geological characteristics" that the EPA decides are necessary to protect water quality. Modifications may be obtained by dischargers of sewage receiving less-than-primary treatment as well as dischargers currently meeting effluent limitations based on secondary treatment. No modification, however, is available to ocean dischargers of sewage sludge.

Section 301(h), with its water quality-based variance for municipal marine dischargers, has been, and continues to be, highly controversial. Its critics argue that POTWs currently discharging into fresh water, and new POTWs that do not yet have discharge points, will be encouraged to switch to marine waters or locate their new discharge pipes in marine waters. Second, dischargers currently without primary treatment will be discouraged from installing it, and dischargers currently doing secondary treatment will be encouraged to "backslide." Third, critics of 301(h) contend that the water quality-based approach is inadequate to protect marine waters unless minimum depths for outfalls are established. Finally, they feel that EPA has been allowed too much discretion under 301(h), and will find it difficult to resist political pressures from cities and sewerage authorities to grant variances. Nearly 150 POTWs, located on or near coasts, applied for section 301(h) variances by the December 31, 1982, application deadline.

Another category of municipal point sources is stormwater overflow outlets [27] that, in combined storm and sanitary sewer systems, bypass the treatment plant during storm events [28]. Stormwater outlets must be controlled not by secondary treatment but by best practicable technology currently available [29]. Little has been done by EPA or states to regulate overflow points, but effective regulation is particularly necessary here because the common law drainage theories described in Part I are inadequate to protect victims of stormwater runoff confronted with restrictive state tort claims acts [28]. Separate storm sewers that do not carry sanitary wastes are also point sources, but are of lesser importance in controlling water pollution.

Chapter 29

THE CLEAN WATER ACT: CONSTRUCTION GRANTS PROGRAM

Unlike air, water can be centrally treated. A program of federal grants for the construction of publicly owned treatment works was established in 1956 and has been greatly expanded by the CWA [30]. The federal government has thus far obligated over $37 billion in construction funds, and state and local contributions have increased total spending for POTWs under the CWA to over $50 billion. Some 4,000 new facilities are already operating, and almost 3,000 more are under construction. At its height, $5 billion per year was authorized by Congress for the construction grants program. Federal funding has been reduced, but Congress has still authorized $2.4 billion per year through fiscal 1985. President Reagan has announced that he intends to phase out the construction grants program after 1985. However, the political pressure for its continuation will be strong.

ELIGIBILITY AND THE FEDERAL SHARE

Various kinds of POTW construction-related projects have been eligible for funding under the act: secondary treatment; AWT where necessary; new interceptor sewers; infiltration-inflow correction; new collector sewers; replacement and rehabilitation of sewers; correction of combined sewer overflow; facilities for storage and recycling of wastes; and acquisition of lands needed for the facilities themselves or for sludge or effluent disposal. In 1977, recognizing that in some areas community managed septic systems are an environmentally sound and cost-effective alternative to sewage treatment plants, Congress authorized grants for privately owned systems in existing communities where a public agency agrees to control the design, installation, and operation of septic systems constructed with grant funds.

Although these categories have been legally grant-eligible, they have not been funded equally. For example, the Environmental Protection Agency has funded few projects to correct combined sewer overflow and, in recent years, has restricted advanced waste treatment funding to projects on water quality-limited stretches which will produce significant water quality benefits. In 1977, Congress declared that each state must use at least 25 percent of its allotted construction grant funds for major sewer rehabilitation, new collector sewers, new interceptors, and correction of combined sewer overflows if projects in these categories appear on a state's priority list. However, in 1981 Congress again changed the eligibility rules with regard to grants approved after October 1, 1984. After that date only secondary treatment, AWT, new interceptor sewers, and infiltration-inflow correction will be directly eligible. But a state governor may use up to 20 percent of a state's allotment for other kinds of projects. The 1981 amendments also instituted a separate grants program, authorized at $200 million annually, to correct combined sewer overflows from urban areas into marine bays and estuaries.

One of the controversies manifested by these shifts in funding priorities is over the extent to which the federal government should be subsidizing community growth. Section 204 of the CWA makes it clear that projects funded by construction grants should include "sufficient reserve capacity." Since early in the administration of the construction grants program, environmentalists have charged that the 75 percent federal share encourages sewerage officials, in the name of speculative growth, to overbuild treatment plants and construct far-flung sewer systems which cause energy-intensive, environmentally destructive, and infrastructure-demanding "leap-frog development." Before 1981, all environmentalist attempts to have Congress limit funding for reserve capacity were defeated by development interests. But in 1981 a combination of environmentalist pressure and the Reagan administration's fiscal policies persuaded Congress to place restraints on federal funding of reserve capacity. All segments and phases of treatment plants and interceptor lines funded prior to October 1, 1984, will be funded based on a twenty-year reserve capacity, instead of the maximum forty-year reserve capacity applicable to earlier projects. After 1984, no grant may be made to provide reserve capacity in excess of the needs existing on the date of the award or those existing on October 1, 1990, whichever comes first. In short, after 1984 states and municipalities must finance their own POTW facilities for anticipated growth.

Restrictions on POTW-induced growth can also be found in section 316 of the Clean Air Act. Before awarding a construction grant, EPA must be satisfied that the direct and indirect air pollution emissions likely to result from the construction of a POTW will conform to the requirements of a state implementation plan. Moreover, grants may be withheld in nonattainment areas. Grants have been withheld by EPA from applicants in both California and Kentucky under this policy.

Decreasing the federal share will also cause local governments to be more cautious in planning for growth. The 1972 CWA increased the federal share of POTW financing from 55 to 75 percent. After October 1, 1984, the 55 percent ceiling will be reinstated, except for the later stages of projects funded before that date. Because a number of municipalities will find it increasingly difficult to raise their local shares of POTW construction costs, the CWA was amended to authorize federal guarantees of municipal financing where necessary.

INNOVATIVE AND ALTERNATIVE WASTE TREATMENT

Environmentalists have criticized conventional secondary treatment for wastefulness because, for one thing, secondary plants discharge water derived from groundwater aquifers to rivers flowing into an ocean or the Great Lakes. Instead, environmentalists have recommended alternatives such as spraying effluent, after primary treatment and chlorination, on land and allowing the "living filter" to remove impurities while groundwater supplies are replenished.

In 1977 Congress passed a number of amendments to stimulate innovative and alternative (I/A) waste treatment. No construction grant can be made unless the applicant demonstrates that

> innovative and alternative wastewater treatment processes and techniques which provide for the reclaiming and reuse of wastewater, otherwise eliminate the discharge of pollutants, and utilize recycling techniques, land treatment, new or improved methods of waste treatment management . . . and the confined disposal of pollutants . . . have been fully studied by the applicant taking into account . . . the more efficient use of energy resources.

I/A projects which conform to EPA guidelines may be funded even though they cost up to 15 percent more than the most cost-effective alternative. Moreover, the federal grant share for I/A projects is 85 percent instead of 75 percent for conventional treatment works, and extra grant monies will be available for modification or replacement of the funded facilities if they do not meet design specifications, except where negligence has occurred. After 1984, I/A projects can be funded at 75 percent, 20 percent higher than projects using standard treatment methods. Furthermore, a minimum of 4 percent and a maximum of 7.5 percent of each state's allotment must be set aside for I/A bonuses. There is also a 4 percent mandatory "set aside" for funding alternatives to conventional treatment works in communities of fewer than 3,500 people located in states with rural populations of 25 percent or more. Private industrial firms are also rewarded for using innovative technology. Any company proposing to install innovative production processes or techniques that would achieve significantly greater effluent reductions than called for by the applicable effluent limitations, or that would achieve categorical effluent limitations at a significantly lower cost than existing systems, may be granted an extension of its date for compliance with BAT-based effluent limitations until 1987 if the innovative systems possess the potential for industry-wide application.

Innovative and alternative waste treatment processes involve replenishing natural systems or recycling and reusing water by POTWs or industry. Either way, discharges to waterbodies will be diminished and downstream or lacustrine diversion rightholders may lose their supplies. As mentioned in Parts I and III, downstream appropriators have no rights to the continuation of a POTW discharge. However, the rule may not be the same for industrial discharges, which may be treated as irrigation return flows. The issue is further complicated by the presence in the CWA of section 101(g): "It is the policy of Congress that the authority of each State to allocate quantities of water within its jurisdiction shall not be superseded, abrogated, or otherwise impaired by this Act." Does this mean that effluent limitations cannot interfere with prior diversion rights? Is it merely an unenforceable affirmation of state primacy as to water allocation? Subsection 101(g)'s legislative history is so sparse that courts may find these issues difficult to resolve.

THE FUNDING PROCESS AND ITS ADMINISTRATION

There has been a trend since 1972 toward state administration of the construction grants program. Prior to 1977, each state developed a "priority list" of needed projects and submitted it to EPA. In turn, EPA made the final decisions about how the state's allotment was to be spent among the priority projects and supervised the planning and construction of POTWs with the assistance of state officials. But in 1977 Congress declared a policy "that the States manage the construction grants program," and authorized delegation of program administration to states. EPA was empowered to reserve up to 2 percent of a state's allotment for making program administration grants to a state accepting delegation. In 1981 the "administration set aside" was increased to 4 percent. State priority lists are now binding on EPA, unless "the administrator, after a public hearing, determines that a specific project will not result in compliance with the enforceable requirements" of the CWA; in other words, unless the project as designed will not meet its effluent limitations. Where a state has been delegated management authority, EPA must approve or disapprove a state grant certification within forty-five days or the grant application is deemed approved. The details of delegation, including how and when EPA will exercise its powers of review and supervision, are included in a "delegation agreement" between EPA and the state. From time to time it is recommended that EPA be eliminated from the construction grants program completely, and that allocations be made directly to states.

The construction grants funding process was significantly changed in 1981. Before that, except for very small projects, POTWs were funded in advance by EPA in three steps: (1) facilities plans; (2) engineering studies, architectural designs, drawings, and specifications; and (3) construction. Each of these three steps was considered as a separate project and had to be funded individually by EPA. In order to encourage local responsibility for POTWs and discourage overbuilding, Congress amended the CWA in 1981 to require local financing of steps 1 and 2, with federal reimbursement for the reasonable amount of these costs if and when EPA approves a step 3 grant. For small communities that need assistance in financing steps 1 and 2, states are required to make loans of up to 10 percent of their allotted funds, with the amount of each loan subsequently deductable from construction grants if any are received.

Facilities planning has assumed an importance unforeseen in 1972. The drafters of the CWA intended that siting and sizing of POTWs be consistent with comprehensive "water quality management plans" required by section 208 of the act. However, because of delays in the 208 areawide planning process, facilities plans have become the major instruments for evaluating the considerable environmental impacts of regional treatment facilities.

The term "facilities planning" does not appear in the act. It is derived from section 201(c), which stipulates that "to the extent practicable, waste-treatment technology shall be on an areawide basis and provide control or treatment of all point and nonpoint sources of pollution." Municipal facilities must also be cost-effective, and EPA is required to encourage the construction of revenue-producing POTWs. As a result, the facilities plan has become an often uneasy combination of cost-effectiveness and environmental impact evaluation.

A facilities plan must be prepared for the entire service area under consideration. The components of a facilities plan are:

1. A description of the complete waste-treatment system, as well as a description of the specific collection and treatment works for

which construction plans and specifications are to be prepared during step 2.

2. An extensive analysis of any infiltration/inflow problems that might be present in the existing system and a plan for rehabilitating the leaking sewers.

3. An analysis of the cost-effectiveness both of the waste-treatment system of which the proposed project is a part and of alternative systems, including innovative systems. This analysis must describe the relationship of the capacity of the system to the needs to be served, and the degree to which effluent quality could be improved by upgrading existing facilities rather than by constructing new ones. Alternative methods of effluent and sludge disposal must also be considered.

4. An environmental impact assessment of all foreseeable impacts of the project and reasonable alternative projects.

Facilities plans are prepared by consulting firms retained by the applicant. Fees of these consulting firms are based on a percentage of the project cost. Environmentalists have cited these percentage fee arrangements as one reason for enacting statutory limitations on POTW size and reserve capacity.

The facilities plan must be approved by the construction grants management agency, either EPA or a state, before a project can move forward. Public participation is mandated during facilities planning, and comments elicited at public hearings have frequently drawn the attention of state and federal officials to defects in the plan. A federal construction grant is one of the two EPA water quality-related actions which are covered by the National Environmental Policy Act.* Frequently, the facilities plan is the core of EPA's environmental assessment and negative declaration, or in some cases of a full-fledged environmental impact statement.

USER CHARGES, INDUSTRIAL USERS, AND PERFORMANCE SAFEGUARDS

Two features of the CWA as originally enacted, "user charges" and "industrial cost recovery," provoked controversy almost immediately. In order to obtain a federal construction grant a municipality must adopt a system of user charges ensuring that all recipients of waste-treatment services pay

---

*The other is EPA issuance of a new source discharge permit.

their proportionate share of operating and maintenance expenses. Under the 1972 act, a user charge system had to be based on volume and concentration of wastes entering the POTW. However, many municipalities were unable to set user charges based on influent volume and concentration because they lacked metering capability, especially for residential and commercial users. In 1977 the CWA was amended to allow user charges for residential and commercial establishments to be based on property value. In order to qualify, an ad valorem levy must have been in effect before 1977, must produce revenues dedicated to operation and maintenance of the POTW, and must allocate the burden proportionately both within and among classes of users. Quantity discounts for large-volume users are unacceptable. Metering, however, is still required for industrial users whose flows exceed 25,000 gallons per day. Indirect dischargers of toxic materials must pay for increased treatment and sludge-handling costs.

Originally, an industrial user of a POTW (indirect discharger) was required to repay a portion of the federal grant corresponding to its percentage use of the system's total capacity. "Industrial cost recovery" was intended to provide funds for reconstruction and repair, and to encourage industries to choose the most cost-effective solution to their waste treatment problems, whether it was indirect or direct discharge. After prolonged and concerted opposition from municipalities and sewerage authorities, industrial cost recovery was first suspended, then limited to large indirect dischargers, and finally repealed entirely. Thus, as the CWA now stands, there is a major federal subsidy for industries that "plug in" to POTWs, because they pay only user charges and therefore save on construction costs. Furthermore, direct dischargers that contract to plug in have been granted extensions of time to meet applicable effluent limitations. These major incentives for indirect dischargers emphasize the need for an effective industrial pretreatment program.

Industrial waste overloads are one reason why many POTWs built under the construction grants program are not performing up to expectations [31]. Other problems have been design deficiencies, equipment deficiencies, infiltration/inflow problems, and deficiencies in operation and maintenance. In its 1981 amendments to the CWA, Congress took the first steps in dealing with this embarrassing situation. Before a construction grant is made, EPA "shall determine that the facilities plan . . . constitutes the most economical and cost-effective combination of treatment works over the life of the project to meet the requirements of [the CWA]." Water conservation methods are to be considered in determining cost-effectiveness. A "value engineering review" must also accompany each application.

The CWA's most powerful safeguard against POTW inadequacy involves continuing responsibilities of the prime engineering consultant. Grant funds are provided to retain the prime consultant on the site for one year after startup to supervise operations and train personnel. At the end of that time, the consultant must assist the POTW's owner or operator in certifying whether or not the POTW meets design specifications as well as applicable effluent limitations. If the plant does not comply, remedial measures must be taken "in a timely manner" at the grantee's expense. However, compliance after one year does not ensure that compliance will continue. The General Accounting Office has found that user charges are often insufficient to pay for operation and maintenance, and they are almost always insufficient to pay for replacement [33]. In addition, the shortage of trained plant operators has been a dilemma. EPA could revise its user charge regulations to improve POTW self-sufficiency and integrity. As for operator shortages, EPA could request and allocate more funds for operator training and scholarship grants to universities under sections 109 and 111 of the CWA.

Thus far, Congress has done nothing about problems that are caused by faulty construction, as opposed to faulty design, of POTWs. Where EPA is the management agency it has utilized the Army Corps of Engineers to prevent defective construction, such as improperly laid sewer pipes, which are susceptible to infiltration and inflow. But states that have accepted delegation may not possess the resources to competently supervise plant construction without strong program funding and technical support from EPA. And state laws may not provide effective sanctions to deter contractors from taking shortcuts.

PRIVATIZATION OF SEWAGE TREATMENT

A novel concept that has been bruited recently is the privatization of sewage treatment, that is, allowing the private sector to take over all or part of what has long been a public function. Given the restrictions imposed by municipal bond law, it is doubtful that POTW ownership could be transferred to private firms. But, where POTWs do not already exist, companies might be given public utility status to provide sewerage services. More likely, consulting firms will be retained to manage, operate, and maintain regional POTWs.

Privatization of sewage treatment is one approach to the problem of fulfilling treatment needs with reduced federal funding. EPA estimates that federal funding will cover only one-third of POTW needs between now and the year 2000. We can expect Congress to soon consider alternative methods of funding POTWs.

Chapter 30
THE CLEAN WATER ACT: INDUSTRIAL PRETREATMENT

"Industrial pretreatment" means the treatment of industrial wastes before they are discharged into publicly owned treatment works. Pretreatment is necessary because certain indirect discharges are "incompatible" with a POTW. This means that they interfere with the POTW's operation, contaminate the sewage sludge, or pass untreated through the POTW in quantities so large that the POTW is in violation of its effluent limitations. Estimates vary regarding the number of industries discharging incompatible pollutants into POTWs, but there are probably around 100,000. Although only a small number of POTWs, perhaps 2,500 out of almost 17,000 POTWs nationwide, have problems with incompatible pollutants, these POTWs generally discharge into highly polluted waterways.

Controlling indirect discharges of incompatible pollutants has been one of the CWA's major failures. According to the General Accounting Office, "almost from its inception, the pretreatment program has been surrounded by controversy and has generated considerable uncertainty and confusion" [33]. The pretreatment program's stagnation is a function of two myths which are common among regulators and regulated alike. The first myth is that municipalities and sewerage authorities will regulate incompatibles in order to protect the treatment process. This is undoubtedly true in the case of incompatibles that interrupt the biological process, but does not apply to pollutants that pass through into the effluent or end up as part of the POTW's sludge. The second myth is that POTW owners will impose pretreatment in order to meet POTW effluent limitations and sludge-quality regulations. However, POTWs violate these standards almost with impunity because federal and state enforcement against POTWs is minimal. It must be kept in mind that indirect dischargers are customers of their POTWs, customers that can threaten to move elsewhere or to unplug and switch to direct discharge if pretreatment costs increase substantially. The remainder of this chapter describes the federal pretreatment program as it currently exists [34] and recommendations for reforming it.

NATIONAL PRETREATMENT STANDARDS

There are two types of pretreatment standards, "prohibited discharge standards" and "categorical pretreatment standards." "Prohibited discharge standards" require that pollutants introduced into a POTW not inhibit or interfere with the POTW operations or performance. For example, it is illegal to introduce into a POTW explosives, corrosives, slug discharges, and solids and heat in excessive amounts. These standards apply to all nondomestic (commercial or industrial) users, whether or not they are subject to other national, state, or local pretreatment requirements. "Categorical pretreatment standards" set out national discharge limits for priority pollutants (toxics) based on BAT, as required by the Consent Decree and the CWA. Separate regulations containing pretreatment standards are being developed and promulgated for each of thirty-four specific industrial categories. These national pretreatment standards contain exemptions for small indirect dischargers in each category. Pretreatment standards for combined wastestreams are set by applying a specified formula to mixed wastestreams where at least one of them would otherwise be subject to pretreatment standards. The CWA requires compliance with categorical pretreatment standards within three years from their effective date.

Categorical pretreatment standards are based on the treatment technology available to industry. They do not recognize that conventional secondary treatment is effective in removing some priority pollutants, especially organic chemicals [33]. In order to obviate redundant treatment, the CWA was amended in 1977 to authorize "removal allowances" for indirect dischargers subject to categorical pretreatment standards. Removal allowances are based on the proven ability of a POTW to treat toxic pollutants; dilution in the plant or sewerage system cannot be taken into consideration. Thus, if the POTW consistently removes a pollutant, the industry-wide indirect discharge limits applicable to dischargers to that system may be raised for the removed pollutants. The burden of developing and granting removal allowances is on the POTW. Environmental Protection Agency regulations stipulate that the POTW must demonstrate "consistent removal

of each pollutant" and provide continued monitoring of its removal efficiency in order to qualify for a removal allowance. The CWA conditions a
removal allowance on (1) the POTW removing all or part of the pollutant; (2)
the POTW not violating the effluent limitation for the incompatible pollutant
that would be imposed on the indirect discharger if it were a direct
discharger; and (3) the POTW's sludge not violating CWA standards. The
removal allowance must be discontinued if the POTW ceases to meet the
requirements and fails to take appropriate corrective actions.

The General Accounting Office has sharply criticized removal allowances as being administratively unworkable for POTWs and inequitable to
industry "because companies in the same industry could be required to
meet different standards for the same pollutants—depending on the
POTW's pollutant removal efficiencies and the POTW's willingness to apply
for the allowance" [33].

PRETREATMENT PROGRAMS

The CWA's pretreatment strategy envisions a parallel effort on the part of
federal, state, and local governments to implement pretreatment requirements. Local pretreatment programs, approved by states, are the focus of
this effort. States, through EPA-approved state pretreatment programs, are
to oversee the operation of the local programs, provide backup enforcement
capability, and, where a local progam has not been developed or is not being
enforced, assume primary responsibility for applying pretreatment standards to industrial users. EPA is to supervise state pretreatment programs,
provide backup enforcement to state and local governments, and, in the
absence of a viable local or state pretreatment program, function as the
primary enforcement agency. POTWs with a total design flow of 5 million
gallons per day or greater and receiving incompatible pollutants must have
had a pretreatment program approved by July 1, 1983. No POTW may grant a
removal allowance unless it possesses an approved pretreatment program.
States must also have had their pretreatment programs approved by July 1,
1983. Both program and construction grant funds may be used by states to
develop and implement pretreatment programs. However, the GAO has
concluded that "the ability of POTWs, States, and EPA to meet the substantial resource commitment that the Federal pretreatment program will require is highly questionable" [33].

PROPOSED PRETREATMENT AMENDMENT

The Reagan administration is supporting a CWA amendment that would
authorize modifications of categorical pretreatment standards where there

will be no interference with attainment or maintenance of designated uses in the receiving waters to which a POTW discharges and where sludge use or disposal will not be impaired. No modification may be granted under this proposal unless the POTW has attained, or is scheduled to attain, secondary treatment. If a modification is granted, the POTW must establish a monitoring program and submit an annual report. The modification could be rescinded where receiving waters are not adequately protected.

It is not clear that this water quality-based approach will alleviate the difficulties that have plagued pretreatment regulation from the outset: lack of POTW resources and enforcement incentives. In fact, calculating the effects of indirect discharges on receiving water quality would be even more complex than the present system. Moreover, the proposal does not indicate how water quality-based modifications would relate to removal allowances.

Chapter 31
THE CLEAN WATER ACT: SEWAGE SLUDGE DISPOSAL

With so many new publicly owned treatment works having recently been constructed, and with an ineffectual pretreatment program, sewage sludge disposal has become one of America's foremost environmental problems. The disposal of sewage sludge is regulated under the CWA and other federal laws.

Under the CWA, construction grants are conditioned on EPA approval of the applicant's sludge disposal plan included in the facilities plan. The industrial pretreatment program is intended to prevent the introduction into POTWs of pollutants that could contaminate sewage sludge and impair opportunities for its use or disposal. Section 405(e) of the CWA makes it unlawful for the owner or operator of a POTW to dispose of sludge in a manner inconsistent with Environmental Protection Agency regulations containing guidelines for sludge disposal and use. EPA has promulgated regulations regarding sludge disposal [35], but guidelines describing the allowable procedures for distributing, marketing, and using composted sludge have not yet appeared. This lacuna is troubling to owners and operators of POTWs, who have hesitated to institute sludge compost utilization programs because of fears about public acceptance and potential lawsuits by consumers of sludge-fertilized crops.

Disposal of sludge by incineration invokes the Clean Air Act. Emissions from sludge incinerators must comply with applicable state and federal regulations.

If a sludge contains hazardous pollutants above specified limits, a

Resource Conservation and Recovery Act (RCRA) permit must be obtained from EPA [36]. The RCRA permit will describe in detail required treatment, storage, or disposal measures. Sludge disposal in violation of regulations is punishable under RCRA as well as the CWA.

Ocean disposal of sewage sludge is practiced by many coastal communities, including Boston, Los Angeles, Philadelphia, and New York. Sludge disposal in the ocean is regulated in part by the CWA and in part by Title I of the Marine Protection, Research and Sanctuaries Act (MPRSA) [37]. The CWA covers all discharges into the ocean from pipes, such as those used by Boston and Los Angeles for sludge disposal. MPRSA regulates the dumping of sludge from barges anywhere in the ocean if the barges originate from an American port.

Both the CWA and MPRSA establish EPA permit systems for the regulation of sludge disposal in the ocean. Under MPRSA, permits can only be issued if EPA determines that the disposal will not "unreasonably degrade or endanger human health . . . or the marine environment." Factors bearing on the reasonableness of dumping include need, environmental impact, and alternative disposal locations or methods. The CWA directs EPA to promulgate guidelines for evaluating the degradation of ocean waters. Once these guidelines are issued they are to control the issuance of ocean discharge permits [38]. Like the MPRSA, the CWA lists the factors to be considered in determining degradation, including environmental impact, social effects, and alternative locations or methods. The required CWA guidelines were published in 1980 [39]. "What sets the [CWA's] scheme apart from the MPRSA's is that [CWA] permits impose technology-based effluent limitations on ocean discharges in addition to the ocean degradation criteria" [40].

In 1977 Congress amended the MPRSA to provide that EPA "shall end the dumping of sewage sludge into ocean waters . . . as soon as possible . . . but in no case may the Administrator issue any permit or renewal . . . which authorizes any such dumping after December 31, 1981." Almost everyone, including EPA and the amendment's congressional sponsors, believed the amendment to mean that all ocean dumping of sewage sludge had to be curtailed by the end of 1981. However, in a lawsuit brought against EPA by New York City, a federal district court ruled that EPA cannot prohibit ocean dumping of sewage sludge unless it finds that sludge dumping will unreasonably degrade the marine environment, taking into consideration the need for ocean disposal, environmental impacts, and the economic and environmental costs of alternative disposal methods [41]. EPA did not appeal this decision, and is revising its strategy to allow continuation of ocean disposal in certain cases where unreasonable degradation is not occurring. Indeed, it appears that ocean dumping of sewage sludge will, and perhaps should, continue for some time to come [42].

Chapter 32

CLEAN WATER ACT: NATIONAL POLLUTANT DISCHARGE ELIMINATION SYSTEM

Effluent limitations are not in themselves enforceable against industrial or municipal point source dischargers. The CWA's effluent limitations for direct dischargers are implemented through the NPDES permit program administered by either a state agency or an Environmental Protection Agency regional office. Discharges of certain pollutants are absolutely prohibited by the CWA or EPA regulations. Examples of prohibited pollutants are radiological, chemical, or biological warfare agents, high-level radioactive wastes, polychlorinated biphenols (PCBs), and certain pesticides. But where there is no outright prohibition, a discharger may lawfully discharge only if he possesses a valid discharge permit and if the discharge is in compliance with permit limitations.

In 1980 EPA promulgated consolidated permit regulations [43] governing the issuance of permits for five EPA programs: (1) the NPDES program under the CWA; (2) the hazardous waste management program under the Resource Conservation and Recovery Act; (3) the underground injection control program under the Safe Drinking Water Act; (4) state dredge or fill permit programs under section 404 of the CWA; and (5) the prevention of significant deterioration program under the Clean Air Act. However, as part

174

of a recent settlement agreement, these regulations are presently being deconsolidated.

Every operator of an existing discharger or potential operator of a new source must apply for an NPDES permit either to the EPA regional office or to a state that is authorized to administer the program. The application must contain accurate discharge information, including the results of tests specified in the regulations. Once a permit application is complete, the permit authority must decide whether to deny the permit or to prepare a draft permit. A draft permit must be accompanied by a fact sheet and a public notice that specifies how comments can be made and how a public hearing can be obtained if there is sufficient public interest. Once a decision is made to issue a permit, the agency must issue a final written decision that responds to comments. Only new source permits issued by EPA are subject to the National Environmental Policy Act. Interested persons who have filed comments may take an administrative appeal if they are dissatisfied with the result. Unlike the public hearing, this evidentiary hearing is what lawyers refer to as "on the record," that is, limited cross-examination of witnesses is allowed. Further appeals may be taken to the administrator and the federal courts.

Discharge permits may be granted for a maximum of five years. EPA is supporting a proposed amendment to the CWA that would increase the maximum term to ten years. When a permit expires the permittee must apply for a renewal. Permits may be modified or revoked and reissued during the permit period. Common grounds for modification or revocation and reissuance are alterations to permitted facilities, new information, supervening federal regulations, unforeseen events, and procurement of a variance. Permits may also be terminated before the scheduled expiration date for nondisclosure, noncompliance, or alleviation of an emergency situation.

Only point source dischargers must apply for NPDES permits. Although the term "point source" must be liberally interpreted, EPA has discretion to define "point source" administratively. In addition to industrial and publicly owned treatment works outfalls, animal feedlots above a certain size and separate storm sewers carrying contaminants are considered to be point sources. There is a strong presumption that any other discharge through a discrete conveyance, pipe, or ditch is a point source. The following do not require discharge permits under the CWA: vessel sewage, discharges of dredged or fill material subject to section 404 permits, indirect discharges, irrigation return flows, groundwater discharges, land discharges, and runoff from nonpoint sources. However, some states managing the NPDES program, under their own state statutes, require discharge permits for some of these types of discharges. Where issuing individual permits would be inconvenient and superfluous, as in the case of some separate storm sewers within a particular area, general permits may be issued if environmental harm will not result.

NPDES permits contain three major parts: effluent limitations, compliance schedules, and reporting requirements. Where technology-based or water quality-based effluent limitations do not exist for an applicant, for example, where technology-based limitations have not yet been promulgated, permit limitations are based on best professional judgment (BPJ) of the permit writer. Otherwise, the applicable categorical limitation or a more stringent one based on water quality must be included in the permit. The compliance schedule will set out interim requirements for dischargers on the way to ultimate compliance. Before and after compliance, a permittee must carry out extensive self-monitoring and reporting, including reporting some violations within twenty-four hours and others on a periodic discharge monitoring report (DMR). The permit will also set out the conditions under which a treatment process may be "bypassed," and what must be done in case of an "upset" (breakdown). An NPDES permit for a POTW may include pretreatment and sludge disposal requirements.

There is one situation where best management practices (BMPs) for a nonpoint source can be included in a discharge permit. Where industrial point sources in a category or subcategory discharge a toxic pollutant, EPA is authorized to include within categorical effluent limitations BMPs "to control plant site runoff, spillage or leaks, sludge or waste disposal, and drainage from raw material storage which . . . are associated with or ancillary to the industrial manufacturing or treatment process . . . and may contribute significant amounts of such pollutants to navigable waters" [44].

Thirty-three states are currently administering NPDES permit programs under agreements with EPA. As the CWA now stands, EPA can only delegate an entire permit program to a state, but a proposed amendment would allow partial delegation. Basically, in order to obtain delegation of the NPDES program from EPA, a state must convince EPA that its program is consistent with the CWA and EPA regulations, and that the state possesses the resources and statutory authority to implement it. The state issues future discharge permits once having obtained EPA program approval. State discharge permits are final subject only to EPA veto of a permit as being "outside the guidelines and requirements" of the CWA. Conditions in a state-issued permit may not be less stringent than EPA regulations, for example, EPA's categorical effluent limitations, but may be more stringent. If the state does not adequately administer the permit program, EPA may rescind program approval and resume primary enforcement responsibility. However, this is a hollow threat in light of philosophical changes and funding cuts at EPA. In theory at least, a state can also lose its permit program for failure to develop an acceptable pretreatment program.

Where EPA is still the permitting authority, a state must be afforded an opportunity to "certify" to more stringent permit conditions. If the state denies certification, the permit may not be issued; and the more stringent conditions of a state certification are binding on EPA. If the state waives certification, or fails to certify within a reasonable time, EPA is free to issue the permit as drafted. State certification decisions, as well as all state permit decisions where the state is the permitting authority, must be contested in state administrative tribunals and state courts.

Section 313 of the CWA waives federal sovereign immunity in the water pollution control area. Federal facilities and the federal personnel operating them must comply with all federal, state, interstate, and local water pollution control requirements "in the same manner, and to the same extent as any nongovernmental entity including the payment of reasonable service charges." This means that federal facilities must obtain discharge permits, comply with effluent limitations and reporting requirements, and respond to enforcement just as any other discharger. Innovative or alternative wastewater treatment must be used in new construction at federal facilities unless the cost of innovative treatment exceeds the life cycle cost of the most cost-effective alternative by more than 15 percent.

There are, however, some potential variances for federal facilities and their operators. The president may grant a variance from CWA requirements to any federal facility if he determines it to be in the "paramount interest of the United States" to do so. No variance can be granted to new sources, indirect dischargers, or dischargers of toxic pollutants. Variances run for one year subject to an unspecified number of one-year extensions. In addition to variances for particular dischargers, the president may also issue variances to "any weaponry, equipment, aircraft, vessels, vehicles, or other classes or categories of property . . . which are uniquely military in nature." Exemptions for classes of military property may run for three years, subject to extension. Finally, EPA may waive the innovative and alternative treatment requirement "in the public interest."

Chapter 33

THE CLEAN WATER ACT: ENFORCEMENT

Enforcement credibility is critical to the success of any regulatory strategy for controlling water pollution. Prior to 1972 federal water quality statutes were inherently unenforceable, and little progress was made in cleaning up America's waterbodies [4]. The CWA provided a new arsenal of enforcement sanctions to deter potential violators and punish illegal conduct. The question is no longer whether the CWA is enforceable, but whether it is actually being enforced.

The Environmental Protection Agency has been given broad powers of inspection, monitoring, and entry of discharger premises in implementing the CWA [45]. A discharger can be required to keep records, make reports, install and maintain monitoring equipment, sample in accordance with EPA instructions, and provide information on request. Moreover, EPA has the right to enter discharger premises and, at reasonable times, inspect and copy records, inspect monitoring equipment, and sample effluent. Because of recent federal court decisions qualifying administrative rights of entry under federal regulatory statutes, EPA routinely obtains a search warrant whenever the discharger refuses entry. All EPA records, including discharger reports, are available to the public unless the discharger demonstrates that the information should be treated as a confidential trade secret; but effluent data cannot be kept confidential.

The most important thing to remember about enforcement is that it is discretionary. Whether, when, and how to enforce are decisions to be made by the enforcement authority. These decisions are further complicated where, as in water pollution control law, a state and the federal government have concurrent enforcement power. "Who will enforce?" becomes the first order of business.

Where a state is administering an approved permit program, it is the primary enforcement authority. Its enforcement powers arise from state law. EPA has the authority to immediately bring enforcement action in an administering state, but it generally does not exercise it. Instead, where EPA finds a violation in an administering state, it either contacts the state informally or issues a thirty-day notice of violation to the discharger and the state. If the state does not take "appropriate enforcement action" within the thirty-day period, EPA can pursue its own enforcement. When a state is apparently neglecting its entire enforcement program, EPA can give notice to the state and assume enforcement of state-issued permits until the state rectifies the situation.

GOVERNMENTAL ENFORCEMENT REMEDIES

The EPA's formal enforcement remedies are administrative compliance orders, civil suits, and criminal actions. These remedies need not be sought in any particular order, but in practice criminal sanctions are a last resort.

The compliance order sanction is vitiated by EPA's inability to impose administrative fines under the CWA. Most state agencies have this power, and EPA can levy administrative fines under the Clean Air Act, but Congress unaccountably omitted administrative fines from the CWA. Consequently, EPA can only go to court in order to recover fines from violators. In a civil action brought in federal court, EPA may seek an injunction, a civil penalty of up to $10,000 per day of violation, or both. The U.S. Supreme Court recently held that a court need not automatically grant an injunction against every CWA violation; it can "balance the equities" and determine whether an injunction would be in the public interest [46].

Any person, including a "responsible corporate officer," who "willfully or negligently" violates the CWA, can be punished criminally by a fine of not less than $2,500 nor more than $25,000 per day of violation, or by up to one year in prison, or both. A second conviction risks a fine of up to $50,000 per day of violation, or up to two years in prison, or both. Persons making false statements in applications or reports, or tampering with monitoring devices, can be fined up to $10,000 and imprisoned for up to six months. Because of the difficulty of obtaining criminal convictions, the criminal sanction is reserved for obvious and heinous cases of water pollution. However, it is used more freely against persons submitting false information and sabotaging monitoring devices. Although still a rarity, jail sentences for water polluters are being imposed with increasing frequency.

If a discharger accidentally discharges in violation of his permit, he cannot be held civilly or criminally liable for his conduct. A legitimate treatment plant upset is an affirmative defense to a civil enforcement action. Moreover, in order to impose criminal liability on a person who violates a regulatory statute such as the CWA, it must be shown that he intended to perform the violating act, even if he did not know it was illegal.

Thus far we have been discussing enforcement options under section 309 of the CWA. But other parts of the act also have a bearing on enforcement. Section 504 authorizes EPA to immediately sue for an injunction "or to take such other action as may be necessary" where a discharge "is presenting an imminent and substantial endangerment to the health . . . or to the welfare of persons." Section 508 prohibits federal agencies from contracting with, or making loans or grants to, listed violators of the CWA. This potentially powerful sanction, however, has only been used in a few cases. Section 401(h) authorizes EPA or a state with an approved program to seek a court order barring new indirect discharges where a POTW is overloaded and violating its permit. These orders, called "sewer bans," are prominent features of many state enforcement efforts, but EPA has generally avoided them.

CITIZEN SUITS

Citizen suits are vital adjuncts to governmental enforcement of the CWA. Section 505 of the CWA gives any citizen standing to bring a civil action in federal district court against a discharger violating an effluent limitation or compliance order, or against EPA for failure to perform a nondiscretionary duty. Most citizen suits have been brought against EPA for failing to issue regulations by dates specified in the CWA. But environmentalists are beginning to sue permittees directly because of EPA's poor enforcement record and because, enforcement being discretionary, EPA cannot be sued to compel enforcement. The court can, if it is in the public interest, grant an injunction in a citizen suit. It can also impose a civil fine on a violating permittee, with the fine being paid into the federal treasury. Damages, however, cannot be awarded to a citizen plaintiff under the CWA.

No citizen suit can be brought unless a sixty-day notice of intent has been given to EPA, the relevant state, and the alleged violator, or to EPA alone if it is the defendant. The sixty-day waiting period is waived in suits against new sources and dischargers of toxics. A citizen suit is barred if EPA or the state is "diligently prosecuting" a civil or criminal action to enforce the standard or order. But if a citizen suit is barred on this ground, the citizen has a right to "intervene" (be included as a plaintiff) in the governmental lawsuit. Thus, the sixty-day notice and citizen suit can be used to stimulate governmental agencies to bring new enforcement actions and proceed seriously with existing actions.

One incentive for meritorious citizen suits is that the court may award costs of litigation, including reasonable attorney and expert witness fees, to any party (plaintiff or defendant) "whenever the court determines such award is appropriate." The plaintiff does not have to win the entire case in order to recover costs, as long as there is some success on the merits. Costs can also be awarded to defendants harassed by frivolous lawsuits.

MUNICIPAL VIOLATORS

Perhaps the most perplexing enforcement problem under the CWA involves municipal violators. Publicly owned treatment works are responsible for meeting effluent limitations in National Pollutant Discharge Elimination System permits even though construction grants have been refused by a state or EPA, or promised grant funds have been delayed. But how effective can a civil suit be against a POTW which cannot raise the funds to bring about compliance? And how effective can it be to threaten incarceration of overburdened and underfunded public officials? Except where fraud or other wrongdoing is present, POTWs cannot be brought in compliance, or encouraged to maintain compliance, by civil or criminal sanctions. Subsidy programs such as construction grants, operation and maintenance grants (which the CWA does not currently authorize), technical assistance, and operator training grants must be funded and implemented. Plant designers and construction contractors must be held responsible for faulty POTW design and construction. In serious cases, as with the city of Detroit, EPA or a state may be forced to seek a court-appointed receiver to operate the POTW and raise construction and maintenance funds by issuing bonds or raising user charges. But it is certain that POTWs cannot be treated as industrial dischargers.

EPA ENFORCEMENT

Even where industrial violators are concerned, EPA's enforcement record is poor. A 1978 report by the General Accounting Office [47] indicated that permittees were reporting a high degree of noncompliance with permit conditions in their discharge monitoring reports to EPA. Some instances of noncompliance involved significant violations of permit limitations for toxic substances. Where EPA responded at all to these violations reported by the permittees themselves, its response was neither timely nor strong in most cases. The General Accounting Office recommended a thorough reevaluation of EPA's enforcement system. But there is no evidence that EPA enforcement has improved since 1978. Indeed, a 1983 GAO report reveals that noncompliance remains widespread, frequent, and significant [48].

Not all blame for this failure can be laid at EPA's door. Administrative fines, if authorized by Congress, could activate EPA enforcement. As things now stand, if EPA determines that a permittee should be fined for violating permit conditions, it must refer the case and its recommended penalty amount to the Justice Department, which represents EPA in court. These referrals are time-consuming and complex. Nevertheless, the GAO found that EPA was not using the tools it already possessed, such as informal contacts and compliance orders. Perhaps even more worrisome were the GAO's conclusions that EPA did not adequately supervise state-managed permit programs, and that state quarterly noncompliance reports (QNCRs) were insufficient. Reduced EPA funding since 1978 can only have further impaired its oversight activities.

Chapter 34

THE CLEAN WATER ACT: ROLE OF INTERSTATE WATER POLLUTION CONTROL COMPACTS

There are currently ten viable interstate compacts that actively deal with water pollution control [49]: Bi-State Metropolitan Development District Compact (Missouri and Illinois); Delaware River Basin Compact (Delaware, New Jersey, New York, Pennsylvania, and the United States); Great Lakes Basin Compact (Illinois, Indiana, Michigan, Minnesota, New York, Ohio, Pennsylvania, and Wisconsin); Klamath River Basin Compact (California and Oregon); New England Interstate Water Pollution Control Compact (Connecticut, Maine, Massachusetts, New Hampshire, Rhode Island, and Vermont); New York Harbor (Tri-State) Interstate Sanitation Compact (New York, New Jersey, and Connecticut); Ohio River Valley Water Sanitation Compact (Illinois, Indiana, Kentucky, New York, Ohio, Pennsylvania, Tennessee, and West Virginia); Potomac Valley Conservancy District Compact (District of Columbia, Maryland, Pennsylvania, Virginia, and West Virginia); and Susquehanna River Basin Compact (New York, Maryland, Pennsylvania, and the United States). Each compact establishes an Interstate Water Pollution Control Compact Commission (IWPCCC) made up of representatives of the signatories. On the international level, the Great Lakes Water Quality Agreement (1972, 1978, 1983) between the United

States and Canada authorizes the International Joint Commission to perform pollution control functions in addition to its water diversion functions mentioned in Part I.

All ten IWPCCCs were formed before 1972, and the subsequent CWA placed them in a subordinate position. Section 101 of the act declares the policy of Congress "to recognize, preserve, and protect the primary rights of *States* to prevent, reduce, and eliminate pollution" (emphasis added). Congress avoided creating an additional bureaucratic layer in water pollution control, perhaps because IWPCCCs cover a relatively small portion of the United States. IWPCCCs do not administer construction grants programs or issue discharge permits, although they provide input to EPA and states that administer these programs [50]. Where IWPCCCs possess enforcement powers they exercise them sparingly [50], because they are cautious about intruding on state prerogatives. Similarly, under the Great Lakes Water Quality Agreement, the International Joint Commission can set standards and perform monitoring, but enforcement is left to the two nations themselves. Although some IWPCCCs have authority to regulate land use in their basins, they concentrate on large, individual projects and do not conduct comprehensive programs of nonpoint source pollution control. Finally, the basinwide planning carried out by IWPCCCs is on a larger scale than the CWA's water quality management planning process.

Either exclusively or jointly with basin states, most IWPCCCs set water quality standards, perform water quality monitoring, undertake research projects, and especially do modeling and wasteload allocations on interstate waters [50]. Perhaps most importantly, IWPCCCs provide a coordinating mechanism and a forum for the exchange of information among basin states.

Existing IWPCCCs will probably survive despite their minor, somewhat duplicative role under the CWA. In the first place, a number of them, for example, the Delaware and Susquehanna commissions, perform other functions such as flood control and water supply management. Second, IWPCCCs are so helpful to basin states as negotiation and communication facilitators that the states continue to fund the IWPCCCs with state and passthrough federal monies. In short, existing IWPCCCs are functional and established.However, given the CWA's structure, it is improbable that new IWPCCCs will be formed. One possibility, nevertheless, is that interstate water supply commissions in the west will be given water pollution control functions by their constituent states.

Chapter 35
THE CLEAN WATER ACT: NONPOINT SOURCE CONTROL

The drafters of the CWA considered point sources to be not only the primary causes of water pollution but also the most easily regulated. Therefore, they emphasized the construction and regulation of publicly owned treatment works and the issuance to them and to industrial dischargers of permits embodying technology-based effluent limitations, two programs specifically aimed at point source control. Early implementation activities reflected this emphasis [51]. Since 1972, however, nonpoint sources have come to be recognized as the major contributors to many waterbodies of such pollutants as biochemical oxygen demand, suspended solids, and toxics such as pesticides from agricultural runoff and lead from urban stormwater runoff. In early 1981, thirty-seven states reported to EPA that they would be unable to meet the CWA's fishable-swimmable goal by 1983 because of nonpoint source pollution [52]. Despite their effectiveness in controlling point sources, technology-based effluent limitations are usually less effective in regulating nonpoint sources than the nontechnological approaches of land use controls and land management practices. In the context of the CWA, these nontechnological methods are dealt with in sections devoted primarily to planning. This has led to an enforceability problem for nonpoint source control programs.

The term "water quality management planning" refers specifically to sections 208, 303(e), and 106(c) of the CWA, as interpreted by federal planning regulations [53]. However, where nonpoint sources are concerned, section 208 is the focal point.

SECTION 208

Entitled "Areawide Waste Treatment Management," section 208 establishes a procedure whereby states or designated regional agencies are required to formulate and implement strategies to control both point and nonpoint source pollution. The relationship of section 208 to point source control is discussed in the next chapter. The mandate for this type of planning can be found in subsection 101(a)(5) of the act, which sets forth the "national policy that areawide waste treatment management planning processes be developed and implemented to assure adequate control of sources of pollutants in each State." Consistent with this policy, section 201 of the CWA further directs: "To the extent practicable, waste treatment management shall be on an areawide basis and provide control or treatment of all point and nonpoint sources of pollution, including in place or accumulated pollution sources."

Under section 208, the governor of each state is required to designate areas with "substantial water quality control problems" and to name for each area "a single representative organization, including elected officials from local government or their designees." By and large, 208 planning agencies have been councils of government or county governmental units. These organizations or their planning agencies must then formulate and institute "a continuing areawide waste treatment management planning process" which "shall contain alternatives" for waste treatment management applicable to "all wastes generated within the area involved." Federal planning grants provide funds for planning studies and the planning process. Plans prepared under this process must be submitted for certification by the governor and approval by the Environmental Protection Agency. Section 208 provides for interstate cooperation where the relevant area lies in more than one state, and authorizes local officials to form their own planning agency if the governor fails to act. Finally, the state itself is the planning agency for all portions of the state not designated by the governor or local authorities as areawide waste treatment management areas.

In its water quality management plan, each planning agency must identify and recommend for designation by the governor "one or more waste treatment *management agencies* (which may be an existing or newly created local, regional, or State agency or political subdivision)" to implement the plan (emphasis added). EPA may reject the governor's designation of a management agency if the designated agency does not have authority to carry out the plan. Water quality management plans must be submitted to

EPA within three years after receipt of EPA's planning grant. Over 200 state and areawide plans have been completed.

Water quality management planning for nonpoint sources requires the identification of nonpoint sources of pollution and the development of "procedures and measures (including land use requirements)" for control-ling them "to the extent feasible." Each plan must address itself to the following nonpoint sources where they are relevant: agricultural and silvi-cultural nonpoint sources; mine-related sources; construction-related sources; saltwater intrusion resulting from reduction of freshwater flow; disposal of residual wastes; disposal of wastes on land or in subsurface excavations; hydrologic modifications due to construction of dams and other flow diver-sion mechanisms; and urban stormwater runoff.

Two aspects of this list deserve attention. First, the protection of ground-water quality is mentioned with regard to several of these sources. Section 208 is the only major part of the CWA which specifically relates to ground-water. Thus, it can serve as a useful instrument for conjunctive manage-ment of groundwater and surface water resources. Second, section 208 recognizes relationships among water diversions, water resources develop-ment, and water quality. In this sense it can enhance comprehensive water resources management.

Nonpoint source control features best management practices as estab-lished by planning agencies and implemented by management agencies. BMPs are intended to control nonpoint pollution "to the extent feasible." According to EPA:

> The term Best Management Practice (BMP) means a practice, or combination of practices that is determined by a State (or designated areawide planning agency) after problem assessment, examination of alternative practices, and appropriate public participation to be the most effective, practicable (including technological, economic, and institutional considerations) means of prevent-ing or reducing the amount of pollution generated by nonpoint sources to a level compatible with water quality goals [54].

These acceptable BMPs must then be applied by management agencies to particular sites in the most expedient and feasible combination, based on site-specific factors. Thus, a water quality management plan, whether de-veloped by a designated areawide planning agency or the state in a nondesig-nated area, contains ranges of BMPs for different kinds of nonpoint sources, not specific BMPs for particular sources. With this in mind, it is not surpris-ing that most water quality management plans resemble abstract studies rather than enforceable mandates.

Furthermore, planning agencies are not required to develop regulatory programs for implementing BMPs [53]. For this reason, and because of the controversial nature of many BMPs, plans are dominated by voluntary programs such as subsidies and voluntary compliance [52]. Even if a water quality management plan contains enforceable requirements, the CWA does not authorize adequate sanctions against management agencies which do not implement them because of lack of authority or fear of political repercussions [51]. EPA regulations raise the possibility of withholding federal planning grant funds from states and areawide agencies that do not ensure that management agencies, which may be the states or areawide agencies themselves, actually control nonpoint sources. However, this is quickly becoming an empty threat. During the life of the water quality management program, EPA has awarded about $1.5 billion in planning and management grants [52]. But planning grant funding has all but disappeared in recent years. A 1981 amendment to the CWA requires that 1 percent of a state's annual construction grants allotment or $100,000, whichever is greater, be set aside to be used by the state to carry out water quality management planning. But how can a state be legally compelled to control nonpoint sources when it hesitates because of the thorny political problems involved [51]? And how much of this funding will be given to areawide agencies, which many state planning officials regard as rivals?

The EPA planning regulations do offer one possibility for compelling state nonpoint source control action. States are required to prepare and submit to EPA annual "work programs" containing specific outputs for implementing the state water quality management plans and the continuing planning process of subsection 303(e). The work programs are incorporated into an annual state/EPA agreement, which must be formulated with public participation. In other words, the state/EPA agreement ties state water quality planning to management and implementation. As yet, however, the legal status of the state/EPA agreement and its enforceability by citizens has not been tested in the courts.

Section 208 contains a cost-sharing provision, called the Rural Clean Water Program (RCWP), for encouraging control of agricultural nonpoint sources of pollution. The secretary of agriculture, acting through the Soil Conservation Service (SCS), is authorized to enter into contracts of between five and ten years with "owners and operators having control of rural land" to install and maintain BMPs in those areas where water quality management plans are in effect. The control practices specified in the contracts must have been certified by the appropriate management agencies as consistent with water quality management plans. If a particular landowner or operator fails to substantially carry out the schedule outlined in the contract, it can be terminated. The owner can then be compelled to forfeit future payments and refund prior payments with interest. Alternatively, the SCS can demand refunds and adjustments instead of terminating the contract. Forfeit and refund are required where the land is transferred, unless the transferee agrees to be bound by the contract. The SCS is authorized to provide technical assistance and a matching share not greater than 50 percent of the total cost of BMPs. This matching share may be increased when "(1) the main benefits to be derived from the measures are related to improving offsite water quality, and (2) the matching share requirement would place a burden on the landowner which would probably prevent him from participating in the program." Some funding was provided for the RCWP between 1977 and 1980, but there is currently no appropriation for the program. This may be just as well, because there is nothing to suggest that the RCWP would be more successful than other Department of Agriculture soil conservation subsidy programs [55].

Although section 208 is virtually toothless, many state and local governments have acted on their own to curb nonpoint sources of pollution. For example, New Jersey regulates construction-related runoff by its Soil Erosion and Sediment Control Act [56] that requires governmental and private project developers to obtain approval of their erosion control plans by local soil conservation districts or participating municipalities. "Stop work orders" can be issued to prevent construction without, or in violation of, an approved plan [57]. New Jersey also requires all permits issued by its Department of Environmental Protection to be "consistent with" water quality management plans [58], assuming that there is something in the plans with which to be consistent. Disposal of residual wastes as well as surface or subsurface waste disposal require permits in New Jersey and many other states. Coal-mining states regulate acid mine drainage to the best of their abilities. Sand and gravel mining and stormwater runoff are generally covered by municipal ordinances. Almost all states closely regulate hydrologic modifications. On the other hand, agricultural and silvicultural runoff are almost never subject to regulation.

Much of this state and local regulatory activity has been generated by the consciousness-raising and information-producing effects of section 208 planning. The 208 process is replete with legal and administrative flaws [59], but it has set America to thinking about nonpoint sources and the complex technical, institutional, and economic issues raised by nonpoint source control. In this sense, 208 nonpoint source planning has succeeded.

POINT AND NONPOINT SOURCE CONTROL SUMMARY

Point sources are subject to direct federal regulation through uniform national technology-based effluent limitations incorporated in discharge permits. A state may administer its own permit program, but only if EPA decides that the state program is substantially equivalent to EPA's, and only if the state-imposed effluent limitations are no less stringent than those included in federal regulations. At least in theory, if state administration is inadequate, EPA can selectively enforce against violators or, in extreme cases, rescind state permit program authorizations.

Nonpoint source control "was specifically reserved to state and local governments through the section 208 process" [12]. Congress treated nonpoint sources differently because (1) nonpoint source control is basically nontechnological, and (2) BMPs should be administered by the level of government closest to the sources of the problem. But initially deferring to state and local control of nonpoint sources does not preclude Congress, in the future, from requiring these governmental units to institute regulatory programs or, if they do not, to forfeit enforcement responsibility or federal aid: "Section 208 . . . may not be adequate. It may be that the States will be reluctant to develop [adequate] control measures . . . and it may be that some time in the future a Federal presence can be justified and afforded" [12]. Congress looked upon section 208 as an experiment. Where this experiment will lead remains to be seen.

Chapter 36
THE CLEAN WATER ACT: 208 POINT SOURCE PLANNING

POTW PLANNING

Section 208 planning is controversial because every program area of a water quality management plan entails land use planning. Decisions about whether or where publicly owned treatment works are to be constructed are particularly controversial, because the location of sewerage and treatment facilities is a major factor in an area's growth and development. Thus, it is significant that each water quality management plan must identify "treatment works necessary to meet the anticipated municipal and industrial waste-treatment needs of the area over a 25-year period." Planning agencies are responsible for establishing construction priorities and time schedules for the initiation and completion of treatment works and for instituting a regulatory program to implement the construction of treatment works and assure their adequate functioning. This program must "regulate the location, modification, and construction of any facilities within such area which may result in any discharge in such area."

In view of these requirements, one of the critical outputs of the water quality management planning process is a land use plan encompassing time-related population and land use projections which the planners consider compatible with water quality goals. These land use projections should govern decisions regarding the phased development of systems and the modular construction of individual facilities to meet future needs, thus avoiding initial overdesign of waste treatment systems and consequent distortion of growth patterns. Crucial to this aspect of the regulatory program is the formulation of a sewer-hookup schedule, described by federal guidelines as "important in managing the system over time in order to prevent growth from exceeding the designed capacity of the system." Where section 201 facilities planning has not been completed, therefore, water quality management planning should establish growth limitations for a particular region by determining the size and location of municipal treatment works.

The CWA requires that facilities planning be consistent with existing areawide water quality management plans. However, many facilities plans were under way before water quality management plans were begun. This problem of coordination has resulted in part from the goals and deadlines of the act and in part from EPA's changing priorities in administering it. In any event, the difficult question of the "accountability" of existing facilities planning to subsequent water quality management planning is unresolved, and this uncertainty clouds the full importance of water quality management planning as a land use planning tool.

One commentator observes that, in contrast to nonpoint source planning, completed water quality management plans offer a strong POTW planning framework [52]. Many POTWs have been planned or constructed in accordance with 208 plans.

> But in some states the WQM plans do not provide enough data on problems and alternative controls to support the establishment of water quality-based priorities for [POTW] construction. Also, many POTWs are experiencing serious operation and maintenance difficulties and permit compliance problems [52].

As POTWs are completed, planning for their adequate functioning will assume top priority.

POTW planning under section 208 can provide a forum for achieving political consensus, but it cannot compel communities in an area to agree on siting POTWs. The GAO relates a horror story involving attempted cleanup of the Potomac River. Washington, D.C., metropolitan communities, working cooperatively for over ten years, have been unable to site needed regional treatment facilities or to develop permanent sites for the disposal of sludge produced by an advanced waste treatment plant, despite EPA's expenditure of over $5 million in 208 planning funds [60].

INDUSTRIAL POINT SOURCE PLANNING

The CWA attempts to integrate industrial discharge permit issuance with water quality management planning by prohibiting the issuance of a discharge permit which is "in conflict" with an approved plan [61]. Theoretically, water quality management plans should provide for the maintenance of effluent-limited stretches and should set wasteload allocations and water quality-based effluent limitations on water quality-limited stretches. However, this aspect of 208 planning is generally a dead letter because areawide planning agencies do not possess the technical resources to cope with prescribing industrial control technology or performing water quality modeling and wasteload allocations. Perhaps the most glaring deficiency of 208 planning has been lack of technical data and expertise on the part of areawide planning agencies [61]. Moreover, as we have seen, even states cannot reliably set water quality-based effluent limitations.

Chapter 37

OCEAN DUMPING

Ocean disposal of sewage sludge is discussed in Chapter 31. Here the ocean disposal of industrial wastes and dredged spoil is discussed. The applicable statute is the Marine Protection, Research, and Sanctuaries Act (MPRSA) [38]. This statute prohibits all transportation of material from the United States for the purpose of ocean dumping, unless authorized by a permit. "The Act provides maximum coverage over both the content and manner of dumps, without duplicating other environmental statutes" [62]. It controls the dumping of any kind of matter except vessel sewage and oil, both regulated under the Clean Water Act.* MPRSA extends to any manner of dumping except effluents discharged from outfall pipes regulated under the CWA or the Atomic Energy Act, routine operational discharges from vessels, and placement of devices or structures in ocean waters for navigation or fisheries purposes.

MPRSA provides for the regulation of all dumping by a permit program. Power to issue permits is divided between the Environmental Protection Agency and the Army Corps of Engineers. EPA sets criteria for evaluation of all permit applications, whatever the material to be dumped, and issues permits for the dumping of all materials except dredged spoils. The Corps, using EPA criteria, issues permits for dumping of dredged spoils. EPA is also responsible under MPRSA for designating and managing approved dump sites, and for limiting all dumping to designated sites. "Critical areas" can be protected by EPA's declaring them off limits to ocean dumping. EPA can also designate "marine sanctuaries" and regulate activities within them.

---

*Section 312 of the CWA relates to marine sanitation devices. Section 311 and oil discharges are analyzed in Chapter 39.

EPA PERMIT SYSTEMS

MPRSA lists the following factors to be considered by EPA in establishing and applying its ocean-dumping criteria: (1) the need for ocean dumping and the land disposal or recycling alternatives available; (2) the effects of ocean dumping on human health and welfare and on alternative uses of the oceans; and (3) the effects of ocean disposal on the marine environment and marine ecosystems. Under MPRSA, dumping may be permitted if it does not "unreasonably degrade or endanger" the environment, using the above factors to determine reasonableness.

EPA regulations [63] set up various categories of wastes and types of permits. A particular class of waste can only be dumped after the permit appropriate for that class has been issued.

Prohibited Materials

These are high-level radioactive wastes, radiological, chemical, or biological warfare agents, materials of unknown components and properties, and materials which float or remain in suspension so as to cause risks to navigation, fishing, or recreation. Prohibited materials cannot be dumped under any circumstances.

Constituents Prohibited as Other Than Trace Contaminants

These are organohalogens, mercury, cadmium, oil not covered by the CWA, and known or suspected carcinogens, mutagens, and teratogens. "Trace amounts" are determined by listed concentrations for some wastes and bioassay results for others. If the trace contaminant levels are exceeded, these constituents can be dumped only by authority of "emergency permits" ("unacceptable risk relating to human health and . . . no other feasible solution"), "research permits" under certain conditions, and "incineration at sea" permits.

Specially Regulated Wastes

Some of these are liquid wastes immiscible with or slightly soluble in seawater, wastes containing living organisms, highly acidic or alkaline wastes, and oxygen-demanding wastes. Restrictions on their disposal are stipulated in the regulations; but these restrictions can be exceeded in dumped materials under the terms of an emergency permit, a research permit, an incineration at sea permit, or an "interim permit." An interim permit can only be granted for otherwise nonconforming wastes if there is a need to ocean dump the material and the adverse environmental effects of the dumping are outweighed by this need or by the adverse effects of alternate disposal methods. The interim permit can only last for one year, and it can only be issued to an existing dumper. Each interim permit must include an environmental assessment and a plan for eliminating the ocean disposal or bringing the waste into compliance with EPA criteria "as soon as practicable." Many former industrial dumpers have already implemented their plans. Sewage sludge is dumped under interim permits.

Toxic Materials

These are defined as wastes that exceed the "limiting permissible concentration" (LPC). The LPC is

> That concentration of waste or dredged material in the receiving water which, after allowance for initial mixing . . . , will not exceed a toxicity threshold defined as 0.01 of a concentration shown to be acutely toxic to appropriate sensitive marine organisms in a bioassay carried out in accordance with approved EPA procedures.

Wastes exceeding LPC limits can be dumped under the same conditions as specially regulated wastes.

Other Materials

These can be dumped for three years under a "special permit" or indefinitely under a "general permit," unless ocean dumping is clearly unnecessary or environmentally harmful.

CORPS PERMIT PROGRAM

Congress has been sharply criticized for placing "regulatory control in an agency which is the major producer and dumper of dredged spoils" [62]. No permit is needed for dumping spoils from dredging operations performed by or for the Corps. If a permit is necessary for another spoil dumper, EPA can object to its issuance and the Corps can respond under a complex procedure for dispute resolution. "These procedures for dispute resolution have never been fully utilized, even though EPA occasionally disagreed with the Corps' issuance of permits" [63]. EPA has been sued because its criteria treat dredged wastes as inherently less harmful than nondredged wastes [64]. There has also been extensive litigation over EPA's choice of dumpsites for dredged and nondredged wastes [64].

ENFORCEMENT

The Coast Guard is responsible for conducting surveillance activities to ensure compliance with MPRSA. It refers apparent violations to EPA for enforcement action. In a 1977 report the General Accounting Office found serious deficiencies in Coast Guard surveillance of ocean dumpers [65]. Unlike the CWA, EPA has the authority to assess administrative fines against MPRSA violators, as much as $50,000 for each offense depending on its gravity and the violator's good faith and subsequent compliance. Any person who knowingly violates MPRSA can be held liable for a criminal fine of up to $50,000 per violation and a prison term of up to one year. Citizens may sue under the same circumstances as found in the CWA. Another distinction between MPRSA and the CWA involves the role of states. States cannot adopt or enforce any rule relating to ocean dumping. They can only propose to EPA special criteria for dumping within state waters (three miles from shore baselines) or dumping that may affect state waters. Unlike permit responsibilities under the CWA, MPRSA regulation cannot be delegated to states.

Chapter 38

GROUNDWATER DISCHARGES

There is nothing comparable for groundwater to the comprehensive federal legislation regarding discharges to surface water.

> Groundwater is a vitally important renewable resource that has been taken for granted and given little protection. Despite the fact that 45% of the nation's drinking water comes from the ground, efforts to abate and even monitor pollution of groundwater have been limited. The massive national clean-up efforts associated with the landmark environmental legislation of recent years largely ignored groundwater and, in fact, increased groundwater contamination by encouraging diversion of pollutants from the air and surface waters to the ground. . . .
>
> Spurred by the emerging awareness of groundwater contamination and its dangers, Congress recently enacted statutes that provide an initial framework for control of groundwater pollution, and some state and local agencies are undertaking their own protection efforts. Unfortunately, the federal framework is a confusing hodgepodge and the state and local ventures are far from comprehensive [67].

Controlling groundwater pollution will be the first priority of future water pollution control law.

The sources of groundwater pollution fall into four general categories [66]: (1) the direct discharge of liquid waste into the ground through septic tanks and injection wells; (2) leachate from municipal and industrial land-fills, pits, ponds, and lagoons, and land application of sludges; (3) ground-water contamination resulting from activities other than direct waste disposal, for example, oil and gas exploration and development, mining, agriculture, leaky sewerage systems, and surface runoff; (4) overdrafting of aquifers, which exacerbates existing pollution, causes subsidence, and induces intrusion of salt or polluted water. Regulation of these sources of groundwater pollution is examined, along with land use controls in critical recharge areas.

DIRECT INJECTION

Federal regulation of direct discharges into groundwater is limited because EPA interprets the Clean Water Act as inapplicable to groundwater discharges. There is, however, subtitle C of the Safe Drinking Water Act of 1974 [67], directing EPA to promulgate regulations containing minimum standards for state underground injection control (UIC) programs. EPA standards are intended to "prevent underground injection which endangers drinking water sources" [67]. "Well injection" means the subsurface disposal of fluids through a bored, drilled, or driven well; or through a dug well "where the depth of the dug well is greater than the largest surface dimension." Thus, the UIC program does not cover industrial pits, ponds, and lagoons. It also does not apply to cesspools or septic systems that serve individual families or fewer than twenty persons a day in a nonresidential setting. Injection of brine or other fluids from oil and gas operations and underground injection for secondary or tertiary recovery of hydrocarbons can only be regulated where "essential" to protect drinking water.

The definition of "underground source of drinking water" (USDW) is central to the UIC program. An USDW is an aquifer that (1) supplies or could supply a public water system, (2) currently supplies drinking water for human consumption, or (3) contains fewer than 10,000 milligrams per liter total dissolved solids [68]. However, an aquifer that meets one of these criteria may still be exempted from the program if it does not presently serve as a source of drinking water and could not because (1) it is actually or potentially mineral, hydrocarbon, or geothermal energy producing, (2) it is situated at a depth or location that makes recovery of water for drinking water purposes economically or technologically impractical, (3) it is untreatably contaminated, (4) it is located over a mining area subject to subsidence or collapse, or (5) the total dissolved solids content is more than 3,000 and less than 10,000 milligrams per liter and the groundwater is not reasonably expected to supply a public water system.

EPA regulations [69] establish five classes of injection wells, based on purpose and degree of threat to an USDW. Each class of injection well is subject to requirements for construction, operation, monitoring and reporting, plugging and abandonment, financial responsibility, and mechanical integrity. All injection wells must be authorized by permit or regulation. If a state does not have an approved UIC program, EPA will carry out a program for the state. Wells that inject hazardous waste directly into, above, or near an USDW are to be phased out, and new wells of this type are prohibited. Each permit applicant bears the burden of showing that his discharge will not endanger an USDW.

The UIC program is characterized by its emphasis on protecting potable water. Its approach of classifying each aquifer as either an USDW or non-USDW has been criticized "because it allows no differentiation of, or setting of priorities among, aquifers used for water supply, and because it completely disregards ecological needs" [66]. Furthermore, the USDW exemptions may be too broad to protect future drinking water supplies. For example, the fact that an aquifer is or could be commercially valuable for its mineral or energy resources does not mean that it will not be more valuable in the future as a potable water source. Moreover, simply because it is now impracticable to recover drinking water from an aquifer does not mean that technological advances or increased demand will not make recovery practicable in the future.

Most septic systems are not regulated under the UIC program, and state and local regulation of septic systems and septage disposal is spotty. Overconcentrations of septic systems can be prevented by central sewering, which depletes groundwater and encourages growth-related runoff, or density restrictions imposed through state critical area legislation or local zoning ordinances. The adequacy of individual septic systems can be assured by performance standards and pumpout requirements enforced by local governments or septic tank management districts. Septage should, where possible, be disposed of into POTWs, and some states mandate this.

LEACHATE FROM WASTE DISPOSAL ACTIVITIES

The primary federal statute in this area is the Resource Conservation and Recovery Act (RCRA) [70]. RCRA extends federal regulation to land disposal of municipal waste and generation, transportation, treatment, storage, and disposal of hazardous waste. RCRA's definition of "disposal" specifically refers to groundwater. However, RCRA does not apply to storage of hazardous raw materials or products.

With regard to municipal solid waste disposal, RCRA requires EPA to promulgate regulations distinguishing sanitary landfills from "open dumps." New open dumps are prohibited and existing dumps must be closed or upgraded within five years. Sanitary landfills located above USDWs must not endanger the quality of groundwater.

RCRA's approach to hazardous waste management consists of four major elements: (1) federal identification of hazardous wastes; (2) a manifest system for tracing hazardous wastes from generator, to transporter, to treatment, storage, or disposal facility; (3) federal minimum standards for hazardous waste treatment, storage, and disposal, enforced through a permit system; and (4) state implementation of hazardous waste management programs at least equivalent to the federal program.

EPA is responsible for issuing regulations containing criteria for identifying hazardous wastes and listing particular hazardous wastes. One of EPA's hazardous waste criteria, the so-called extraction procedure (EP) toxicity test, simulates the leaching action that occurs in poorly managed landfills. The initial hazardous waste list may be revised by EPA whenever appropriate. State governors may petition EPA to identify or list a material as a hazardous waste, and EPA must either grant or deny the petition within ninety days. Moreover, any person may petition EPA "for the promulgation, amendment, or repeal of any regulation" under RCRA. EPA must take action on a citizen petition "within a reasonable time" and publish in the *Federal Register* its reasons for taking such action.

Regulations have also been promulgated with regard to generators and transporters of hazardous wastes. It is the responsibility of generators to determine whether the wastes they produce are hazardous under RCRA. Generators of hazardous wastes must (1) keep records and report to the federal government, (2) initiate a manifest system "to assure that all such hazardous waste generated is designated for treatment, storage, or disposal in . . . facilities . . . for which a permit has been issued" [70], and (3) properly label and containerize hazardous wastes delivered to transporters and treatment, storage, and disposal facilities. The duties of a transporter involve (1) record keeping and reporting, (2) accepting only properly labeled and containerized wastes, (3) complying with the manifest system, and most important, (4) transporting all hazardous waste only to the permitted facility that the generator identifies on the manifest. The manifest system terminates with the receipt of the wastes by the owner or operator of the disposal facility and his notification to the generator.

Permits are not required of generators or transporters of hazardous wastes, but disposal, treatment, or storage of these wastes are prohibited except in accordance with a permit. In order to obtain and retain a permit, an owner or operator of a disposal, treatment, or storage facility must meet EPA performance standards governing location, design, construction, operation, and maintenance of such a facility. The applicable performance standards become permit conditions, in addition to the record keeping and reporting requirements.

A state is authorized to administer and enforce a hazardous waste regulatory program in lieu of the federal program if EPA finds that the state program is equivalent to the federal program and is consistent with the programs of neighboring states. No state may impose less stringent requirements than those included in federal law, but a state may elect to be more stringent. EPA is the primary enforcement authority where a state program has not been approved. Even subsequent to approval, EPA can enforce directly against a violator after giving notice to the state. If an approved program is later determined to be inadequate, EPA may withdraw program authorization and reinstitute the federal program in that state.

RCRA provides EPA with a broad range of enforcement mechanisms, including compliance orders, administrative fines, civil actions for injunctions, civil penalties of up to $25,000 per day of violation, permit suspension or revocation, and criminal indictments for knowing transportation to an unpermitted facility, unpermitted disposal, and making false statements in applications, manifests, labels, and reports. State programs must ensure adequate enforcement, but state enforcement tools may be weaker than those which RCRA provides EPA.

EPA has promulgated regulations applicable to facilities that treat, store, or dispose of hazardous wastes [71]. These regulations cover facility performance standards, preparedness and prevention, contingency plans and emergency procedures, the manifest system, closure and postclosure measures, financial responsibility, and the management of containers, tanks, surface impoundments, waste piles, land treatment units, landfills, incinerators, thermal treatment units, and chemical, physical, and biological treatment units. An entire subpart of these regulations is devoted to ground-water protection. The facility permit must contain conditions to ensure that hazardous constituents from a regulated unit do not exceed certain concentration limits at the downgradient facility boundary for the active life of the facility and during postclosure if the site has not been decontaminated on closure. A "hazardous constituent" is a constituent on the RCRA list which has been detected in the underlying aquifer or "that [is] reasonably expected to be in or derived from waste contained in a regulated unit" [71]. However, EPA may grant a variance if it "finds that the constituent is not capable of posing a substantial present or potential hazard to human health or the environment" [71]. "Concentration limits" are background levels, drinking water standards where they exist, or alternate concentration limits based on the variance criterion for "hazardous constituent." In other words, permit limitations are set on a site-specific basis. Moreover, a site is exempt from regulation if EPA finds "that there is no potential for migration of liquid from a regulated unit to the uppermost aquifer during the active life . . . and the post-closure care period" [71].

All facilities treating, storing, or disposing of hazardous wastes must perform detection monitoring. Any waste found beyond the actual waste management area is presumed to originate from the regulated unit. When a hazardous constituent is detected in excess of permit limits, the owner or operator must take "corrective action" to remove the waste constituents or treat them in place. A compliance monitoring system is also required.

One of the most controversial aspects of these regulations is their approval of hazardous waste disposal in so-called secure landfills and surface impoundments. The groundwater protection provisions are inapplicable to double-lined surface impoundments and landfills which are located, including the liners, entirely above the seasonal high water table, as long as leak detection and reporting requirements are met.

ACTIVITIES OTHER THAN WASTE DISPOSAL

If a pesticide is found to contaminate groundwater, its registration may be disapproved or cancelled under the Federal Insecticide, Fungicide, and Rodenticide Act [72]. Leaking underground storage tanks, e.g., gasoline storage tanks, may be regulated by EPA under the Toxic Substances Control Act [73].

Nonpoint source pollution, if regulated at all, is under the control of state and local governments. An exception that proves the rule is the Surface Mining Control and Reclamation Act of 1977 (SMCRA) [74]. This act, administered by the Department of the Interior and participating states, requires operating permits, mining and reclamation plans, reclamation bonds, and monitoring. It also establishes minimum standards to prevent water diminution and pollution, acid mine drainage, and hydrologic disturbance. Thus far, enforcement of SMCRA has been desultory.

DEPLETION AND POLLUTION

SMCRA is based on the recognition that groundwater must be managed comprehensively.

> Rational management of the groundwater resource requires consideration of the effects of pollution-control measures on depletion and depletion-control measures on pollution. For instance, preventing contaminated water from recharging an aquifer—to avoid pollution—may cause depletion problems, such as reduced stream flows or saltwater intrusion. An example is replacement of septic systems by central sewering. Similar dilemmas result from diversion of contaminated runoff from developed areas and contaminated irrigation return flows [66].

As pointed out in Part I, facilitating comprehensive water resources management is the greatest challenge to future water law. This challenge will be particularly formidable in states that follow the "absolute ownership" or "reasonable use" rules of groundwater diversion rights.

GROUNDWATER POLLUTION AND LAND USE

Although utilization of best available technology and best management practices can prevent some groundwater pollution, the close relationship between land development and groundwater quality necessitates land use controls in critical recharge areas. According to Tripp and Jaffe, the water quality objective for high-quality aquifers should be nondegradation, and the major mechanism for achieving this objective should be state and local regulation of land use to prohibit polluting activities within critical recharge zones [66].

A model for state and local land use regulation is the "sole source aquifer" provision of the federal Safe Drinking Water Act [75]. EPA, either by petition or on its own initiative, may designate an aquifer as the "sole or principal source of drinking water" for an area. After designation, "no commitment for federal financial assistance may be entered into for any project which [EPA] determines may contaminate such aquifer through a recharge zone so as to create a significant hazard to public health" [75]. EPA has made a number of "sole source aquifer" designations, including the Edwards Aquifer in Texas and the Pinelands Aquifer in New Jersey.

FUTURE OF GROUNDWATER POLLUTION CONTROL LAW

In 1980 EPA released its "Proposed Groundwater Protection Strategy," a document which can be interpreted as representing EPA's maximum potential involvement in groundwater pollution control. EPA's strategy contains three major elements: (1) groundwater classification, (2) state groundwater protection strategies, and (3) minimum national requirements for selected high-priority problems.

EPA would develop a set of groundwater classes based on present and projected future uses. Important criteria would be present water quality, yields, aquifer vulnerability, and source value relative to alternative sources of water supply in an area. The classification system developed by EPA would be accompanied by recommended control approaches. It would be up to individual states whether or not to accept EPA's model classification system, whether and how to classify specific aquifers, and whether and how to implement any control measures. EPA would override state program decisions only where they were in conflict with existing federal statutes and regulations. Other than enforcing existing laws, EPA's role would be advisory and coordinative.

In other words, the future of groundwater pollution control law lies with the states. State groundwater protection programs differ widely in approach, institutional structure, and quality. New Jersey law is particularly well developed in this area because New Jersey generates more hazardous waste than any other state and because groundwater furnishes almost half of the state's potable water.

All New Jersey water pollution control statutes refer specifically to groundwater. Discharge permits are required for: (1) groundwater discharges; (2) well injection; (3) land application of wastewater, septage, and sludge; (4) landfills; (5) storage of liquid or solid pollutants, including raw materials and products; and (6) the disposal of waste into surface impoundments [76]. There is a comprehensive statute for siting hazardous waste facilities, and it prohibits siting in an area where the seasonal high water table rises to within one foot of the surface [77]. New Jersey also possesses an active hazardous waste management program under RCRA. The Spill Compensation and Control Act [78] provides funds for spill cleanups and requires major facilities to prepare and implement spill prevention and control plans. Septic systems are regulated by a program administered by the state in cooperation with local governments. Much of the state, including the shore and Pinelands regions, is covered by critical areas legislation that is sensitive to protection of groundwater quality. Large groundwater diversions require a permit, and the relationship between depletion and pollution, especially saltwater intrusion, receives close attention. Runoff from construction is regulated [56], and some municipalities are receiving state funds to prepare stormwater control plans. Lastly, in 1981 the state adopted a system of groundwater quality standards including a prohibition on the introduction of toxic pollutants into groundwater and a strong antidegradation element [79].

Nevertheless, New Jersey's groundwater is still vulnerable to pollution. New Jersey law does not adequately regulate pollution of freshwater wetlands, agricultural runoff, urban stormwater runoff, individual septic systems, and leaky sewer systems. Most important, there is no systematic protection of aquifer recharge areas in New Jersey, despite the presence of two designated sole source aquifers. Moreover, a regulatory structure is no better than its enforcement credibility, and New Jersey, along with all other states, is feeling the pinch of reduced federal program funding. The success or failure of groundwater pollution control in New Jersey may well depend upon whether sufficient monies can be raised through discharge fees to cover program costs.

Chapter 39
OIL AND HAZARDOUS SUBSTANCES CLEANUP

The law of oil and hazardous substances control and cleanup merits a book unto itself. In the words of Jeffrey Trauberman, director of the Environmental Law Institute's Toxic Substances Program:

> The control of oil and hazardous substances releases reflects a complex interweaving of regulatory and liability mechanisms at the international, federal, and state levels. Part of the reason for this intricate array of controls is the pervasive nature of the problem. Each year there are an estimated 3,500 chemical incidents that pose a significant risk of harm to the environment. In addition, almost 11,000 oil pollution incidents occur annually in U.S. waters alone. These events can occur at nearly every stage in the production, storage, transportation, and use of oil and hazardous substances; they involve accidental spills, continuing discharges, intentional dumping, and leaching waste sites [80].

Chapters 23–36 deal with regulation of point and nonpoint source discharges under the Clean Water Act. This chapter concentrates on cleanup liability.

Trauberman believes that regulatory efforts must be supplemented by liability mechanisms:

> Because of the perceived inadequacies of control strategies relying exclusively on regulation, a number of alternative international, federal, and state mechanisms have been developed which emphasize liability as an economic disincentive to pollution. These approaches foster the internalization of "social" costs of pollution by those responsible for oil and hazardous substances re-

leases. By incorporating the "polluter pays" principle, such legal mechanisms are intended both to deter harmful conduct and to redress pollution-caused harm [80].

This chapter primarily examines federal law dealing with oil and hazardous substances cleanup. The active international law in this field is beyond the scope of this book [81]. However, the New Jersey Spill Compensation and Control Act is summarized as an example of state liability legislation.

OIL AND HAZARDOUS SUBSTANCES SPILLS

Liability for oil spills is covered under four federal statutes. Section 311 of the CWA is the most comprehensive of these statutes. The others were enacted to control oil pollution in specific areas. They are the Outer Continental Shelf Lands Act Amendments [82], the Deepwater Port Act [83], and the Trans-Alaska Pipeline Authorization Act [84]. These four statutes are similar in that they establish trust funds to pay for cleanup of oil spills. However, they differ in many ways, and Congress has been considering a comprehensive oil pollution control statute [80].

Section 311 of the CWA deals with oil and hazardous substance liability. However, with regard to hazardous substances it must be read together with the Comprehensive Environmental Response, Compensation, and Liability Act of 1980 (CERCLA) [85].

The coverage of section 311 is limited to "spilling, leaking, pumping, pouring, emitting, emptying, or dumping" oil and hazardous substances from vessels, onshore facilities, and offshore facilities into fresh or marine navigable waters of the United States seaward to the 200-mile limit. It does not cover groundwater discharges or point source discharges under CWA discharge permits. Section 311 is administered by the Environmental Protection Agency and the Coast Guard.

The first step in the 311 process is for EPA to determine "those quantities of oil and any hazardous substances the discharge of which may be harmful to the public health or welfare." In 1979, EPA promulgated regulations designating approximately 300 substances as hazardous and establishing a "reportable quantity" for each [86]. Virtually all discharges of oil are reportable. Any person in charge of a vessel or an onshore or offshore facility is required to "immediately notify" the Coast Guard or EPA "as soon as he has knowledge" of the discharge of a reportable quantity of oil or a hazardous substance. Failure to notify is punishable by fines and imprisonment.

Apart from the notification requirement, discharge of a reportable quantity gives rise to responsibility for both penalties and the costs of removal. There is an alternative set of procedures to assess civil penalties for hazardous waste spills: an administrative assessment by the Coast Guard of up to $5,000 or a civil lawsuit by EPA to assess a penalty of up to $50,000 for each discharge of a reportable quantity. Where EPA can show that the discharge was the result of "willful negligence or willful misconduct within the privity and knowledge" of the responsible person, the maximum penalty is $250,000. Lesser penalties apply to oil spills.

As for cleanup liability, whenever any oil or a hazardous substance is discharged the Coast Guard and EPA are authorized by section 311 "to remove or arrange for the removal of such oil or substance at any time" unless they determine that "such removal will be done properly by the owner or operator" of the vessel or onshore or offshore facility from which the discharge occurs. In addition to removal, the federal government "may act to mitigate the damage to the public health or welfare caused by such discharge." An owner or operator is liable to reimburse the federal government "for the actual costs" incurred by federal officials or their contractors for the removal of oil or a hazardous substance that is discharged in reportable quantities, including the costs of mitigation. Limitations on liability differ among onshore facilities, offshore facilities, and vessels and among dischargers of oil and hazardous substances. However, an owner or operator is liable for the full amount of the costs where the United States can show that the discharge "was the result of willful negligence or willful misconduct within the privity and knowledge" of the responsible person. Removal costs include restoration or replacement of natural resources damaged or destroyed by the discharge. Under section 311, a discharger is exempt from cleanup liability only if he can prove that the discharge "was caused solely by (a) an act of God, (b) an act of war, (c) negligence on the part of the United States Government, or (d) an act or omission of a third party without regard to whether such act or omission was or was not negligent, or any combination of the foregoing causes." This is often referred to as "strict liability" because the exercise of care is no defense.

In order to prevent oil spills before they occur, owners and operators of large oil storage facilities must develop, implement, and maintain spill prevention, control, and countermeasure (SPCC) plans. SPCC plans are not yet required under federal law for hazardous waste transfer and storage facilities. Vessels are encouraged to take preventive measures by requiring them to establish proof of financial responsibility to meet potential liability under section 311.

Section 311 includes a revolving fund, financed by fine receipts and congressional appropriations, to support federal oil spill cleanup efforts where financially responsible dischargers that are willing to undertake cleanup cannot be located. The 311 fund may not be used to compensate "third-party" spill victims, that is, owners of shorefront property, fishermen, and others damaged by spills. But the U.S. Supreme Court has held that states can enact stricter oil spill liability statutes [87].

CERCLA AND HAZARDOUS WASTES

CERCLA, also known as "Superfund," applies to "releases" of "hazardous substances" from "facilities" and vessels. The term "release" is extraordinarily comprehensive, covering "any spilling, leaking, pumping, pouring, emitting, emptying, discharging, injecting, escaping, leaching, dumping, or depositing into the environment" [85]. Unlike section 311, CERCLA applies to groundwater discharges. "Release" does not include specified discharges of nuclear materials, workplace emissions, most engine exhausts, and "normal" fertilizer applications. Moreover, the releases of pollutants under federal permits, releases from the applications of registered pesticides, and releases mentioned in environmental impact statements are exempt from CERCLA.

"Hazardous substances" are any substances listed as toxic or hazardous under any federal pollution control statute. Oil and gas are not "hazardous substances." A "facility" is

> (A) any building, structure, installation equipment, pipe or pipeline (including any pipe into a sewer or publicly owned treatment works), well, pit, pond, lagoon, impoundment, ditch, landfill, storage container, motor vehicle, rolling stock, or aircraft, or (B) any site or area where a hazardous substance has been deposited, stored, disposed of, or placed, or otherwise come to be located; but does not include any consumer product in consumer use or any vessel.

Abandoned hazardous waste sites are covered by this definition.

CERCLA contains spill notification provisions that are similar to those of section 311. Moreover, owners and operators of vessels or facilities handling hazardous wastes must show proof of financial responsibility. Unless the Coast Guard and EPA determine that the person responsible for the spill will clean it up, the federal agencies may arrange for pollution removal and remedial operations whenever "any hazardous substance is released or there is a substantial threat of such a release into the environment."

CERCLA establishes a $1.6 billion "Hazardous Substances Response Fund" financed jointly by industry and government. Almost $1.4 billion is derived from a tax on oil, specified organic chemicals, and certain heavy metals [80]. The remainder comes from the federal treasury. The Response Fund can be used to pay for governmental cleanup costs and for "restoring, replacing, rehabilitating, or acquiring the substantial equivalent of damaged [natural] resources" [80]. Only natural resources belonging to, managed by, or protected by a state or the federal government are eligible. Moreover, funds are not available for resource damage occurring "wholly before" CERCLA's enactment, or for losses arising from "long-term exposure to ambient concentrations of air pollutants from multiple or diffuse sources" (e.g., acid rain). Like section 311, CERCLA does not provide compensation for private victims of hazardous waste spills.

Federal hazardous substances response must, "to the greatest extent possible," be consistent with the National Contingency Plan (NCP) begun under section 311 and updated under CERCLA. The NCP includes preferable removal methods, cost-effectiveness criteria, the roles of governmental units, and criteria for determining cleanup priorities. Perhaps most important, the NCP shall "list . . . national priorities among the known releases or threatened releases throughout the United States," subject to annual revision. Except in an emergency, federal payments from the Response Fund cannot continue beyond six months or $1 million, whichever comes first, unless the appropriate state agrees to bear at least 10 percent of the cleanup costs and all future site maintenance expenses. The state must also agree to "assure the availability" of an approved hazardous waste disposal site within the state.

Payment of remedial expenses and natural resource damages by the Response Fund entitles its representatives to proceed against the responsible parties for compensation. CERCLA makes the following persons strictly liable, without regard to fault, for costs sustained by the fund:

1. Current owners or operators of facilities.
2. Owners or operators of facilities at the time the hazardous substances were discarded.
3. Persons who arranged by contract, agreement, or otherwise for disposal, treatment, or transport for disposal or treatment of their hazardous substances by others.
4. Persons who accept or accepted hazardous substances for transport to disposal or treatment facilities of their selection [88].

Since CERCLA applies to releases from inactive sites, it "implies that strict liability can be imposed to recover response costs even though the acts upon which liability is based occurred before the enactment of Superfund" [88].

Like section 311, CERCLA provides certain defenses to liability (e.g., an act of God), but the CERCLA defenses are fewer and narrower than their 311 counterparts. By the same token, CERCLA's dollar limitations on liability are considerably higher than those under section 311. CERCLA applies where it and section 311 conflict.

There is a second fund created by CERCLA, the "Post-Closure Liability Fund." This $200 million fund, financed by a tax on hazardous wastes treated at approved facilities, assumes liability for hazardous waste sites that have been issued federal permits and that have been closed in accordance with these permits. The Post-Closure Liability Fund, unlike the Hazardous Substances Response Fund, can be called upon to pay compensation for personal injury and property damage to third-party victims of releases from an inactive site [88].

CERCLA authorizes both judicial and administrative action where an actual or threatened release of a hazardous substance causes "an imminent and substantial endangerment to the public health or welfare or the environment." Willful violations of EPA's administrative orders are punishable by fines of up to $5,000 per day of violation. Persons who unjustifiably fail to follow these orders may be liable for punitive damages of up to three times the response costs.

STATE SPILL STATUTES

State spill compensation and control statutes are important because (1) they impose liability where CERCLA does not (for example, for third-party damage), and (2) they provide extra money to finance the state share of CERCLA cleanup, or to clean up sites which are not National Contingency Plan priorities. An estimated twenty-three states have statutory funding mechanisms to cover cleanup costs. Moreover, thirteen states have reportedly enacted statutes allowing private citizens to recover for damages caused by hazardous substance spills [80].

The New Jersey Spill Compensation and Control Act [78] was enacted in 1976, four years before CERCLA. The act establishes a revolving $50 million New Jersey Spill Compensation Fund, financed by a tax on major facilities that "refine, produce, store, handle, transfer, process, or transport" oil or hazardous substances. The fund may be used to remove actual discharges or threatened discharges if hazardous materials are dangerously stored or transported. Discharges that occurred prior to the act's passage may also be cleaned up, but a maximum of $3 million may be spent to clean up preenactment sites in any one year.

The fund is "strictly liable, without regard to fault, for all cleanup and removal costs and for all direct and indirect damages, no matter by whom sustained." Compensable damages include (1) costs of restoring and replacing natural resources, (2) costs of restoring, repairing, or replacing private property, (3) loss of income due to property or resource damage, (4) loss of tax revenues by state or local governments for one year due to property damage, and (5) interest on loans taken out by a claimant pending fund payments. The act does not mention personal injury costs, but would probably be construed to cover them.

"Any person who has discharged a hazardous substance or is in any way responsible for any hazardous substance which the department has removed" is strictly liable for all cleanup and removal costs. Where damage costs are concerned, there are dollar liability limitations similar to those in section 311. The only defenses to liability are acts of war, sabotage, and acts of God. The act has been held to apply retroactively, that is, to impose liability for preenactment discharges that are still a threat to public health.

There is some question about whether, or to what extent, state spill funds have been "preempted" (replaced) by Superfund. Thus far, courts have held that state funds retain their viability as adjuncts to the Hazardous Substances Response Fund.

Chapter 40
DRINKING WATER PROTECTION

Ambient water quality and tap water quality are regulated by different federal statutes. The Clean Water Act has as its goal fishable-swimmable, not potable, waters. Nevertheless, state antidegradation policies are intended to maintain the quality of some surface waters that are of potable quality or could be after treatment. The underground injection control program and the Resource Conservation and Recovery Act have been used to protect some aquifers that do or could serve primarily as drinking water sources. But these statutes cannot assure that tap water is fit to drink. Background contamination, incomplete regulation, nonpoint sources, and permit violations make it necessary to create another layer of protection for the public. This is the function of the Safe Drinking Water Act (SDWA) [67] and, to a lesser extent, the Saline Water Conversion Program.

SAFE DRINKING WATER ACT

SDWA was enacted in 1974 in response to the discovery of toxic substances in the drinking water supplies of major American cities. The Environmental Protection Agency is required to promulgate national primary and secondary drinking water regulations applicable to "public water systems," defined as systems that have at least fifteen service connections or regularly serve at least twenty-five individuals at least sixty days per year [67]. "Pri-

213

mary drinking water regulations" identify potential toxic contaminants and for each contaminant set a maximum contaminant level (MCL) if the contaminant can feasibly be measured or a treatment technique if it cannot. Secondary drinking water standards set MCLs for nontoxic contaminants that affect, for example, color and taste. As with the CWA or RCRA, states may assume primary enforcement responsibility under SDWA and receive federal program grants.

EPA development of primary drinking water regulations is a three-step process. In the first step, the National Interim Primary Drinking Water Regulations [89] became effective in 1977 and are still in effect. EPA based the MCLs contained in these interim regulations in large part on the 1962 U.S. Public Health Service drinking water standards. In the second step, EPA must develop and publish recommended maximum contaminant levels (RMCLs). The RMCLs are nonenforceable health goals for public water systems. They are to be set at a level which, in the administrator's judgment, "no known or anticipated adverse effects on the health of persons occur and which allows an adequate margin of safety" [67]. EPA has recently announced its intention to initiate this second step. As the third step, EPA must propose and promulgate RMCLs and National Revised Primary Drinking Water Regulations that would include MCLs and monitoring and reporting requirements for those contaminants that may have an adverse effect on human health. MCLs in the revised regulations must be set as close to RMCLs as feasible. "Feasible" means "with the use of the best technology, treatment techniques, and other means, which the Administrator finds are generally available (taking costs into consideration)" [67]. The revised regulations must then be reviewed and, if feasible, strengthened every three years.

EPA and states may authorize variances and exemptions from primary regulations. Variances for unspecified lengths of time can be granted to public water systems that, despite the application of best available technology economically achievable, cannot comply with primary regulations because of impurities in their raw water sources. Exemptions until 1984 or seven years after promulgation of a new primary regulation may be awarded if "due to compelling factors (which may include economic factors), the public water system is unable to comply" [67]. Neither a variance nor an exemption may be granted where there would be "an unreasonable risk to health."

Enforcement against public water systems is subject to the same infirmities as enforcement against publicly owned treatment works under the CWA because legislatures, courts, and agencies are reluctant to impose heavy fines and jail sentences on public bodies and their officials. Thus, under the SDWA, court-imposed civil penalties are limited to $5,000 per day, and can be imposed only on "willful" violators. Enforcement is supposedly accomplished by injunctions and public exposure of violators. All violators of the SDWA or a comparable state statute must publish notices of violation in local newspapers and include violation notices with water bills. Citizens can use this information to work for compliance through local political channels or to bring citizen suits for injunctions. Once again, this system presupposes a high degree of citizen vigilance and litigation capability.

The MCLs established under the interim regulations cover chemical contaminants, microbiological contaminants, radionuclides, and turbidity. However, MCLs for only ten organic and six inorganic chemicals have been listed under the SDWA [89]. In 1978 EPA proposed regulations setting an MCL for trihalomethanes, formed by the chlorination of water, and requiring large public systems with significant levels of synthetic organics in their source water to install granular activated carbon (GAC) filters as a treatment technique [90]. The trihalomethane MCL was finally promulgated, but the GAC requirement was abandoned after vehement protests by water purveyors.

Instead of setting MCLs for compounds that frequently contaminate drinking water, EPA has prepared "suggested no adverse response levels" (SNARLs) that can be used by state and local governments to regulate drinking water quality. At some point, EPA may use a SNARL in setting an RMCL. Under the SDWA, states are authorized to set additional and stricter MCLs, but few states have done so due to insufficient resources and pressure from water purveyors. Another major problem in state regulation of drinking water is coping with the variety of institutions that provide drinking water (see Part I).

Implementation of the SDWA has encountered heavy criticism. In the first place, except for microbiological contaminants, EPA monitoring requirements are not particularly demanding. Drinking water must be tested for inorganics annually by those suppliers using surface water sources, and every three years by public water systems using groundwater sources. For organics, testing of surface sources is required every three years, and there is no federal requirement that groundwater be tested for organics. "These monitoring schedules are too infrequent to offer public protection and produce an adequate data base" [90].

In the second place, there is widespread failure to comply with even these limited testing requirements [91]. Moreover, EPA and state enforcement actions studied by the General Accounting Office "ranged from none to minimal, followed no particular patterns, and [were] not as timely as [they] could or should have been" [91]. Finally, "failure to notify water system users when a violation occurs appears to be the norm rather than the exception" [91]. As sporadic as enforcement has been, it will decrease even further as the forty-eight states granted primary enforcement responsibility lose program funds.

SALINE WATER CONVERSION

Since 1952 the Department of the Interior has been conducting a research program for the development of processes for economically converting saline water into fresh water. The present Saline Water Conversion Program was authorized by Title II of the Water Research and Development Act of 1978 [92]. The GAO has concluded that "a practical, low-cost desalting method has not been achieved" [93]. GAO recommends that the program be thoroughly reevaluated, and future funding is uncertain.

Chapter 41
COMMON LAW REMEDIES

This part has justifiably concentrated on the statutory law of water treatment. However, the common law still plays an important role in achieving and maintaining clean water in the United States. Common law litigation is generally the first response of our legal system to an emerging issue. Then, as the issue evolves and grows more complex, municipal ordinances and state legislation are brought to bear on the problem. Finally, federal legislation establishes the partnership between federal and state administrative agencies that is the characteristic of a mature regulatory system responding to a significant national issue [94].

The replacement of common law actions for injunctions and damages by administrative regulation is inevitable because of severe limitations on the common law as a pollution control strategy. Private litigation is sporadic in place and time, while administrative regulations are universally applicable and often uniform in effect. Second, many private actions are inhibited by restrictive rules of standing and the expense of bringing litigation. On the other hand, administrative agencies automatically possess standing and agencies, with their professional enforcement staffs, are far less sensitive to expense than the average citizen. Third, in deciding whether an injunction should be granted, courts "balance the equities" between the interests of a plaintiff and society as a whole. The balance is more likely to be in favor of pollution control where a public agency, also representing society as a whole, is the plaintiff. Lastly, a plaintiff in an environmental common law action is inherently at a grave disadvantage because he must prove, by a preponderance of the evidence, that a particular discharger, or group of dischargers acting independently, caused his injury. The difficulty of fulfilling this burden under the conditions of scientific uncertainty that characterize environmental problems is illustrated by the fifteen-year struggle to curtail Reserve Mining Company's discharge of taconite tailings into Lake Superior [95].

Although they cannot bear the brunt of modern pollution control, common law actions still play an important part in regulatory systems. Lawsuits based on legal theories such as nuisance, trespass, negligence, abnormally dangerous activities, and interference with riparian rights "fill in the gaps" left by water pollution control statutes and regulations. For this reason, most of the federal statutes discussed in this part include "savings clauses" similar to section 505(e) of the Clean Water Act: "Nothing in this section shall restrict any right which any person (or class of persons) may have under any statute or common law to seek enforcement of any effluent standard or limitation or to seek any other relief."

Where a discharger is violating his permit limitations, an action for an injunction may be brought under the "citizen suit" section of CWA. Section 505 provides access to federal courts and allows for recovery of legal fees and expert witness fees, awards which an ordinary common law court cannot make. But section 505 does not provide for (1) damage actions; (2) private actions against indirect dischargers; and (3) private actions against dischargers that are in compliance with their permits but are still injuring downstream riparians, fishermen, boat owners, etc. Here are statutory gaps that common law actions can fill.

The recent case of *Village of Wilsonville* v. *SCA Services, Inc.* [96] shows the interactions between a permit system and private litigation. As a rule, permit compliance will insulate a discharger against common law actions, but this is not always so. In *Wilsonville*, the Illinois Supreme Court affirmed a trial court judgment ordering the defendant to close its hazardous chemical waste landfill in Wilsonville, to remove all toxic waste and contaminated soil at the disposal site, and to restore and reclaim the site. The Illinois Supreme Court was impressed by evidence that groundwater contamination was inevitable, despite engineering techniques, because the site was located over an abandoned coal mine that was already settling and causing subsidence at the landfill site. Moreover, there was convincing testimony that hazardous materials had been buried in such a sloppy manner that an explosion was likely if oxygen could reach the chemicals. The court rejected the defendant's argument that the landfill site and each batch disposal had been permitted by the Illinois Environmental Protection Agency, because IEPA had granted the permits based on the defendant's inaccurate data. The U.S. Environmental Protection Agency appeared as *amicus curiae* (friend of the court) and filed affidavits claiming that removal and transportation of wastes from the site would be riskier than allowing the site to remain open and operate in a "clean" mode, but the court could not understand how safe operation was possible in light of the subsidence. The court acknowledged the need for hazardous waste disposal sites, but declared that they must be located in suitable locations where they will not pose a threat to public health. In "balancing the equities" the Illinois Supreme Court firmly held that in Illinois the rights of a private landowner are presumptively superior to the public benefit or convenience from having a business operate at a particular location.

Private litigation such as *Wilsonville* allows our legal system to go beyond statutes and regulations in protecting the public against pollution. In addition, common law actions call attention to issues that legislatures may not have adequately addressed. For example, *Wilsonville* emphasizes the need for hazardous waste facility-siting legislation in order to forestall building hazardous waste sites over abandoned coal mines. The decision deals with water resources and land use in a comprehensive manner. This enlightened approach should be taken by legislatures, administrative agencies, and other courts in addressing future water resource problems.

REFERENCES FOR PART IV

1. Dworsky, L. B. *Water and Air Pollution* (New York: Chelsea House Publishers and Van Nostrand Reinhold Co., 1971) p. 33.
2. 33 U.S.C. 1251 et seq.
3. Rose-Ackerman, S. "Market Models for Water Pollution Control: Their Strengths and Weaknesses," *Public Policy* 25(3):383–406 (1977).
4. Benstock, M. and L. Zwick. *Water Wasteland* (New York: Grossman Publishers, 1971), ch. 14.
5. "Many Water Quality Standard Violations May Not Be Significant Enough to Justify Costly Preventive Actions," USGAO Report CED-80-86 (1980), p. 6.
6. Ackerman, B. A., S. Rose-Ackerman, J. W. Sawyer Jr., and D. W. Henderson. *The Uncertain Search for Environmental Quality* (New York: The Free Press, 1974), Part IV.
7. *EPA v. California*, 426 U.S. 200 (1976).
8. "National Accomplishments in Pollution Control: 1970–1980," U.S. EPA Report (1980).
9. "Cleaning Up the Environment: Progress Achieved but Major Unresolved Issues Remain," USGAO Report CED-82-72 (1982).
10. Goldfarb, W. "Better Than Best: A Crosscurrent in the Federal Water Pollution Control Act Amendments of 1972," *Land and Water Law Review* 11(2):1–26 (1976). Reprinted in Lamb, B. L., ed. *Water Quality Administration: A Focus on Section 208* (Ann Arbor, MI: Ann Arbor Science Publishers, 1980), pp. 115–125.
11. CWA § 301.
12. "A Legislative History of the Federal Water Pollution Control Act Amendments of 1972 and the Clean Water Act of 1977," Congressional Research Service, U.S. Government Printing Office (1973, 1978).
13. Comment: "Nondeterioration and the Protection of High Quality Waters Under Federal Water Pollution Control Law," *Utah Law Review* 1977(4):737–757.
14. 40 CFR § 131.1 et seq. 48 FR 51400–51413.
15. CWA § 301.
16. CWA § 306.
17. CWA § 304.
18. EPA policy in this regard was upheld by the U.S. Supreme Court. *National Crushed Stone Assn v. EPA*, 101 S. Ct. 295 (1980).
19. *DuPont v. Train*, 430 U.S. 112 (1977).
20. *NRDC v. Train*, 8 ERC 2120.
21. CWA § 307.
22. *National Assn of Metal Finishers v. EPA*, 18 ERC 1785 (CA 3, 1983). EPA is

recommending that the CWA be amended to make the FDF variances available to dischargers of toxics.
23. *Train* v. *Colorado PIRG*, 426 U.S. 1 (1976).
24. "Quality Criteria for Water," EPA Office of Water and Hazardous Materials (1976).
25. CWA § 510.
26. BNA *Environment Reporter Current Developments*, January 21, 1983, p. 1630.
27. *City of Milwaukee* v. *Illinois*, 101 S. Ct. 1784, 68 L. Ed. 2d 114 (1981).
28. Goldfarb, W., and B. King. "Urban Stormwater Runoff: The Legal Remedies," *Real Estate Law Journal* 11(1):3−46 (1982), p. 7.
29. *Montgomery* v. *Castle*, 15 ERC 1118.
30. CWA Title II.
31. "Costly Wastewater Treatment Plants Fail to Perform as Expected," USGAO Report CED-81-9 (1980), p. 15.
32. "User Charge Revenues for Wastewater Treatment Plants—Insufficient to Cover Operation and Maintenance," USGAO Report CED-82-1 (1981).
33. "A New Approach Is Needed for the Federal Industrial Wastewater Pretreatment Program" USGAO Report CED-82-37 (1982), p. 14.
34. CWA section 307 and 40 CFR pt. 403.
35. 40 CFR pt. 257.
36. 42 U.S.C. § 6922.
37. 33 U.S.C. § 1401 et seq.
38. CWA § 403.
39. 40 CFR pt. 125.
40. Reuter, M. "Ocean Pollution" in *Air and Water Pollution Control Law: 1982*, P. D. Reed and G. S. Wetstone, eds. (Washington D.C.: Environmental Law Institute, 1982), p. 537.
41. *City of New York* v. *EPA*, 17 ERC 1181 (1982).
42. Lahey, W. L. "Ocean Dumping of Sewage Sludge: The Tide Turns from Protection to Management," *Harvard Environmental Law Review* 6(2):395−431 (1982).
43. 40 CFR pt. 122.
44. CWA § 402(e).
45. CWA § 308.
46. *Weinberger* v. *Romero-Barcelo*, 17 ERC 1217 (1982).
47. "More Effective Action by the Environmental Protection Agency Needed to Enforce Industrial Compliance with Water Pollution Control Discharge Permits," USGAO Report CED-78-182 (1978).
48. "Wastewater Dischargers Are Not Complying with EPA Pollution Control Permits," USGAO Report RCED-84-53.
49. Curlin, J. W. "The Interstate Water Pollution Compact—Paper Tiger or Effective Regulatory Device?" *Ecology Law Quarterly* 2(2):333−356 (1972), pp. 345, 356.
50. Blaser, Zeni, and Company. "Role of Interstate Water Pollution Control Commissions," NTIS PB-257 759 (1975), p. 16.
51. Goldfarb, W. "Water Quality Management Planning: The Fate of 208," *University of Toledo Law Review* 8:105−134 (1976).

52. Henderson, T. "Water Quality Management Planning," in *Air and Water Pollution Control Law*, see reference 41.
53. 40 CFR pt. 35.
54. "Legal and Institutional Approaches to Water Quality Management Planning and Implementation," USEPA Report (1977), p. VI-4.
55. Williams, C. L. "Soil Conservation and Water Pollution Control: The Muddy Record of the United States Department of Agriculture," *Boston College Environmental Affairs Law Review* 7(3):365–421 (1979).
56. N.J.S.A. 4:24–39 et seq.
57. Goldfarb, W., and J. Heenehan. "Legal Control of Soil Erosion and Sedimentation in New Jersey," *Rutgers Camden Law Journal* 11(3):379–422 (1980), p. 412.
58. N.J.S.A. 58:11A-10.
59. "Water Quality Management Planning Is Not Comprehensive and May Not Be Effective for Many Years," USGAO Report CED-78-167 (1978).
60. "Environmental, Economic, and Political Issues Impede Potomac River Cleanup Efforts," USGAO Report GGO-82-7 (1982).
61. CWA 402(e).
62. Lumsdaine, J. A. "Ocean Dumping Regulation: An Overview," *Ecology Law Quarterly* 5(4):753–792 (1976), p. 762.
63. 40 CFR §§ 220–225, 227–229.
64. O'Halloran, R. L. "Ocean Dumping: Progress Toward a Rational Policy of Dredged Waste Disposal," *Environmental Law* 12(3):745–772 (1982).
65. "Problems and Progress in Regulating Ocean Dumping of Sewage Sludge and Industrial Wastes," USGAO Report CED-77-18 (1977), pp. 17–25.
66. Tripp, J. T. B., and A. B. Jaffe. "Preventing Groundwater Pollution: Towards a Coordinated Strategy to Protect Critical Recharge Zones," *Harvard Environmental Law Review* 3:1–47 (1979), pp. 1,2.
67. 42 U.S.C. § 300(f) et seq.
68. 40 CFR pt. 146.
69. 40 CFR pts. 122, 146.
70. 42 U.S.C. § 6901 et seq.
71. 40 CFR pts. 264, 265, 267.
72. 7 U.S.C. § 135 et seq.
73. 15 U.S.C. § 2601 et seq. especially § 2606 (a) (6).
74. 30 U.S.C. § 1201 et seq.
75. 42 U.S.C. § 300(h)-3(e).
76. N.J.A.C. § 7:14A-1 et seq.
77. N.J.S.A. 13:1E-57.
78. N.J.S.A. 58:10-23.11 et seq.
79. N.J.A.C. § 7:9-6.4 et seq.
80. Trauberman, J. "Oil and Hazardous Spills Control," in *Air and Water Pollution Control Law*, see reference 41.
81. See Schoenbaum, T. J. *Environmental Policy Law* (Mineola, NY: The Foundation Press, 1982), pp. 869–873, 880–881.
82. 43 U.S.C. § 1801 et seq.
83. 33 U.S.C. § 1501 et seq.

84. 43 U.S.C. § 1651 et seq.
85. 42 U.S.C. § 9601 et seq.
86. 40 CFR § 117 et seq.
87. *Askew* v. *American Waterways Operators, Inc.*, 411 U.S. 325 (1973).
88. Hinds, R. de C. "Liability under Federal Law for Hazardous Waste Injuries," *Harvard Environmental Law Review* 6(1):1−33 (1982), p. 25.
89. 40 CFR pt. 141.
90. Singer, G. L. *Public Policies Toward Chemical Contamination of Drinking Water* (Princeton, NJ: Princeton University Center for Energy and Environmental Studies, 1982), p. 24.
91. "States' Compliance Lacking in Meeting Safe Drinking Water Regulations," USGAO Report CED-82-43 (1982).
92. 42 U.S.C. § 7801 et seq.
93. "Desalting Water Probably Will Not Solve the Nation's Water Problems, But Can Help," USGAO Report CED-79-60 (1979), p. i.
94. Laitos, J. G. "Legal Institutions and Pollution: Some Intersections between Law and History," *Natural Resources Journal* 15:423−451 (1975).
95. Bartlett, R. V. *The Reserve Mining Controversy* (Bloomington: Indiana University Press, 1980).
96. 16 ERC 1105 (1981).

AFTERWORD

Law is dynamic, and water law is more active than most legal fields because of the intense stress on limited water resources. Thus, the reader should make an effort to keep abreast of water law developments after the currency date of this book.

The Clean Water Act, for example, will be reauthorized and amended. Its basic structure will not be changed, but some proposed amendments, if enacted, will influence the CWA's administration in important ways.

The author's "Litigation and Legislation" commentary in the *Water Resources Bulletin* analyzes recent developments in water law. There are also other informative water resources journals and newsletters. The reader is urged to subscribe to one of these publications and consult it on a regular basis.

Index